The ASEAN Charter

A COMMENTARY

The ASEAN Charter
A COMMENTARY

by *Walter Woon*

NUS PRESS
SINGAPORE

Published by:

NUS Press
National University of Singapore
AS3-01-02, 3 Arts Link
Singapore 117569
Fax: (65) 6774-0652
E-mail: nusbooks@nus.edu.sg
Website: http://nuspress.nus.edu.sg

ISBN: 978-981-4722-08-7 (Paper)
978-9971-69-867-6

National Library Board, Singapore Cataloguing-in-Publication Data

Woon, Walter C. M., author.
The ASEAN Charter : a commentary / by Walter Woon. - Singapore : NUS Press, National University of Singapore, [2016]
pages cm
ISBN : 978-981-4722-08-7 (paperback)
ISBN : 978-9971-69-867-6 (hardcover)

ASEAN - Charters. 2. ASEAN – History. I. Title.

KNE173
341.2473 -- dc23 OCN908013064

Designed by: Nelani Jinadasa
Printed by: Mainland Press Pte Ltd

CONTENTS

FOREWORD

ASEAN has come a long way since the signing of its founding Bangkok Declaration on 8 August 1967. The conclusion of the ASEAN Charter in 2007 marks an important milestone in ASEAN's 40-year evolution. The ASEAN Charter does not only set out purposes for ASEAN to chart its future direction and to build an ASEAN Community, but also codifies ASEAN's principles that are important to ASEAN and its member states. The ASEAN Charter, as a constituent treaty, has also established the legal and institutional framework for ASEAN to support and facilitate its community-building and integration initiatives and the work towards a rules-based community.

Following the entry into force of the ASEAN Charter in 2008, ASEAN has focused efforts on ensuring its effective operationalisation and implementation. Required ASEAN Organs/Bodies were set up, and numerous legal instruments, as well as rules and procedures have been concluded and/or are being developed in pursuance of the ASEAN Charter. Likewise, the successful conclusion of the Protocol to the ASEAN Charter on Dispute Settlement Mechanisms in 2010, in addition to the existing Treaty of Amity and Cooperation in Southeast Asia and the Protocol on Enhanced Dispute Settlement Mechanism (EDSM), is a significant achievement of ASEAN in establishing reliable and trustworthy dispute settlement mechanisms as provided for in the ASEAN Charter.

This *Commentary* is a timely publication with useful information and can serve as a helpful source of reference.

Le Luong Minh
Secretary-General of ASEAN

PREFACE

As I write these words, the world is reminded of the echoes of the Guns of August. The assassination of the Austrian Archduke Franz Ferdinand in Sarajevo in July 1914 lit the European powder keg. The resultant explosion set off a second Thirty Years' War (1914–45) which devastated the Continent (and much of the rest of the world) more thoroughly than the first Thirty Years' War (1618–48) did. After dragging themselves out of the rubble and ashes, the Europeans forswore war as a continuation of policy by other means and consciously set out to build a system that would preclude such a cataclysm ever happening again. They created the most successful regional organisation on earth, the European Union.

Despite common misconception, ASEAN is not patterned after the European Union. There has never been any feeling that political integration is necessary for survival. ASEAN was a child of the decolonisation process as the European powers were progressively ejected from their colonies, and of the proxy wars that erupted as the Communist and Western Blocs contended against one another. Southeast Asia in 1967 – the year ASEAN was born—was politically unsettled and beset with suspicions amongst the newly-independent countries of the region. The Cold War had turned hot in Indochina and the spectre of Communist domination loomed large. ASEAN was founded in order to foster trust among Southeast Asian countries and preclude foreign meddling in local affairs. It was never meant to be a supranational organisation, much less an embryonic United States of Southeast Asia.

Nearly four decades on, Southeast Asia had been transformed. The Indochina wars were over. Communism had collapsed. The countries of ASEAN were at peace. It was felt that the time had come to move to a higher plane. As an organisation, ASEAN has been propelled by a mixture of hot air and idealism. That idealism came to the fore when the ASEAN leaders took the decision in December 2005 to promulgate an ASEAN Charter. They established an Eminent Persons Group to reimagine ASEAN and make 'bold and visionary' recommendations.

The Eminent Persons Group fulfilled their mandate to dream dreams and see visions, but it was left to the High Level Task Force on the ASEAN Charter to translate these into something that would work in the hard, cold world. The result of their efforts is the ASEAN Charter. It is said that a camel is a horse designed by a committee. The ASEAN Charter is the diplomatic equivalent of a camel. It does not have the looks of a thoroughbred, but it is serviceable and will survive in hard going where a thoroughbred would die.

I should say at the outset that this is not a law book. It is impossible to write a legal text when there is so little law involved. What I have tried to do is explain how the provisions of the Charter came to be drafted and how they relate to the realities of diplomatic practice. ASEAN is above all still a political animal. For all the fine statements about rule of law and creating a rules-based community, when push comes to shove, *realpolitik* and not legal principle will likely prevail. Nonetheless, the ambition is laudable. Progress towards the goal of a rules-based, democratic, people-oriented community will not be linear. ASEAN, in its time-honoured way, will waltz towards that objective with two steps forward and one step back, meandering around the dance floor. That should not detract from the fact that ASEAN has come such a long way from its modest beginnings. The Charter is a living document, and like all living organisms will have to evolve to adapt to its changing environment.

Note: I have used material in this book that I have previously written for other works, notably *Towards a Rules-Based Community: An ASEAN Legal Service* (2014). Readers should therefore not be surprised to find similarities in expression to other books and articles written by me. I hope that this practice may be forgiven, as it would have been unnecessarily tedious to have had to recast in different words everything I have published on the subject before.

Walter Woon
Singapore, August 2014

ACKNOWLEDGEMENTS

This book could not have been written without the assistance of a host of persons who spoke to me about their interactions with ASEAN over the years, ranging from legal officers, officials in ministries and diplomats from various countries, private sector business people and officials of the ASEAN Secretariat. From the ASEAN Secretariat I would specially acknowledge my debt to former Director for Political and Security Affairs Dr Termsak Chalermpalanupap; former Deputy Secretary-General (AEC) Pushpanathan Sundram; former Deputy Secretary-General (Community and Corporate Affairs) Bagas Hapsoro; and Mr Un Sovannasam and Ms Sendy Hermawati of the Legal Services and Agreements Division. Their input regarding the reality (as opposed to the theory) of how ASEAN works has been extremely valuable.

I would like in particular to put on record my thanks to my friends for sharing their insights and experiences of working with ASEAN: former ASEAN Secretary-General Ong Keng Yong; former ASEAN Secretary-General Rodolfo Severino; former Indonesian Permanent Representative Ngurah Swajaya; former Thai Permanent Representative Manasvi Srisodapol; former Singaporean Permanent Representative T. K. Lim; and from the Ministry of Foreign Affairs, Singapore, Deputy-Secretary Vanu Gopala Menon, Ambassador Jai Sohan Singh, Director-General Kok Li Peng and Director-General Dominic Goh.

I am also extremely grateful to the staff of the Singapore Permanent Representation to ASEAN and Permanent Representative Tan Hung Seng for their help and support during my visits to Jakarta.

Finally, I owe a debt of gratitude to Ms Chan Sze Wei and Dr Hao Duy Phan of the Centre for International Law, National University of Singapore, for their assistance in looking through the manuscript, contributing their own perspectives and chasing down obscure points. To Sze Wei in particular, I would like to express my warm appreciation. She was present from the start with the Eminent Persons Group, throughout the drafting process with the High Level Task Force and finally as a researcher at the Centre for International Law. Her help has been both valued and invaluable.

I apologise that I am unable thank every single one who has assisted me by name, as there have been so many. I hope that this will not be taken as a lack of appreciation. I am grateful to one and all for their help.

Although I have presumed to name several people as having contributed to this book, what I have written should not to be taken as representing their views. The responsibility for any conclusions and interpretations is mine alone.

INTRODUCTION

The Association of Southeast Asian Nations was founded on 8 August 1967 by means of the Bangkok Declaration (officially, the ASEAN Declaration), a modest document that did not even purport to be a treaty. The Bangkok Declaration did not create an organisation in the mould of the United Nations or the European Economic Community. What it sought to do was to set up a mechanism to foster mutual trust among the original five founder-states, viz, Indonesia, Malaysia, the Philippines, Singapore and Thailand. This mechanism initially envisaged annual meetings of the Foreign Ministers known as the ASEAN Ministerial Meeting (AMM).[1] The AMM was supported by National Secretariats in each member state and a Standing Committee under the chairmanship of foreign minister of the host country of the next AMM.

A Short History of ASEAN[2]

At the time of ASEAN's founding Southeast Asia was in an unsettled state. The countries of ASEAN had all been colonies of various European powers,[3] except for Thailand. Decolonisation had occurred recently;[4] in the case of

---

1 *See* the ASEAN Declaration signed on 8 Aug. 1967 in Bangkok, Thailand. It was signed by the Foreign Ministers of Indonesia (Mr Adam Malik), Malaysia (Tun Abdul Razak, who was Deputy Prime Minister rather than Foreign Minister), the Philippines (Mr Narciso Ramos), Singapore (Mr S. Rajaratnam) and Thailand (Mr Thanat Khoman).

2 Material in this section has been used in other published works by the author, notably in W. Woon & J-C Piris, *Towards a Rules-Based Community: An ASEAN Legal Service* (Cambridge: Cambridge University Press, 2014).

3 Indonesia is not a natural country, but rather the old Dutch empire in Asia, viz the Netherlands East Indies. The Philippines was a colony first of Spain and later of the United States of America. Malaysia is a federation of former British colonies and protectorates. Singapore was similarly a British colony.

4 For a general overview, *see* M. C. Ricklefs et al., *A New History of Southeast Asia,* (London: Palgrave Macmillan, 2010), chapter 11. The Philippines became independent

Indonesia, only after a bitter war against the Dutch to prise the archipelago from their grip. Malaysia was formed in 1963, comprising the Federation of Malaya and the former British colonies in Southeast Asia, namely Singapore, British North Borneo (Sabah) and Sarawak.[5] Indonesia had opposed this, seeing it as a neo-colonialist plot and an impediment to unification of the Malay archipelago.[6] The idea of an Indonesia Raya (Greater Indonesia) had germinated during the Japanese occupation of 1942–45. Indeed, Indonesia's success in incorporating Dutch New Guinea in 1963[7] may have given fresh life to the ambition to realise an Indonesia Raya. The Philippines too opposed the formation of Malaysia because of its claim to Sabah (British North Borneo).[8] Indonesian hostility to Malaysia led to an undeclared war (euphemistically termed *Konfrontasi*, from the Dutch word for 'confrontation'). Though fighting took place primarily along the jungle border between East Malaysia and Indonesian Kalimantan, there were repeated attempts to infiltrate Peninsular Malaysia (including a paratroop drop in the southern state of Johore) and one notorious incident where Indonesian marines detonated a bomb at

---

from the United States on 4 Jul. 1946. *See* Britannica Online, 'Philippines: World War II': www.britannica.com/EBchecked/topic/456399/Philippines/23718/World-War-II. Indonesia proclaimed its independence from the Netherlands on 17 Aug. 1945 in the immediate aftermath of the Japanese Surrender. *See* Britannica Online, 'Indonesia: Japanese Occupation': www.britannica.com/EBchecked/topic/286480/Indonesia/22819/Japanese-occupation. The Federation of Malaya became independent from Great Britain on 31 Aug. 1957. *See* Britannica Online, 'Malaysia: Political Transformation,' Britannica Online, online: www.britannica.com/EBchecked/topic/359754/Malaysia/52562/Political-transformation#ref509484.

5 Brunei, a British protectorate, declined to join Malaysia and remained under British protection until 1984, becoming a member of ASEAN that same year. *See* the Declaration of the Admission of Brunei Darussalam into ASEAN, signed in Jakarta on 7 Jan. 1984.

6 The history of the Malay independence movement and its Pan-Indonesian ambitions is recounted in B. K. Cheah, *Red Star Over Malaya*, 3rd ed. (Singapore: Singapore University Press, 2003), chapter 4. The suspicions of the independence generation of Indonesians regarding the British are understandable, given the part that British and Indian troops played in restoring Dutch rule in the East Indies after the Japanese surrender from Sept. 1945.

7 After the success of the Indonesian revolution, the only portion of the Dutch East Indies to remain under the suzerainty of the Netherlands was western New Guinea. This was placed under United Nations administration in 1962 and transferred to Indonesia in 1963. *See* 'Papua: History,' Britannica Online: global.britannica.com/EBchecked/topic/293960/Papua/303094/History.

8 *See* R. C. Severino, *Southeast Asia in Search of an ASEAN Community* (Singapore: ISEAS Publishing, 2006), chapter 2, 164–6. The Philippines has never formally abandoned its claim. The issue again came to prominence in early 2013 when a group of armed Filipinos landed in Sabah near the town of Lahad Datu claiming to be the Royal Army of Sulu, which supposedly exercised sovereignty over Sabah. This incursion ended in bloodshed. *See* 'Malaysia boosts Sabah security after Lahad Datu clashes,' 4 Mar. 2013, BBC News Asia, online: www.bbc.co.uk/news/world-asia-21656732.

MacDonald House in Singapore, killing three civilians. *Konfrontasi* came to an end with the fall of President Soekarno in October 1965 after an abortive communist coup.

However, all was not well even within Malaysia. Tensions between the state government of Singapore and the federal government in Kuala Lumpur came to a head in 1965 over the incendiary issue of whether the new Malaysian federation would be multiracial (a line espoused by the People's Action Party in Singapore) or communal (which was the *leitmotiv* of Malayan politics ever since the demise of the short-lived Malayan Union in 1948). These tensions led to the ejection of Singapore from the Malaysian federation in August 1965.[9] On the northern border of Peninsular Malaysia, the remnants of the communist Malayan People's Liberation Army continued to lurk in the jungles of Thailand, continuing to pose a sporadic danger even after the end of the Malayan Emergency.[10] Relations between Singapore and Indonesia were fraught after the conviction for murder in 1966 of Indonesian marines who had infiltrated Singapore in civilian clothes and bombed MacDonald House, killing several civilians.[11]

Looming over all these disputes was the shadow of the Vietnam War. The unspoken motive for the formation of ASEAN was fear of Communist expansion. It was felt that cooperation among the five non-Communist states of Southeast Asia was essential to meet the challenge. Four of the five founders were aligned to the Western bloc. As US allies, the Philippines and Thailand played host to American bases. Singapore was home to the major British naval base in the Far East, while the Training Depot for the British Brigade of Gurkhas was in Sungei Patani in West Malaysia. Indonesia was non-aligned and determined to remain so. ASEAN was not conceived as a military or security organisation. Given the unhappy history of international relations amongst the five original member countries, the primary objective of ASEAN

---

9 *See* M. Turnbull, *A Short History of Malaysia, Singapore and Brunei* (Singapore: Graham Brash, 1980), chapter 18. The story is told in more detail (albeit from only one side) in K. Y. Lee, *The Singapore Story: Memoirs of Lee Kuan Yew* (Singapore: Times Editions, 1998). For an interesting view from a non-English-speaking historian, *see* H. S. Kubitscheck, *Geschichte Malaysias und Singapurs* (Berlin: VEB Deutscher Verlag der Wissenschaften, 1984), 159–62.

10 This was a communist insurrection lasting from 1948 until 1960, when it was officially declared to be over. *See* R. Clutterbuck, *The Long, Long War: The Emergency in Malaya 1948–1960* (London: Cassell & Co, 1966).

11 The Indonesian marines were tried and convicted of murder, the Federal Court in Singapore holding that they had forfeited the right to be treated as prisoners of war. See *Osman v Public Prosecutor* [1965–67] Singapore Law Reports (Reissue) 402. The Decision of the Federal Court was affirmed on appeal by the Privy Council [1968–70] Singapore Law Reports (Reissue) 117.

was the fostering of trust amongst the member states in order to meet the Communist threat and keep Southeast Asia free of big power rivalries.[12]

The initial idea for ASEAN arose in early 1966 when Thailand was brokering reconciliation among Malaysia, the Philippines and Indonesia.[13] Thai Foreign Minister Thanat Khoman floated the idea to Indonesian Foreign Minister Adam Malik at a banquet marking the reconciliation of the three parties.[14] Mr Malik agreed but asked for time to normalize relations with Malaysia. The initial draft was prepared by the Thai Foreign Ministry. According to Mr Thanat Khoman,[15] the initial idea was that the association would comprise only the members of the Association of Southeast Asia (ASA)[16] plus Indonesia. Singapore asked to join and was included in the discussions. In August 1967, ministerial representatives[17] of the five countries met in the Thai coastal resort of Bang Saen, where they negotiated in the informal manner over golf and dinner in what became something of an ASEAN tradition.[18] The negotiations took four days. The ASEAN Declaration was signed in the Saranrom Palace in Bangkok on 8 August 1967.

The foundation of ASEAN did not lead to an immediate outburst of fraternal feeling. In an assertion of newly independent Singapore's prickly sovereignty, the Indonesian marines who had perpetrated the MacDonald House bombing were hanged in October 1968, an act which provoked severe anti-Singapore riots in Indonesia.[19] Also in 1968, information surfaced about

---

[12] See the Preamble to the 1967 ASEAN Declaration, signed on 8 Aug. 1967 by the Foreign Ministers in Bangkok, Thailand. The first four paragraphs emphasise the need for regional cooperation, solidarity and partnership while the final two paragraphs make plain the desire to exclude external meddling in the politics of the member states. The aims and purposes of the organisation listed in the operative paragraphs emphasise the economic growth and social development of the member states, the promotion of regional peace and stability and the development of mutual cooperation in various fields.

[13] Both the Philippines and Indonesia had opposed the formation of Malaysia. Indonesia had just ended its undeclared war against Malaysia and Singapore (euphemistically called *Konfrontasi*, from the Dutch word for 'confrontation').

[14] *See* 'The Founding of ASEAN', in J. M. Flores and J. Abad, *ASEAN at 30* (Jakarta: ASEAN Secretariat, 1997), chapter 1, available at www.asean.org/news/item/asean-at-30.

[15] Ibid.

[16] This was formed in 1961, the members being Thailand, the Philippines and the Federation of Malaya. *See* 'ASEAN,' Britannica Online, global.britannica.com/EBchecked/topic/556542/ASEAN#ref227052.

[17] These were the Foreign Ministers of Indonesia (Mr Adam Malik), the Philippines (Mr Narciso Ramos), Singapore (Mr S. Rajaratnam) and Thailand (Mr Thanat Khoman) and the Deputy Prime Minister of Malaysia (Tun Abdul Razak).

[18] *See* Severino, *In Search of an ASEAN Community*, chapter 2, quoting the former Thai Foreign Minister Thanat Khoman.

[19] Lee, *From Third World to First*, 37–8. The issue is not dead even after nearly half a century. In Feb. 2014, Indonesia named a frigate after the two marines, who had been

a Filipino plot to infiltrate saboteurs in Sabah.[20] Continued tensions between Malaysia and the Philippines over Sabah eventually led to the postponement of the Fourth ASEAN Ministerial Meeting (AMM), which was supposed to have been held in 1970 in Manila.[21] Meanwhile, North Vietnam had launched the Tet Offensive in 1968, which demonstrated to the world that the Vietnam war would not be won by America. Racial riots racked Malaysia in May 1969, threatening to spill over into Singapore.[22] It was against this backdrop that in 1971 ASEAN issued the ZOPFAN Declaration,[23] which was 'inspired by the worthy aims and objectives of the United Nations, in particular by the principles of respect for the sovereignty and territorial integrity of all states, abstention from threat or use of force, peaceful settlement of international disputes, equal rights and self-determination and non-interference in affairs of States,' according to its Preamble. The five founder members declared that Southeast Asia should be a 'zone of peace, freedom and neutrality, free from any form of interference by outside powers.'

North Vietnam's victory over South Vietnam in 1975 gave a new impetus to regional cooperation. The Heads of State/Government[24] of ASEAN met for the first time in Bali in February 1976. Two major results of the First ASEAN

---

elevated to the pantheon of national heroes. This act elicited a strong protest from Singapore, which announced that visits from the frigate *KRI Usman-Harun* would not be welcome. *See* 'Indonesian warship Usman Harun disallowed from calling at Singapore ports and naval bases', www.straitstimes.com, 18 Feb. 2014, *The Straits Times*, online: www.straitstimes.com/microsites/parliament/story/indonesian-warship-usman-harun-banned-singapore-ports-and-naval-bases-20.

[20] Severino, *In Search of an ASEAN Community*, 164. *See also* 'Philippines: Relations with Asian Neighbours,' *Federal Research Division of the Library of Congress Country Studies*, online: 'Philippines: Relations with Asian Neighbours,' countrystudies.us/philippines/93.htm. This website contains online versions of books previously published by the Federal Research Division of the Library of Congress.

[21] The ASEAN Ministerial Meeting (AMM) is a meeting of the Foreign Ministers of the ASEAN member states. The very first AMM was the one at which the ASEAN Declaration was adopted on 8 Aug. 1967. It was only in 1969 at the Third AMM in the Cameron Highlands, Malaysia (Dec. 1969) that normalisation of relations between Malaysia and the Philippines had been announced. See the Joint Communiqué of the Third ASEAN Ministerial Meeting, issued on 16–17 Dec. 1969 in Cameron Highlands, Malaysia, para 2. The fourth AMM finally took place in Mar. 1971.

[22] Lee, *From Third World to First,* 38–40.

[23] Officially, the Zone of Peace, Freedom and Neutrality Declaration, signed in Kuala Lumpur on 27 Nov. 1971 in Kuala Lumpur, Malaysia, by the Foreign Ministers. This was signed by the Foreign Ministers of Indonesia (Mr Adam Malik), Malaysia (Tun Abdul Razak, who was by then Prime Minister and Foreign Minister), the Philippines (Mr Carlos Romulo), Singapore (Mr S. Rajaratnam) and Thailand (Mr Thanat Khoman, then Special Envoy of the National Executive Council). For the background to this, *see* Severino, *In Search of an ASEAN Community*, 166–7.

[24] ASEAN Summits are meetings of the heads of government. Ceremonial heads of state (e.g., the King of Thailand, the President of Singapore and the Yang di-Pertuan Agong of Malaysia) do not attend.

Summit were the Declaration of ASEAN Concord (or the Bali Concord, as it is known) and the Treaty of Amity and Cooperation (commonly referred to as the TAC).[25] The Bali Concord solemnly declared that 'Member states, in the spirit of ASEAN solidarity, shall rely exclusively on peaceful processes in the settlement of intra-regional differences.' It established a meeting of the Heads of Government 'as and when necessary'. ASEAN Summits were held irregularly to begin with. The second, in Kuala Lumpur, took place the following year. After that ten years elapsed until the next Summit. It was only in the nineties that Summits became a regular feature of the ASEAN calendar. The Bali Concord emphasised the need for greater cooperation in the political, economic, social and cultural fields. The member states also committed themselves to improving the ASEAN machinery, *inter alia* by studying the desirability of a new constitutional framework. This desire was only fulfilled three decades later when the ASEAN Charter was adopted. The member states renounced the use of force and committed themselves to settlement of differences or disputes by peaceful means in Article 2 of the Treaty of Amity and Cooperation in Southeast Asia (TAC). The UN General Assembly at its 47th session in 1992 endorsed the TAC, recognising that it provides a strong foundation for regional confidence-building and cooperation.[26]

The end of the Vietnam War posed a challenge to ASEAN. The fall of South Vietnam, followed shortly by communist takeovers in Cambodia and Laos, created a fear that Thailand would be next. However, despite the gloomy prognostications of doomsayers at the time, it was Cambodia and not Thailand that provided the stage for the next act of the drama. In December 1978 Vietnamese forces invaded Cambodia and overthrew the Khmer Rouge regime. This placed the members of ASEAN in a quandary: Pol Pot and the Khmer Rouge were odious, but it would be an unfortunate precedent to acquiesce to a regime change imposed by Vietnamese bayonets. The ASEAN Foreign Ministers held a special meeting to 'deplore' the Vietnamese invasion.[27] The fear was of an escalation of fighting and an

---

[25] Both of which were signed on 24 Feb. 1976 in Denpasar, Bali by the President of Indonesia (Mr Soeharto), the Prime Minister of Malaysia (Dr Hussein Onn), the President of the Philippines (Mr Ferdinand Marcos), the Prime Minister of Singapore (Mr Lee Kuan Yew) and the Prime Minister of Thailand (Mr Kukrit Pramoj). Brunei ratified the Treaty of Amity and Cooperation in Southeast Asia (TAC) on 6 June 1987. Accession to the TAC has become a first step towards membership of ASEAN.

[26] A/Res/47/53B adopted by consensus on 9 Dec. 1992.

[27] *See* the Joint Statement of the Special ASEAN Foreign Ministers' Meeting on the Current Political Development in the Southeast Asia Region, issued on 12 Jan. 1979 in Bangkok, Thailand.

incursion across the Thai border.[28] The situation in Indochina would occupy the political attention of ASEAN for more than a decade.[29]

The diplomatic struggle over recognition of the new Cambodian government was a defining experience for ASEAN. ASEAN diplomats worked together in the United Nations and other international forums to ensure that the use of force to change a government was not legitimised. This cooperation forged close relationships among the members of that generation of diplomats who were on the front line of the campaign to deny recognition of the Vietnamese-installed Cambodian government.[30]

After more than a decade, the Cambodian imbroglio ended in 1991 with the withdrawal of Vietnamese forces and the election of a new government in Cambodia. At that point, it was felt that the inclusion of the Indochinese countries was necessary to ensure that there would be no recurrence of hostilities.[31] The end of the Cambodian problem marked a shift in focus to ASEAN economic cooperation and integration, in addition to political and security cooperation.[32] In 1992, ASEAN member states concluded two major economic agreements: the Framework Agreement or Enhancing ASEAN Economic Cooperation and the Agreement on the Common Effective Preferential Tariff (CEPT) Scheme for the ASEAN Free Trade Area (AFTA). Since 1992 the majority of ASEAN agreements deal with the economic sphere.[33]

---

[28] See the Joint Communiqué of the Twelfth ASEAN Ministerial Meeting, issued on 30 June 1979 in Bali, Indonesia, paras 13, 16–17.

[29] An account of ASEAN's involvement in this period can be found in M. Leifer, *ASEAN and the Security of Southeast Asia* (London: Routledge, 1989), chapter 4, 89-121. This stops short of the final dénouement, when elections were held after the Vietnamese withdrawal in 1991.

[30] Former Singapore Foreign Minister Wong Kan Seng at the S. Rajaratnam Lecture, Shangri-la Hotel, Singapore, 23 Nov. 2011.

[31] *See* the Singapore Declaration, signed on 28 Jan. 1992 by the Heads of State/Government in Singapore, para 2, which states that 'ASEAN shall forge a closer relationship based on friendship and cooperation with the Indochinese countries, following the settlement on Cambodia.' The Joint Communiqué of the 28th ASEAN Ministerial Meeting, issued on 30 July 1995 in Bandar Seri Begawan, Brunei Darussalam, and the Bangkok Summit Declaration, adopted on 15 Dec. 1995 by the Heads of State/Government in Bangkok, Thailand, also refer to a vision of ASEAN that would include all Southeast Asian countries.

[32] *See* the Singapore Declaration, signed on 28 Jan. 1992 by the Heads of State/Government in Singapore.

[33] *See* the ASEAN Legal Instruments list maintained by the ASEAN Secretariat on its website: agreement.asean.org.

Rapprochement with former foes came quickly. Vietnam joined ASEAN in 1995,[34] followed by Laos[35] in 1997. At the same time, Myanmar[36] also joined the organisation despite the chorus of international criticism following the military crackdown on civilian protesters after the general election. Cambodia's accession was delayed due to a coup by Second Prime Minister Hun Sen against First Prime Minister Prince Norodom Ranariddh.[37] The process of rounding out the membership of ASEAN was finally completed with the accession of Cambodia in 1999.[38]

The accession of the four new members (commonly referred to by the acronym CLMV) demonstrated the inclusiveness of the ASEAN ideal. There were no preconditions as to form of government or political system, only that candidates should be in the Southeast Asian region and subscribe to the aims, principles and purposes of ASEAN.[39] There was no shared history or culture binding the new members to the old, no common language or religion. The governing philosophy was entirely pragmatic. These were countries within Southeast Asia and had to be brought within the family group, warts and all.

It is easy in the light of this history to understand the aversion to outside interference in the internal affairs of member states. Suspicion of former

---

[34] Declaration of the Admission of the Socialist Republic of Viet Nam into the Association of Southeast Asian Nations, signed on 28 July 1995 in Bandar Seri Begawan, Brunei Darussalam. Vietnam had acceded to the Treaty of Amity and Cooperation in Southeast Asia (TAC) on 16 June 1992.

[35] Declaration on the Admission of the Lao People's Democratic Republic into the Association of Southeast Asian Nations, signed on 23 July 1997, in Subang Jaya, Malaysia. Laos had acceded to the Treaty of Amity and Cooperation in Southeast Asia (TAC) on 29 June 1992.

[36] Declaration on the Admission of the Union of Myanmar into the Association of Southeast Asian Nations, signed on 23 July 1997, in Subang Jaya, Malaysia. Myanmar ratified the Treaty of Amity and Cooperation in Southeast Asia (TAC) on 10 July 1996.

[37] *See* 'Cambodia: Cambodia since 1990,' Britannica Online: global.britannica.com/EBchecked/topic/90520/Cambodia/52491/Cambodia-since-1990.
The Joint Statement of the Special Meeting of the ASEAN Foreign Ministers on Cambodia issued on 10 July 1997 in Kuala Lumpur, Malaysia, glosses over this completely. Cambodia had made a formal application to join ASEAN, which was accepted at the Twenty-ninth ASEAN Ministerial Meeting, 20–21 July 1996 in Jakarta, Indonesia. *See* Joint Communiqué of the Twenty-ninth ASEAN Ministerial Meeting, issued on 21 July 1996 in Jakarta, Indonesia, paras 2–3.

[38] Declaration on the Admission of the Kingdom of Cambodia into the Association of Southeast Asian Nations, signed on 30 Apr. 1999 in Hanoi, Vietnam. Cambodia acceded to the Treaty of Amity and Cooperation in Southeast Asia (TAC) on 23 Jan. 1995.

[39] The ASEAN Declaration, signed on 8 Aug. 1967 by the ASEAN Foreign Ministers in Bangkok, Thailand, para 4. The Cambodian Prime Minister Hun Sen once scathingly joked that the only three criteria for ASEAN leaders were eating durian, playing golf and singing karaoke. *See* 'I Still Need Ranariddh,' 13 June 1997, *Asiaweek*, online: www-cgi.cnn.com/ASIANOW/asiaweek/97/0613/cs4.html.

colonial masters and big powers runs deep.[40] Even within the family suspicions remain.[41] There is a fairly high degree of trust and comfort among the founding members and Brunei (commonly referred to as ASEAN-6), born of the baptism by fire of the Vietnamese invasion of Cambodia. This narrative of ASEAN solidarity is not shared by the newer members. At the S Rajaratnam Lecture 2011,[42] Singapore's former Foreign Minister Wong Kan Seng recounted how ASEAN diplomats had worked closely together for over a decade to deny international recognition of the Cambodian government installed by the Vietnamese after the invasion in 1978. At the end of the lecture the Cambodian ambassador stood up to make the point that the Vietnamese had not invaded Cambodia but had instead liberated the Cambodian people from the horrors of the Pol Pot regime. This lack of a shared narrative is a fault line that separates the CLMV countries from the ASEAN-6. It takes time to forge the habit of working together for the common good. The older members have had nearly half a century to do it; the newer ones barely two decades.[43] The process of building trust still remains a challenge.[44]

---

[40] Foreign Minister Adam Malik expressed Indonesia's vision at the time ASEAN was founded of a Southeast Asia 'that can be on its own feet, strong enough to defend itself from any negative influence from outside the region'. *See* Flores and Abad, *ASEAN at 30*, chapter 1, and D. T. Djani, 'A Long Journey', in Koh, Manalo and Woon, eds., *Making of the ASEAN Charter*, chapter 11, 137. Pak Djani was Indonesia's member on the High Level Task Force for Drafting the ASEAN Charter.

[41] During the drafting of the ASEAN Charter, there was a divide between the newer members (collectively referred to as CLMV) and the older ones. Malaysian HLTF member Tan Sri Ahmad Fuzi bin Abdul Razak alludes to this in his chapter 'Facing Unfair Criticisms', in Koh, Manalo and Woon, eds., *Making of the ASEAN Charter*, chapter 2, 21. Cambodian HLTF member Dr Kao Kim Hourn admits as much in chapter 12, 153, of the same book.

[42] Held at the Shangri-La Hotel, Singapore, on 23 Nov. 2011.

[43] Interestingly, Myanmar HLTF member U Aung Bwa (a former Director-General of the ASEAN Affairs Department in the Myanmar Foreign Ministry) comments: 'When Myanmar first joined ASEAN in 1997, we were a new member state compared to the older members which were already into their thirtieth year as members of the Association. We, as a new member, had to accede to whatever agreements or treaties we were compelled to sign. However, in the drafting of the ASEAN Charter we are now in a stronger position, with equal footing with the other members.' *See* Aung Bwa, 'The Jewel in my Crown', in Koh, Manalo and Woon, eds.,, *Making of the ASEAN Charter*, chapter 3, 27–8.

[44] As illustrated by the very public disagreement between Cambodia on one hand and the Philippines and Vietnam on the other over the latter's disputes with China in the South China Sea. This led to an unprecedented failure to issue a joint communiqué at the conclusion of the Forty-fifth ASEAN Ministerial Meeting held in Phnom Penh in July 2012. Cambodia came under intense criticism and felt it necessary to issue a press statement on 26 July 2012 defending its chairmanship. The lack of fraternal feeling was again evident at the subsequent Twenty-first ASEAN Summit in Phnom Penh, where the Cambodian chair again came in for criticism over the way it handled the South China Sea issue.

ASEAN: A Timeline

1967 Signing of the ASEAN Declaration in Bangkok on 8 August by the Foreign Ministers of Indonesia, Malaysia, the Philippines, Singapore and Thailand, marking the foundation of the association. This counts as the first ASEAN Ministerial Meeting (AMM). The AMM meets annually thereafter. Creation of the ASEAN Standing Committee (ASC) to prepare meetings of the AMM.

1971 ASEAN Senior Officials' Meeting (ASEAN SOM) established to discuss sensitive issues before submission to the ASEAN Ministerial Meeting (AMM). The SOM leader is the permanent secretary or equivalent.

1973 Foreign Ministers decide to establish an ASEAN Secretariat.

1975 End of the Vietnam War with the fall of South Vietnam. ASEAN Economic Ministers meet for the first time in Bali (the next meeting in Kuala Lumpur the following year adopted the name ASEAN Economic Ministers' Meeting). ASEAN Labour Ministers Meeting (ALMM) meet in Jakarta and thereafter biennially.

1976 First ASEAN Summit held in Bali. Issuing of the Declaration of ASEAN Concord (Bali Concord). Signing of the Treaty of Amity and Cooperation in Southeast Asia (TAC). Establishment of the ASEAN Secretariat in Jakarta.

1977 Second ASEAN Summit held in Kuala Lumpur. ASEAN Economic Ministers' Meeting (AEM) formalised. Establishment of the Senior Economic Officials' Meeting (SEOM). The AEM meets annually thereafter. ASEAN Education Ministers (ASED) meet for the first time in Manila; meetings are held irregularly thereafter.

1978 Invasion of Cambodia by Vietnamese forces. Special meeting of ASEAN Foreign Ministers held in January 1979 to deplore the invasion. ASEAN diplomats thereafter work together to deny diplomatic recognition to the new regime in Cambodia.

1980 Establishment of the ASEAN Ministers of Health Meeting (AHMM), ASEAN Ministerial Meeting on Science and Technology (AMMST) and ASEAN Ministers on Energy Meeting (AMEM).

1981 ASEAN Ministerial Meeting on the Environment (AMME) held in Manila for the first time.

1986 ASEAN Law Ministers Meeting (ALAWMM) established, to be held every 36 months thereafter with senior law officials' meetings (ASLOM) in between.

1987 Brunei joins ASEAN. Third ASEAN Summit held in Manila.

1989 Conference of Ministers Responsible for Information (AMRI) inaugurated.

1991 Withdrawal of Vietnamese forces from Cambodia and election of a new government.

1992 Secretary-General of the ASEAN Secretariat redesignated as Secretary-General of ASEAN and given an enhanced role carrying with it ministerial status. ASEAN Secretariat ostensibly professionalised by open recruitment of staff rather than nomination by Member States.

Fourth ASEAN Summit held in Singapore. Signing of the Agreement on Common Effective Preferential Tariff Scheme for the ASEAN Free Trade Area (AFTA) and the Framework Agreement on Enhancing ASEAN Economic Cooperation.

1995 Vietnam joins ASEAN. Fifth ASEAN Summit held in Bangkok. Signing of the Treaty on the Southeast Asia Nuclear-Weapon-Free Zone (SEANWFZ). ASEAN Transport Ministers Meeting (ATM) held for the first time and annually thereafter.

1996	First informal ASEAN Summit held in Jakarta, marking the de facto inauguration of annual meetings of the Heads of State/Government.
1997	Laos and Myanmar join ASEAN. Cambodia's application to join is postponed because of a coup in the country. Second Informal ASEAN Summit held in Kuala Lumpur, marking the 30th anniversary of the founding of ASEAN. ASEAN Vision 2020 adopted. ASEAN Finance Ministers Meeting (AFMM) and ASEAN Ministerial Meeting on Transnational Crime (AMMTC) established. Asian financial crisis impacts ASEAN Member States severely.
1998	Sixth ASEAN Summit held in Hanoi, the first to be hosted by one of the new member states. Hanoi Action Plan launched to realise the Vision 2020. Conclusion of the Framework Agreement on the ASEAN Investment Area (AIA). Establishment of the ASEAN Tourism Ministers Meeting (M-ATM). First meeting of the ASEAN Ministers on Rural Development and Poverty Eradication (AMRDPE).
1999	Cambodia joins ASEAN. This rounds off the current membership of the organisation. Inauguration of the ASEAN Foreign Ministers' Retreat, allowing the Foreign Ministers to discuss issues informally.
2001	From this year ASEAN Summits are held annually. ASEAN Telecommunications and IT Ministers Meeting (TELMIN) established.
2002	Framework Agreement on Comprehensive Economic Cooperation between ASEAN and China. This is the first of several such agreements with external partners. Subsequently, agreements have been entered into with Japan, India, South Korea, Australia and New Zealand.
2003	Ninth ASEAN Summit held in Bali. Adoption of the Declaration of ASEAN Concord II (Bali Concord II). Leaders declare their intention to establish an ASEAN Community consisting of three pillars: political and security cooperation,

economic cooperation and socio-cultural cooperation. Meeting of ASEAN Ministers Responsible for Culture and the Arts (AMCA) established.

2004 Tenth ASEAN Summit held in Vientiane; Protocol on Enhanced Dispute Settlement Mechanism adopted by the economic ministers. Vientiane Action Programme (designed to deepen economic integration and narrow the development gap) replaces the Hanoi Plan of Action. ASEAN Socio-Cultural Community Plan of Action and the ASEAN Security Community Plan of Action adopted, with a commitment to work towards the development of an ASEAN Charter. Legal unit in the ASEAN Secretariat set up. ASEAN Consultation to Solve Trade and Investment Issues (ACT) and the ASEAN Compliance Body (ACB) established.

2005 Eleventh ASEAN Summit held in Kuala Lumpur. ASEAN Heads of State/Government issue the Declaration on the Establishment of the ASEAN Charter. Eminent Persons Group (EPG) formed. ASEAN Ministerial Meeting on Minerals (AMMin) established.

2006 ASEAN Defence Ministers Meeting (ADMM) established.

2007 Twelfth ASEAN Summit held in Cebu in January 2007. Cebu Declaration on the Blueprint for the ASEAN Charter issued endorsing the Report of the Eminent Persons Group and setting up a High Level Task Force (HLTF) for Drafting of the ASEAN Charter. HLTF completes work on the Charter. Completed Charter presented to the Heads of State/Government at the Thirteenth ASEAN Summit in Singapore on 20 November 2007. ASEAN Economic Community Blueprint adopted.

2008 ASEAN Charter comes into force on 15 December 2008. Creation of the ASEAN Political-Security Community Council (APSC), the ASEAN Economic Community Council (AECC) and the Socio-Cultural Community Council (ASCC). ASEAN Coordinating Council (ACC) and Committee of Permanent Representatives (CPR) established.

2009	Declaration on the Roadmap for the ASEAN Community (2009–15) adopted at the Fourteenth ASEAN Summit in Cha-Am, Thailand. The Roadmap for an ASEAN Community replaces the Vientiane Action Programme. ASEAN Intergovernmental Commission on Human Rights (AICHR) established in October 2009 at the Fifteenth ASEAN Summit in Cha-Am, Thailand.
2010	Protocol to the ASEAN Charter on Dispute Settlement Mechanisms (the DSM Protocol) signed by the Foreign Ministers at the Sixteenth ASEAN Summit in Hanoi.
2011	Declaration on 'ASEAN Community in a Global Community of Nations' (Bali Concord III) issued at the Nineteenth ASEAN Summit in Bali.
2012	ASEAN Human Rights Declaration (AHRD) adopted by the ASEAN leaders at the Twenty-first ASEAN Summit in Phnom Penh, Cambodia.

The road to the ASEAN Charter[45]

The idea of a Charter for ASEAN was floated as early as 1974 at the Seventh ASEAN Ministerial Meeting in Jakarta.[46] Mr Carlos Romulo, the Secretary of Foreign Affairs of the Philippines, advanced a proposal for a Charter in order to 'institutionalise the function and structure of ASEAN'. The other members were not enthusiastic and referred the matter to the ASEAN Standing Committee,[47] where the idea languished for two decades. At the Kuala Lumpur informal summit in December 1997, Vision 2020 was promulgated on the occasion of the Thirtieth Anniversary of ASEAN. Vision 2020 pledged the creation of 'a stable, prosperous and highly competitive ASEAN Economic Region in which there is a free flow of goods, services and investments, a freer

---

45 Some material in this section has been used in other published works by the author, notably in Woon and Piris, *Towards a Rules-Based Community*.

46 Joint Communiqué of the Seventh ASEAN Ministerial Meeting, issued on 9 May 1974 in Jakarta, Indonesia, para 9.

47 The ASEAN Declaration provided for an annual meeting of Foreign Ministers, known as the ASEAN Ministerial Meeting (AMM). To support the work of the Foreign Ministers, a standing committee (the ASEAN Standing Committee or ASC) was also created, under the chairmanship of the Foreign Minister of the country hosting the AMM. Initially, this comprised the ambassadors to the host country of the next AMM.

flow of capital, equitable economic development and reduced poverty and socio-economic disparities' by the year 2020. Shortly after that the economic crisis hit ASEAN badly, severely damaging the regional economies. There was a political crisis in Indonesia, which led to the fall of President Soeharto and fears that the country might break up. The economic crisis of 1997 caused ASEAN's share of world GDP to fall from a peak of 4.2 per cent to 3.9 per cent in 1998[48] and its share of world trade declined from 6.5 per cent in 1997 to 5.5 per cent in 1998.[49] The fall in ASEAN's share of world inward foreign direct investment flows was even more drastic: from 7.0 per cent in 1997 to 3.1 per cent in 1998, to a low of 1.7 per cent in 2000.[50] In the meantime, China and later India were posing increasing competition to ASEAN, which until 1997 had been on the economic upswing.

Indonesia and ASEAN survived the economic and political crisis of 1997, but it was a severe jolt to the self-congratulatory mood in which the Thirtieth Anniversary had been celebrated. It was in a more sober frame of mind that the Sixth ASEAN Summit in Hanoi (December 1998) saw the launch of the Hanoi Action Plan to realise the Vision 2020. The Hanoi Action Plan envisaged a host of measures to strengthen macroeconomic and financial cooperation and enhance economic integration. Both the ASEAN Ministerial Meeting and ASEAN Economic Ministers Meeting[51] were involved in implementing the measures. A Special Joint Ministerial Meeting (JMM) among Economic, Finance and Foreign Ministers was convened at the Third Informal Summit (Manila, 1999) to discuss cross-sectoral coordination to aid the regional recovery process.[52] In 2001, following up from an idea mooted at the ASEAN Economic Ministers Meeting Retreat in Siem Reap, Cambodia, the Ministers agreed to commission a reputable international consultant to conduct an ASEAN Competitiveness Study.[53]

The interim report by McKinsey & Company was presented to the ASEAN leaders at the Eighth ASEAN Summit in Phnom Penh (November 2002) and

---

48 P. K. Wong and K. K. Ng, *The Competitiveness of ASEAN after the 1997 Asian Financial Crisis* (Singapore: Asia Competitveness Institute Monograph Series, Aug. 2008), Table 5.

49 Ibid., Table 7.

50 Ibid., Table 21.

51 At the First ASEAN Summit, 14 Feb. 1976 in Bali, Indonesia, the leaders agreed that the economic ministers would meet 'to consider measures to the taken to implement the Decisions of the [ASEAN Summit] on matters of economic cooperation.' ASEAN Economic Ministers Meetings (AEM) took place annually thereafter.

52 Joint Press Statement of the Thirty-first ASEAN Economic Ministers Meeting (AEM), issued on 30 Sept. 1999 in Singapore, para 39. The JMM did not become a regular feature of the ASEAN calendar, despite a call in the Chairman's Statement of the Ninth ASEAN Summit, 7 Oct. 2003 in Bali, Indonesia, that it should be revived.

53 Joint Press Statement of the Thirty-third ASEAN Economic Ministers Meeting, issued on 15 Sept. 2001 in Hanoi, Vietnam, para 12.

the final report was completed the following year. This report was considered by the High Level Task Force on ASEAN Economic Integration (HLTF-EI) in formulating its recommendations. At the Thirty-fifth ASEAN Economic Ministers Meeting in Phnom Penh in September 2003, the economic ministers approved the recommendation of the HLTF on ASEAN Economic Integration to formalise the ASEAN Economic Community (AEC) as the end-goal of ASEAN economic integration. ASEAN would become a single market and production base by 2020, characterised by the free flow of goods, services, investment and skilled labour and a freer flow of capital.[54]

The Ninth ASEAN Summit adopted the Declaration of ASEAN Concord II (also known as the Bali Concord II) in October 2003.[55] The Bali Concord II stated that an ASEAN Community would be established consisting of three pillars, viz, political and security cooperation, economic cooperation and socio-cultural cooperation. The ASEAN Political-Security Community (APSC)[56] was not meant to coordinate the foreign or defence policies of the member states. Indeed, it was explicitly recognised that member states had a 'sovereign right' to pursue individual foreign policies and defence arrangements. What was envisaged was closer cooperation in the political-security field. Similarly, the ASEAN Socio-Cultural Community (ASCC) was meant to foster social development and cultural cooperation. The meat was in the ASEAN Economic Community (AEC). The AEC envisaged economic integration of the economies of the member states by 2020. Integration

---

54 Joint Press Statement of the Thirty-fifth ASEAN Economic Ministers Meeting, issued on 4 Sept. 2003 in Phnom Penh, Cambodia, para 15. Subsequently, the deadline for the establishment of the ASEAN community was accelerated to 2015 at the Twelfth ASEAN Summit, 9–15 Jan. 2007 in Cebu, the Philippines. *See* the Cebu Declaration on the Acceleration of the Establishment of an ASEAN Community by 2015, signed on 13 Jan. 2007 in Cebu, the Philippines. Private sector businessmen have expressed scepticism about the realisation of this grand design; *see* for example, R. Sally, 'The ASEAN Charter and the ASEAN Economic Community: A Watershed for Regional Economic Integration?', E. Pedrosa, 'Implications of an Uncertain Global Economy on Integration Initiatives', and M. Hutagalung, 'ASEAN: An Integrated Market?', chapters 7–9 in Tiwari, ed., *Life After the Charter*. Although these articles were written in 2010, shortly after the entry into force of the Charter, similar doubts have repeatedly been expressed to the author by business leaders in the years leading up to the realisation of the ASEAN Economic Community. The private sector is not optimistic.

55 Declaration of ASEAN Concord II (Bali Concord II), signed on 7 Oct. 2003 by the leaders of the ASEAN member states in Bali, Indonesia.

56 This is referred in Bali Concord II as the ASEAN Security Community, abbreviated ASC. It was later realised that the acronym ASC had already been used for the ASEAN Standing Community. Furthermore, activities under this pillar encompassed political as well as security cooperation. In the ASEAN Charter, the ASEAN Security Community was redesignated as the ASEAN Political-Security Community or APSC. To avoid confusion, the abbreviation APSC will be used henceforward when referring to the (then) ASEAN Security Community.

meant creating a single market and production base and bridging the development gap between the ASEAN-6 and the CLMV countries. Adopted as annex to the Concord was a list of recommendations by the High Level Task Force on ASEAN Economic Integration, proposing the establishment of several bodies: a legal unit in the ASEAN Secretariat, the ASEAN Consultation to Solve Trade and Investment Issues (ACT), and the ASEAN Compliance Body (ACB).[57]

The Tenth ASEAN Summit in 2004 saw the signing of the Vientiane Action Programme (VAP) by the leaders. This replaced the Hanoi Plan of Action.[58] The VAP was a six-year plan designed to deepen economic integration and narrow the development gap between the older members and the CLMV countries. A Framework Agreement for Integration of Priority Sectors was also signed. In addition, the ASEAN Socio-Cultural Community Plan of Action and the ASEAN Security Community Plan of Action were adopted. Buried in the Annex to the latter was a commitment to work towards the development of an ASEAN Charter 'which will *inter alia* reaffirm ASEAN's goals and principles in inter-state relations, in particular the collective responsibilities of all ASEAN Member Countries in ensuring non-aggression and respect for each other's sovereignty and territorial integrity; the promotion and protection of human rights; the maintenance of political stability, regional peace and economic progress; and the establishment of effective and efficient institutional framework for ASEAN.'[59]

In fact, the ASEAN Charter idea had been presented to incoming Secretary-General Ong Keng Yong by senior staff of the ASEAN Secretariat when he took office in January 2003.[60] Malaysia subsequently proposed to reform the institutional framework of ASEAN in a paper entitled 'Review of ASEAN Institutional Framework: Proposals for Change' circulated at the Foreign Ministers' retreat in Ha Long Bay, Vietnam, in March 2004. It was recognised that the existing regime was political rather than legal. There was a lack of coordination, which could only get worse with the proliferation of ASEAN bodies and meetings. The ASEAN Secretariat put up a draft, which was a review of the institutional framework and highlighted the need for a

57 ACT and ACB were formally established by ASEAN Economic Ministers in 2004.

58 The VAP itself was replaced by the Roadmap for an ASEAN Community (2009–15), adopted on 1 Mar. 2009 by the Heads of State/Government at the Fourteenth ASEAN Summit in Cha-Am, Thailand.

59 Annex to the ASEAN Security Community Plan of Action, adopted on 29 Nov. 2004 by the Heads of State/Government in Vientane, Laos, para 2.

60 *See* C. Termsak Chalermpalanupap, 'In Defence of the ASEAN Charter', in Koh, Manalo and Woon, eds., *Making of the ASEAN Charter*, chapter 10, 121. Dr Termsak was a senior official of the ASEAN Secretariat for many years and served as Special Assistant to Secretary-General Ong Keng Yong.

legal personality for the organisation. The Senior Officials Meeting (SOM)[61] produced a draft charter for consideration of the Foreign Ministers. The following year, the ASEAN Ministerial Meeting agreed to work towards the promulgation of an ASEAN Charter which would 'reaffirm the objectives, goals and principles of the ASEAN Community'.[62] Reforming the institutional framework was a principal goal of this endeavour.

The ASEAN leaders issued the Declaration on the Establishment of the ASEAN Charter at the Eleventh ASEAN Summit held in Kuala Lumpur (December 2005). The declared aim of the Charter was to create the legal and institutional framework for ASEAN, which had hitherto been functioning on a totally informal basis. The Charter was also meant to 'codify all ASEAN norms, rules and values' and confer legal personality on ASEAN. To this end, an Eminent Persons Group (EPG) was set up and tasked with reimagining ASEAN as an organisation.[63] The EPG was enjoined to 'put forward bold and visionary recommendations' as well as undertake a thorough review of the ASEAN institutional framework and propose improvements.[64] Apart from institutional streamlining, the EPG was specifically asked to look into effective conflict resolution mechanisms.[65] The Secretary-General was to brief the EPG on ASEAN issues. Two senior staff members of the ASEAN Secretariat were assigned as resource persons. The EPG was given a year to produce its report.

The EPG held extensive consultations with ASEAN stakeholders, including the ASEAN Inter-Parliamentary Organisation (AIPO), the Working

---

61 In 1971 senior officials from the ministries of foreign affairs began meeting regularly at the ASEAN Senior Officials' Meeting (ASEAN SOM), a body which was not specifically created by any agreement but which evolved naturally. SOM was established to discuss political issues, especially sensitive ones, before submission to the ASEAN Ministerial Meeting. The SOM leader was generally the permanent secretary (or his equivalent in countries that did not adopt the British nomenclature) of the ministry.

62 Joint Communiqué of the Thirty-eighth ASEAN Ministerial Meeting, issued on 24–29 July 2005 in Vientiane, Laos, para 6.

63 The EPG consisted of the following: Pehin Dato Lim Jock Seng (Minister of Foreign Affairs and Trade II, Brunei); Dr Aun Porn Moniroth (Advisor to the Prime Minister and Chairman of the Supreme National Economic Council, Cambodia); Mr Ali Alatas (former Minister of Foreign Affairs, Indonesia); Mr Kamphan Simmalavong (Former Deputy Minister, Laos); Tan Sri Musa Hitam (former Deputy Prime Minister, Malaysia); Dr Than Nyun (Chairman of the Civil Service Selection and Training Board, Myanmar); Mr Fidel Ramos (Former President, Philippines); Professor S Jayakumar (Deputy Prime Minister, Singapore); Mr Kasemsamosorn Kasemsri (former Deputy Prime Minister and Minister of Foreign Affairs, Thailand); Mr Nguyen Manh Cam (former Deputy Prime Minister and Minister of Foreign Affairs, Vietnam).

64 Terms of Reference of the Eminent Persons Group (EPG) on the ASEAN Charter, para 3.

65 Ibid., para 4.2(i).

Group for an ASEAN Human Rights Mechanism, ASEAN Institutes of Strategic and International Studies (ASEAN-ISIS), civil society organisations, ASEAN Chambers of Commerce and Industry (ASEAN-CCI) and the private sector. The EPG met eight times over the course of the year. They also made a visit to Brussels to study the experience of the European Union. At the second EPG meeting Mr Ali Alatas of Indonesia produced a paper containing a draft of the ASEAN Charter. He wanted the EPG to draft the charter itself, but the other EPG members disagreed. Their report was ready for presentation at the Twelfth ASEAN Summit, which was scheduled to be held in Cebu, the Philippines, in December 2006. As it happened, the Cebu Summit was postponed on account of a threatened typhoon. It took place finally in January 2007. The Eminent Persons Group Report stated that the ultimate goal was the formation of an ASEAN Union.[66] The EPG also recommended that ASEAN as an organisation should have legal personality.[67] However, the EPG recognised that ASEAN's main problem was not lack of vision; the main problem was following up on the grand declarations, plans of action and roadmaps. This lack of follow-up was a constant refrain in meetings with ASEAN officials. The EPG stated baldly that 'ASEAN must establish a culture of honouring and implementing its decisions and agreements, and carrying them out on time'.[68] To remedy the deficiency in carrying out commitments, the EPG recommended the establishment of dispute settlement mechanisms in all fields of ASEAN cooperation, including monitoring and enforcement mechanisms.[69]

---

[66] Report of the Eminent Persons Group on the ASEAN Charter, para 23. Although the Report was endorsed by the ASEAN leaders, there was little enthusiasm for the creation of such a Union. This was an initiative of the Philippines. In drafting the Charter, no reference was made to the idea of an ASEAN Union.

[67] Ibid., para 43. *See now* Article 3 of the ASEAN Charter. The concern of the drafters of the Charter was to make clear that ASEAN was to have a legal personality in the domestic law of the member states.

[68] Report of the Eminent Persons Group on the ASEAN Charter, para 44. This remains a matter of concern even now; in conversation with this author, this issue was repeatedly raised by ASEAN officials and former Secretaries-General.

[69] Ibid., Executive Summary, para 6.

Drafting the ASEAN Charter[70]

The Cebu Declaration on the Blueprint for the ASEAN Charter[71] endorsed the Report of the Eminent Persons Group (EPG) and set up a High Level Task Force (HLTF) for Drafting of the ASEAN Charter. The leaders' endorsement of the EPG report as a basis for the new Charter was however supplemented by instructions to draft the ASEAN Charter based on the 'directions given at the Eleventh and Twelfth ASEAN Summits, the relevant ASEAN documents, together with the EPG recommendations.'[72] The HLTF was given until ASEAN's Fortieth Anniversary Summit in November 2007 to finish its task – less than the time the EPG had to formulate its 'bold and visionary' recommendations.

The representatives appointed to the HLTF were senior officials from the Ministries of Foreign Affairs of ASEAN member states.[73] In most cases, the delegation leaders were selected for their experience with ASEAN as long-serving representatives in the Senior Officials Meeting or as Directors-General in the ASEAN Standing Committee. This was an advantage in that many of the HLTF members were known to one another because of their interactions on the ASEAN circuit.[74] The HLTF reported at intervals to the ASEAN Foreign Ministers. The negotiations were driven by the foreign

---

[70] In writing this section, the author has relied substantially on his own experiences as Alternate Member of the High Level Task Force (HLTF) for Drafting of the ASEAN Charter. The author became leader of the Singapore delegation in the later part of the process when Singapore's HLTF member Ambassdor Tommy Koh took over the chairmanship Ambassdor Koh's record of the HLTF process may be found in T. Koh, 'The Negotiating Process', in Koh, Manalo and Woon, eds., *Making of the ASEAN Charter*, chapter 5.

[71] Issued at the Twelfth ASEAN Summit, 13 Jan. 2007 in Cebu, the Philippines.

[72] 2007 Cebu Declaration on the Blueprint of an ASEAN Charter, adopted on 13 Jan. 2007 in Cebu, the Philippines, para 2.

[73] The members of the HLTF were: Pengiran Dato Paduka Osman Patra (Permanent Secretary, Ministry of Foreign Affairs and Trade, Brunei); Dr Kao Kim Hourn (Secretary of State, Ministry of Foreign Affairs and International Cooperation, Cambodia); Mr Dian Triansyah Djani (Director-General, ASEAN-Indonesia, Department of Foreign Affairs, Indonesia); Mr Bounkeut Sangsomsak (Deputy Minister, Ministry of Foreign Affairs, Laos); Tan Sri Ahmad Fuzi Haji Abdul Razak (Ambassador-at-large, Malaysia); U Aung Bwa (Director-General, ASEAN-Myanmar, Ministry of Foreign Affairs, Myanmar); Ambassador Rosario Manalo (Special Envoy, Department of Foreign Affairs, Philippines); Ambassador Tommy Koh (Ambassador-at-large, Singapore) [in addition, Ambassador Walter Woon (Solicitor-General, Singapore) functioned as alternate member of the HLTF and Singapore delegation leader when Ambassador Koh took over the Chairmanship of the HLTF from Ambassador Manalo]; Khun Sihasak Phuangketkeow (Deputy Permanent Secretary, Ministry of Foreign Affairs, Thailand) [Khun Pradap Pibulsonggram (Deputy Permanent Secretary, Ministry of Foreign Affairs, Thailand) replaced Khun Sihasak in Mar. 2007]; Mr Nguyen Trung Thanh (Assistant Minister, Ministry of Foreign Affairs, Vietnam) [he was replaced by Mr Pham Quang Vinh in Sept. 2007].

[74] *See* P. Pibulsonggram, 'The Thai Perspective' and T. T. Nguyen, 'The Making of the ASEAN Charter in my Fresh Memories', in Koh, Manalo and Woon, eds., *Making of the ASEAN Charter*, chapters 7 and 8, 87–100.

ministries, with the legal agencies playing a subordinate supporting role. In contrast to the members of the EPG (who were appointed in their private capacities), the members of the HLTF were bound by instructions from the Foreign Ministers.[75] They were there to represent national interests and not to go boldly when none had gone before. It was clear throughout the Charter-drafting process that *realpolitik* rather than legal principle would be the paramount consideration.

While a number of delegations were accompanied by legal experts from either their foreign ministries or their legal agencies, most HLTF delegation leaders were from a diplomatic rather than a legal background. Delegations from some member states did not have the resources to have a legal expert present at every meeting. This caused delays as these countries were obliged to refer negotiated text back to their capitals at the end of each meeting, sometimes reverting with instructions to reopen sections that had been agreed on at prior sessions. On several occasions, there were problems in agreeing on interpretations of common terms in the English language - a consequence of the fact that most ASEAN countries do not use English as an official language.[76] The mix of civil law and common law traditions was a further complication. Later in the process, an Assistants' Group was established to 'scrub' the text and put it in a proper legal form; even then the going was hard on account of linguistic problems. Drafting legal documents is a specialist skill. The HLTF did not have a proper legal drafting group to manage the task, which is why one finds that the finished Charter is not quite a paragon of clarity or coherence. The HLTF would have benefited greatly from the assistance of a group of officials trained in international law and fluent in English for both advice on legal matters as well as on drafting. Fortunately, there were members of certain HLTF delegations and officials from the ASEAN Secretariat who had sufficient legal expertise and linguistic competence to sort things out.[77] Nonetheless, the Charter-drafting process is illustrative of the ad hoc nature of rule-making in ASEAN.

The first informal HLTF meeting took place on 13 January 2007 at the sidelines of the Cebu Summit. All ten HLTF members were present. It was agreed that the goal was to have a draft ready for presentation to the Fortieth

---

[75] *See* Koh, 'The Negotiating Process', in Koh, Manalo and Woon, eds., *Making of the ASEAN Charter,* chapter 5, 51. Ambassador Koh was the Chairman of the HLTF in the latter half of 2007, taking over from the Philippine Chair.

[76] This is corroborated by Vietnamese HLTF member T. T. Nguyen, in 'The Making of the ASEAN Charter in my Fresh Memories', in Koh, Manalo and Woon, eds., Making of the ASEAN Charter, chapter 8,102.

[77] Significant contributions were made by ASEAN Secretary-General Ong Keng Yong (trained as a lawyer, although he spent his career in the diplomatic service), as well as the Malaysian, Filipino, Singaporean and Thai delegations.

ASEAN Ministerial Meeting, scheduled for 31 July 2007 in Manila. That gave the HLTF barely six months to complete the first cut. This was a real challenge. Dreaming dreams and having visions was one thing; translating them into concrete terms was quite another. As Dr Termsak Chalermpalanupap put it: '[The] EPG members were not concerned about how to implement what they recommended ... The drafters, on the other hand, were fully aware of the need to ensure implementation of and compliance with every provision in the Charter. They would be held responsible if they put in something that turned out to be too idealistic and impracticable.'[78] It should be remembered that when negotiations on drafting the Charter were begun in January 2007, ASEAN as an organisation of ten member states was not even eight years old. Now the HLTF was being asked to fundamentally change the structure into a tighter, less informal organisation. The ASEAN Secretariat was requested to produce a draft outline of the Charter based on the EPG report and the 2005 Senior Officials' Meeting draft charter.

Work formally began at the first HLTF meeting in Jakarta (5–6 February 2007), under the Chairmanship of Ambassador Rosario Manalo of the Philippines. The HLTF met with EPG chairman Tan Sri Musa Hitam (Malaysia) and EPG members Dr Aun Porn Moniroth (Cambodia) and Mr Kamphan Simmalavong (Laos). Tan Sri Musa briefed the HLTF on areas where the EPG might have gone further, for example, an ASEAN Parliament, a Court of Justice and a Human Rights Commission. None of these were subsequently accepted by the HLTF. The proposed Human Rights Commission in particular proved sensitive right from the start.

Most of the first session was spent in establishing the *modus operandi*. A suggestion that the work of drafting the Charter could be split up and assigned to the various national delegations was rejected. It was decided that the whole HLTF would work on the Charter together, considering clause by clause the draft put up by the ASEAN Secretariat. The result was that the drafting process proceeded much less quickly than might have otherwise been the case had there been a neutral legally trained drafting group. Negotiations began slowly as the members of the HLTF got the measure of each other. Later, as friendship and confidence grew things speeded up, even though delegations stoutly defended national positions.[79] It is a tribute to

---

[78] *See* Termsak, 'In Defence of the ASEAN Charter', in Koh, Manalo and Woon, eds., *Making of the ASEAN Charter*, chapter 10, 124. Dr Termsak was a senior official of the Secretariat for many years and served as resource person to both the EPG and HLTF.

[79] *See* for example, Myanmar HLTF member U Aung Bwa's comments in his chapter 'The Jewel in my Crown', in Koh, Manalo and Woon, eds., *Making of the ASEAN Charter*, chapter 3, 31. Malaysian HLTF member Tan Sri Ahmad Fuzi bin Abdul Razak also alludes to this in his chapter 'Facing Unfair Criticisms', chapter 2, 21 of the same book.

the patience and diplomatic skill of both Chairpersons – Ambassador Rosario Manalo of the Philippines and Ambassador Tommy Koh of Singapore – that the HLTF was able to complete its work without dissolving into acrimony.

At the first meeting there was discussion of the proposal for an ASEAN Union, which had figured in the EPG Report as a long-term objective.[80] Most members were against the idea. Based on the HLTF's mandate in the Cebu Declaration on the Blueprint of The ASEAN Charter[81] and the notes of the discussions of the Heads of State/Government on the EPG report, it was unclear whether the ASEAN Summit had unequivocally instructed this to be included in the Charter. Concerns were expressed about ASEAN becoming a supranational organisation rather than an intergovernmental one. This concern formed a constant *leitmotiv* during the rest of the Charter-drafting process. Shared sovereignty in the European Union style was never on the agenda. For the young states of Southeast Asia, any erosion of their hard-won sovereignty was not something that could or would be easily accepted.[82]

The second HLTF meeting took place in Siem Reap on 28 February and 1 March 2007. The skeleton of the Charter was agreed upon. Discussion on the Human Rights Commission continued at the insistence of certain delegations, with several other delegations expressing reservations. The HLTF meeting was followed by a Foreign Ministers' Retreat in Siem Reap (1–2 March). Some of the thorny issues that could not be resolved by the HLTF were put to the Foreign Ministers. The Foreign Ministers instructed that suspension, expulsion and withdrawal from ASEAN should not be included in the Charter. Consensus would remain the basic mode of decision making. However, the Foreign Ministers recognised that there would be practical difficulties in achieving a consensus to expel a member, even for an egregious breach of the Charter, and instructed the HLTF to provide an option for the leaders to decide how specific decisions could be made. The Foreign Ministers also agreed to drop any reference to an ASEAN Union. This was a matter to be decided by the leaders at a future time. Significantly, instructions were given that a draft article on a Human Rights organ (though not necessarily a commission, as suggested by some) should be prepared for the Ministers' consideration. It

---

80 Report of the Eminent Persons' Group on the ASEAN Charter, 19, para 23. The ASEAN Union was not mentioned in the body of the draft Charter proposed in the report.

81 Adopted on 13 Jan. 2007 by the Heads of State/Government in Cebu, the Philippines.

82 ASEAN Secretary-General Ong Keng Yong commented that national egos remain strong and bureaucratic agencies in member countries are 'reluctant to commit to region-wide initiatives for fear of losing their national independence of action'; *see* 'At Close Quarters with the Drafting of the ASEAN Charter', in Koh, Manalo and Woon, eds., *Making of the ASEAN Charter*, chapter 10, 108. In chapter 11, 140 of the same book, Indonesian HLTF member Dian Triansyah Djani states that 'the fear of losing an inch of sovereignty and the suspicions of one's neighbour still linger on'.

was also agreed that the dispute settlement provisions should provide an enabling provision for the establishment of new mechanisms, and that the HLTF could make reference to the UN Charter mechanisms for resolution of disputes. At the same meeting, the Foreign Ministers also gave instructions on the nomenclature of ASEAN bodies and decision-making principles. They further instructed that the Charter need not go into specific provisions for resource mobilisation such as the EPG proposal for a Special Fund.[83]

Substantive work on the draft Charter only began with the third meeting in Manila on 28–29 March 2007. Khun Pradap Pibulsonggram took over as Thailand's HLTF member from Khun Sihasak Phuangketkeow. The Preamble and first two articles were settled, an indication of the slow pace of work at the start.[84] A dialogue with non-governmental organisations was held.

At the fourth meeting in Yangon on 9 April 2007 the HLTF met with the High Level Task Force on ASEAN Economic Integration (HLTF-EI),[85] who wanted a stronger commitment to economic integration. Their major concern was that there was neither prompt compliance with economic agreements nor effective implementation. The HLTF-EI wanted the ASEAN minus X formula[86] and the Vientiane Protocol on Enhanced Dispute Settlement Mechanism[87] enshrined in the Charter. Despite the fact that economic integration is probably the key factor in creating an ASEAN community, some of the HLTF members lacked empathy with their colleagues from the economic ministries, as noted by Ambassador Tommy Koh of Singapore.[88]

The fifth meeting took place in Hanoi on 19–20 April. The Chapters on legal personality, membership, decision making and immunities and privileges were considered. The ASEAN Secretariat presented a paper on the proposed organisational structure of ASEAN in preparation for work on Chapter IV, dealing with Organs.

---

[83] Malaysian HLTF member Tan Sri Ahmad Fuzi bin Abdul Razak stated 'many within the HLTF itself were unhappy with its inability to achieve a consensus on this': *see* 'Facing Unfair Criticisms', in Koh, Manalo and Woon, eds., *Making of the ASEAN Charter*, chapter 2, 22.

[84] This was due in a large part to the fact that some HLTF members would insist on reopening text that had been previously agreed. *See* Koh, 'The Negotiating Process', in Koh, Manalo and Woon, eds., *Making of the ASEAN Charter*, chapter 5, 56. This problem would bedevil the negotiation process throughout.

[85] The HLTF on Economic Integration comprises the permanent secretaries of the trade agencies of ASEAN member states, who are also the members of the ASEAN Senior Economic Officials Meeting.

[86] This is now Article 21(2).

[87] *See now* Article 24(3).

[88] *See* Koh, 'The Negotiating Process', 56, 65–6. Ambassador Koh speculated that 'this could have been due to the fact that in some ASEAN countries, coordination between them [viz, the foreign ministries and the economic ministries] is not optimal and there is also considerable rivalry between them'.

The Hanoi meeting was followed by the sixth meeting in Penang on 17–19 May. It was in Penang that the provisions on dispute settlement were finalised. Several delegations presented drafts, which were combined and rationalised. Mindful of the Foreign Ministers' instructions, explicit reference was made to the UN Charter dispute settlement mechanisms. The creation of a proper dispute settlement mechanism was one of the key recommendations of the Eminent Persons Group that the HLTF took up at this meeting.

The seventh meeting was held in Bali from 25–28 June 2007. A start was made on the organisational architecture of ASEAN. The system was to be streamlined. To realise the ASEAN Community, councils for each of the pillars had to be set up. A central coordinating council was also necessary. A Committee of Permanent Representatives was to be established, comprising Permanent Representatives of the member states, based in Jakarta. There was a dialogue session with the heads of the national human rights institutions of Indonesia, Malaysia, the Philippines and Thailand, as well as the Chairman of the ASEAN Human Rights Mechanism Working Group.[89] The Terms of Reference of the Human Rights 'Mechanism' were also discussed by the HLTF. Some delegations pushed for a Human Rights Commission. Others were uncomfortable with the whole idea. The term 'mechanism' was therefore adopted as a compromise.

At the next meeting in Manila on 26 July 2007 the first draft of the Charter was settled for presentation to the Foreign Ministers at the Fortieth ASEAN Ministerial Meeting (29–30 July 2007). Consensus could not be reached on the prickly question of the human rights organ. Cambodia, Laos, Myanmar and Vietnam opposed the creation of a Human Rights Commission, while Indonesia and Thailand pushed for one. Brunei, Malaysia the Philippines and Singapore were caught between the two camps.[90] The guidance of the Foreign Ministers was again sought. The ministers themselves were divided. The ministers from the Philippines, Indonesia, Malaysia and Singapore rejected the formula that the HLTF had put to them as being weaker than the instructions given at the Foreign Ministers' Retreat in Siem Reap in March. A counter-proposal from the Philippines, supported by Indonesia, Malaysia and Thailand, was rejected by Cambodia, Laos, Myanmar and Vietnam.[91]

---

[89] Viz, Mr Marzuki Darusman, a member of the Indonesian parliament and former Attorney-General. Pak Marzuki subsequently chaired a Special Committee of the Indonesian Parliament to consider ratification of the Charter: *see* Djani, 'A Long Journey', in Koh, Manalo and Woon, eds., *Making of the ASEAN Charter*, chapter 11,148.

[90] *See* Koh, 'The Negotiating Process', 58–9. Ambassador Koh took over as Chairman of the HLTF after this meeting.

[91] Secretary-General Ong Keng Yong noted that the CLMV countries 'stamped their own imprimatur' on the Charter. *See* 'At Close Quarters with the Drafting of the ASEAN Charter', in Koh, Manalo and Woon, eds., *Making of the ASEAN Charter*, chapter 9, 113. Cambodian

There were heated exchanges on the subject.[92] Secretary-General Ong Keng Yong suggested a compromise form of words for Article 14, which was finally agreed to by the Ministers. It was instructed that the Terms of Reference of the Human Rights Body, as it came to be called, would be submitted by the HLTF but need not be included in the Charter.[93] The ministers also instructed that the principle of rejecting 'undemocratic and unconstitutional changes of government' (which had been recommended by the Eminent Persons Group) should be replaced with a reference to the principles of democracy and constitutional government.

At the ninth meeting in Singapore from 24–26 August 2007 Ambassador Tommy Koh of Singapore took over the Chairmanship of the HLTF. Ambassador Koh announced that he would sit apart from his national delegation. The role of HLTF member and delegation leader for Singapore was taken over by this author.[94] Discussion was focused on the organisational structure of ASEAN, which had already been considered at the previous meetings in Bali and Manila. The final shape of the organs of ASEAN was settled. It was decided not to 'hard-code' the function and composition of the organs in the Charter so as to allow them to evolve naturally.

The tenth meeting took place in Chiang Mai from 10–14 September. The new HLTF member from Vietnam, Mr Pham Quang Vinh, took over from Mr Nguyen Trung Thanh. This meeting proved to be the most contentious. The negotiations almost broke down at one point as delegations could not agree on the role and Terms of Reference (TOR) of the Human Rights Body (as it had become known by this time). Cambodia, Laos, Myanmar and Vietnam insisted that the TOR be settled together with the Charter. If this could not be done, then there could be no agreement on the Charter as a whole. The Philippines, Indonesia, Malaysia and Thailand disagreed to even have this placed on the meeting agenda. As for the role of the Human Rights Body, some delegations wanted it to have a monitoring function while others were vehemently opposed, insisting that it be consultative only. The Singapore Chair shuttled between the various delegations seeking to broker a compromise.[95] In the end agreement was reached on a form of words for clause 2 of Article 14. This stated that the Terms of Reference would be determined by the Foreign

---

HLTF member Dr Kao Kim Hourn admitted at p. 153 of the same book that the HLTF was split between the 'old members' and 'new members' on the issue of human rights.

92 *See* Koh, 'The Negotiating Process', in Koh, Manalo and Woon, eds., *Making of the ASEAN Charter*, chapter 5, 59.

93 Following the eighth HLTF meeting the ASEAN Secretariat prepared a non-paper on the Terms of Reference of the Human Rights Body.

94 *See* Koh, 'The Negotiating Process', 61.

95 *See* Koh, 'The Negotiating Process' and Pibulsonggram, 'The Thai Perspective', 63, 89–90 in Koh, Manalo and Woon, eds., *Making of the ASEAN Charter*, chapter 5 and 7.

Ministers. It was agreed as a compromise that the Terms of Reference of the Human Rights Body need not be finalised before completion of the Charter. Guidance was to be sought from the Foreign Ministers as to who should settle the Terms of Reference for the Human Rights Body. The ASEAN Secretariat updated its non-paper on the Terms of Reference of the Human Rights Body for further discussion.

The next meeting of the HLTF took place in New York on 26 September 2007, the main focus being the preparation of a third progress report and draft Charter to be submitted to the Foreign Ministers on 27 September. At the informal ASEAN Ministerial Meeting that followed, the laboriously negotiated wording of Article 14(2) was accepted. The Foreign Ministers were divided over the role of the Human Rights Body but nonetheless gave instructions to the HLTF to draft the Terms of Reference (TOR), to be completed if possible in conjunction with the finalisation of the Charter. If that could not be done before the November ASEAN Summit, it would remain a work-in-progress.

It was finally agreed at the twelfth HLTF meeting in Bandar Seri Begawan from 3-5 October that the Terms of Reference of the Human Rights Body would be taken up after the completion of the Charter. The text of the Charter was 'scrubbed' by the legal assistants to the HLTF on the understanding that changes to the wording would be kept to an absolute minimum so as to avoid having to reopen discussion.

The final meeting of the HLTF took place in Vientiane from 18-20 October. As the HLTF had been working on the basis that 'nothing is agreed until everything is agreed' there was a rush to tie up all the loose ends before the deadline.[96] The HLTF was fully conscious that the Charter had to be completed in time for the Thirteenth ASEAN Summit in November. Work carried on literally until midnight on the last day of the HLTF meeting, when the Charter was finally settled.

The completed Charter was presented to the ASEAN Foreign Ministers and Heads of State/Government for signing at the Thirteenth ASEAN Summit in Singapore on 20 November 2007.[97] It came into force on 15 December 2008, one month after the last instrument of ratification was delivered to the Secretary-General by Thailand.

---

[96] *See* Koh, 'The Negotiating Process', in Koh, Manalo and Woon, eds., *Making of the ASEAN Charter,* chapter 5, 65-6.

[97] This author had the honour of doing so as leader of the Singapore delegation and alternate HLTF member, in the absence of HLTF Chairman Ambassador Tommy Koh.

COMMENTARY

2007 CHARTER OF THE ASSOCIATION OF SOUTHEAST ASIAN NATIONS

PREAMBLE

The initial draft of the Preamble was prepared by the ASEAN Secretariat for the first meeting of the HLTF in Jakarta, 5-6 February 2007. After this meeting redrafts of the Preamble, objectives and principles were received from Malaysia, Vietnam, Thailand and Laos. A second draft was presented at the second HLTF meeting in Siem Reap, 28 February-1 March 2007. The Preamble was finalised only at the third HLTF meeting in Manila, 28-9 March 2007. This is indicative of the slow pace of negotiations at the start of the process, as members of the HLTF gradually got the measure of their colleagues. Things speeded up as the comfort level grew.

WE, THE PEOPLES of the Member States of the Association of Southeast Asian Nations (ASEAN), as represented by the Heads of State or Government of Brunei Darussalam, the Kingdom of Cambodia, the Republic of Indonesia, the Lao People's Democratic Republic, Malaysia, the Union of Myanmar, the Republic of the Philippines, the Republic of Singapore, the Kingdom of Thailand and the Socialist Republic of Viet Nam;

The Charter is the first ASEAN document expressly adopted by the ASEAN Heads of State/Government on behalf of the peoples of the member states of ASEAN. Compare the Charter of the United Nations, the Preamble of which also starts with 'we the people of the United Nations'. The UN Charter's Preamble is shorter and less verbose.

See Article 4 listing the member states of ASEAN. Article 5 sets out the rights and obligations of the member states. Article 6 makes provision for admission of new members.

NOTING with satisfaction the significant achievements and expansion of ASEAN since its establishment in Bangkok through the promulgation of The ASEAN Declaration;

The ASEAN Declaration (also known as the Bangkok Declaration) was signed in Bangkok on 8 August 1967 by the Foreign Ministers of Indonesia (Mr Adam Malik), Malaysia (Tun Abdul Razak, who was Deputy Prime Minister rather than Foreign Minister), the Philippines (Mr Narciso Ramos), Singapore (Mr S Rajaratnam) and Thailand (Mr Thanat Khoman). The Heads of State/Government were not involved.

RECALLING the decisions to establish an ASEAN Charter in the Vientiane Action Programme, the Kuala Lumpur Declaration on the Establishment of the ASEAN Charter and the Cebu Declaration on the Blueprint of the ASEAN Charter;

The Vientiane Action Programme (VAP) was signed by the leaders of the ASEAN member states at the Tenth ASEAN Summit held in Vientiane, Laos, in November 2004. The ASEAN Security Community Plan of Action was also adopted. In the Annex to the Plan of Action was a commitment to work towards the development of an ASEAN Charter 'which will *inter alia* reaffirm ASEAN's goals and principles in inter-state relations, in particular the collective responsibilities of all ASEAN Member Countries in ensuring non-aggression and respect for each other's sovereignty and territorial integrity; the promotion and protection of human rights; the maintenance of political stability, regional peace and economic progress; and the establishment of effective and efficient institutional framework for ASEAN'.[1]

The Declaration on the Establishment of the ASEAN Charter was issued at the Eleventh ASEAN Summit held in Kuala Lumpur (December 2005). The declared aim of the Charter was to create the legal and institutional framework for ASEAN, which had hitherto been functioning on an informal basis. The Charter was also meant to 'codify all ASEAN norms, rules and values' and confer legal personality on ASEAN. To this end, an Eminent Persons Group (EPG) was set up and tasked with reimagining ASEAN as an organisation.[2] The EPG was enjoined to 'put forward bold

[1] ASEAN Security Community Plan of Action 2004, adopted 29 Nov. 2004 in Vientiane, Laos, Annex, para 1.2.1.

[2] The EPG consisted of the following: Pehin Dato Lim Jock Seng (Minister of Foreign Affairs and Trade II, Brunei); Dr Aun Porn Moniroth (Advisor to the Prime Minister and

and visionary recommendations' as well as undertake a thorough review of the ASEAN institutional framework and propose improvements.[3] Apart from institutional streamlining, the EPG was specifically asked to look into effective conflict resolution mechanisms.[4] The Cebu Declaration on the Blueprint of the ASEAN Charter[5] endorsed the Report of the EPG on the ASEAN Charter and established the High Level Task Force to complete drafting the ASEAN Charter by the Thirteenth ASEAN Summit in Singapore in November 2007.

MINDFUL of the existence of mutual interests and interdependence among the peoples and Member States of ASEAN which are bound by geography, common objectives and shared destiny;

The ASEAN Declaration of 1967[6] was the first ASEAN instrument to make reference to the mutual interests and interdependence of the member countries, as well as the ties of history and culture. This was reiterated in the first preambular paragraph of the 1976 Treaty of Amity and Cooperation in Southeast Asia.

INSPIRED by and united under One Vision, One Identity and One Caring and Sharing Community;

The ASEAN motto is 'one vision, one identity, one community', which was the theme of the Eleventh ASEAN Summit held in Kuala Lumpur in December 2005: *see* Article 36. The reference to a caring and sharing community reflects the Cebu Declaration Towards a Caring and Sharing Community issued at the Twelfth ASEAN Summit in Cebu, the Philippines,

---

Chairman of the Supreme National Economic Council, Cambodia); Mr Ali Alatas (former Minister of Foreign Affairs, Indonesia); Mr Kamphan Simmalavong (Former Deputy Minister, Laos); Tan Sri Musa Hitam (former Deputy Prime Minister, Malaysia); Dr Than Nyun (Chairman of the Civil Service Selection and Training Board, Myanmar); Mr Fidel Ramos (Former President, Philippines); Professor S Jayakumar (Deputy Prime Minister, Singapore); Mr Kasemsamosorn Kasemsri (former Deputy Prime Minister and Minister of Foreign Affairs, Thailand); Mr Nguyen Manh Cam (former Deputy Prime Minister and Minister of Foreign Affairs, Vietnam).

[3] Terms of Reference of the Eminent Persons Group on the ASEAN Charter, adopted at the First Meeting of the EPG on the ASEAN Charter, 12–13 Dec. 2005 in Kuala Lumpur, Malaysia, para 3.

[4] Terms of Reference of the Eminent Persons Group on the ASEAN Charter, adopted at the First Meeting of the EPG on the ASEAN Charter, 12–13 Dec. 2005 in Kuala Lumpur, Malaysia, para 4.2(i).

[5] Issued at the Twelfth ASEAN Summit in Cebu, the Philippines, on 13 Jan. 2007.

[6] Signed in Bangkok on 8 Aug. 1967 by the Foreign Ministers of the five original member countries.

on 13 January 2007. A reference to a community of caring societies appears in the ASEAN Vision 2020, issued at the Second ASEAN Informal Summit in Kuala Lumpur on 15 December 1997.

UNITED by a common desire and collective will to live in a region of lasting peace, security and stability, sustained economic growth, shared prosperity and social progress, and to promote our vital interests, ideals and aspirations;

Note Article 1(1), which states the first purpose of ASEAN is to maintain and enhance peace, security and stability in the region. This theme of promoting peace, security and stability is a recurring motif of ASEAN instruments from the 1967 ASEAN Declaration[7] and 1976 Treaty of Amity and Cooperation in Southeast Asia.[8] The ASEAN Human Rights Declaration[9] (AHRD) contains a right to 'enjoy peace within an ASEAN framework of security and stability, neutrality and freedom'; *see* Article 38 of the AHRD.

RESPECTING the fundamental importance of amity and cooperation, and the principles of sovereignty, equality, territorial integrity, non-interference, consensus and unity in diversity;

The 1976 Treaty of Amity and Cooperation in Southeast Asia (TAC)[10] is one of the key instruments of ASEAN. Article 2(a) of the TAC declares that 'mutual respect for the independence, sovereignty, equality, territorial integrity and national identity of all nations' is a fundamental guiding principle. This principle is reiterated in Article 2(2)(a) of the Charter.

The fundamental principle of non-interference in the internal affairs of the member states as an ASEAN principle appears for the first time in the preamble of the 1971 Zone of Peace, Freedom and Neutrality Declaration and is subsequently repeated in Article 2(c) of the 1976 Treaty of Amity and Cooperation in Southeast Asia. *See* also Article 2(2)(e) of the Charter, where the principle is again emphasised. This may be seen as

---

7 Signed by the Foreign Ministers on 8 Aug. 1967 in Bangkok, *see* para 2(2).

8 Signed by the Foreign Ministers on 24 Feb. 1976 in Bali, *see* Article 1 (entered into force 21 June 1976).

9 Adopted by the Heads of State/Government at the Twenty-first ASEAN Summit in Phnom Penh, Cambodia, on 18 Nov. 2012.

10 Signed at the First ASEAN Summit in Bali on 24 Feb. 1976 by the Heads of State/Government of the original five member states. Accession to the TAC was a necessary step in order to join ASEAN before the Charter came into force. Other non-ASEAN states may also accede to the TAC without joining the organisation.

one of the core principles of ASEAN. Given the historical circumstances surrounding the birth of ASEAN in 1967 (*see* 'A Short History of ASEAN', p.), it is understandable that the member states are extremely wary of interference in their internal affairs by outsiders.

Consensus is the principle on which all ASEAN decisions are taken; *see* now Article 20(1) of the Charter. This is the only practical way of holding such a diverse grouping together. Any alternative system of voting based on population or size of the economy is unlikely to commend itself to the smaller member states.

The phrase 'unity in diversity' is a nod in the direction of Indonesia, being the translation of the Javanese phrase 'Bhinneka Tunggal Ika', the motto of the Republic of Indonesia inscribed on its coat of arms.

ADHERING to the principles of democracy, the rule of law and good governance, respect for and protection of human rights and fundamental freedoms;

Democracy, rule of law and good governance are constant themes repeated in the Charter. Article 1(7) states that one of the purposes of ASEAN is to 'strengthen democracy, enhance good governance and the rule of law, and to promote and protect human rights and fundamental freedoms'. One again finds reference to 'adherence to the rule of law, good governance, the principles of democracy and constitutional government' in Article 2(2)(h) and 'respect for fundamental freedoms, the promotion and protection of human rights and the promotion of social justice' in Article 2(2)(i). The constant repetition of these themes may not be elegant drafting but it was a conscious decision on the part of the HLTF to do so.

The ASEAN commitment to human rights and fundamental freedoms is now to be found in the ASEAN Human Rights Declaration[11] (AHRD). These are set out in Articles 10 to 32 of the AHRD. Note also AHRD Article 38, which states that there is a right to 'enjoy peace within an ASEAN framework of security and stability, neutrality and freedom'. The member states also affirm all the rights and freedoms contained in the Universal Declaration of Human Rights: *see* AHRD, Preamble, Articles 10 and 26.

See also Article 14 on the ASEAN Human Rights Body (now known as the ASEAN Intergovernmental Commission on Human Rights).

---

[11] Adopted by the Heads of State/Government at the Twenty-first ASEAN Summit in Phnom Penh, Cambodia, on 18 Nov. 2012.

RESOLVED to ensure sustainable development for the benefit of present and future generations and to place the well-being, livelihood and welfare of the peoples at the centre of the ASEAN community building process;

Promotion of sustainable development is one of the purposes of ASEAN: Article 1(9). The ASEAN Socio-Cultural Community Blueprint[12] sets out the elements of the plan to promote sustainable development and environmental protection. The right to development is proclaimed to be an inalienable human right in the ASEAN Human Rights Declaration (AHRD).[13]

CONVINCED of the need to strengthen existing bonds of regional solidarity to realise an ASEAN Community that is politically cohesive, economically integrated and socially responsible in order to effectively respond to current and future challenges and opportunities;

The Report of the Eminent Persons Group had stated that the establishment of an ASEAN Union was an 'ultimate goal' of the organisation.[14] However, the HLTF was instructed by the ASEAN Foreign Ministers not to include this in the Charter. In its place, the Charter envisages the creation of an ASEAN Community. Member states were wary of anything that smacked of supranationality, preferring to keep the organisation inter-governmental in nature.

COMMITTED to intensifying community building through enhanced regional cooperation and integration, in particular by establishing an ASEAN Community comprising the ASEAN Security Community, the ASEAN Economic Community and the ASEAN Socio-Cultural Community, as provided for in the Bali Declaration of ASEAN Concord II;

---

12 Adopted by the Heads of State/Government at the Fourteenth ASEAN Summit in Cha-Am, Thailand, on 1 Mar. 2009 as an annex to the Cha-Am Hua Hin Declaration on the Roadmap for the ASEAN Community (2009–15).

13 Adopted by the Heads of State/Government at the Twenty-first ASEAN Summit in Phnom Penh, Cambodia, on 18 Nov. 2012.

14 Report of the Eminent Persons Group on the ASEAN Charter, 19.

The Declaration of ASEAN Concord II (Bali Concord II) was signed by the leaders of the ASEAN member states in Bali on 7 October 2003 at the Ninth ASEAN Summit.

HEREBY DECIDE to establish, through this Charter, the legal and institutional framework for ASEAN;

The 2005 Kuala Lumpur Declaration on the Establishment of the ASEAN Charter[15] stated that the ASEAN Charter would 'serve as a legal and institutional framework of ASEAN to support the realisation of its goals and objectives'.

AND TO THIS END, the Heads of State or Government of the Member States of ASEAN, assembled in Singapore on the historic occasion of the 40th anniversary of the founding of ASEAN, have agreed to this Charter.

The Heads of State or Government who signed the Charter were: Sultan Hassanal Bolkiah (Brunei); Samdech Hun Sen (Cambodia); Dr Susilo Bambang Yudhoyono (Indonesia); Mr Bouasone Bouphavanh (Laos); Dato' Seri Abdullah Ahmad Badawi (Malaysia); General Thein Sein (Myanmar); Mrs Gloria Macapagal-Arroyo (Philippines); Mr Lee Hsien Loong (Singapore); General (Ret) Surayud Chulanont (Thailand); Mr Nguyen Tan Dung (Vietnam).

[15] Issued by the Heads of State/Government at the Eleventh ASEAN Summit (Kuala Lumpur, Malaysia, 12 Dec. 2005).

CHAPTER I.

PURPOSES AND PRINCIPLES

Chapter 1 follows the structure of the Charter of the United Nations, with the first article covering purposes and the second principles. The difference in length between the ASEAN Charter provisions and the UN Charter is immediately noticeable. The Eminent Persons Group (EPG) on the ASEAN Charter had already recommended 18 objectives and 23 principles.[1] When drafting these two articles, many delegations brought a laundry list of purposes and principles, sometimes with no clear distinction between them. Thus, for example, one finds repeated mentions of democracy, rule of law and good governance in Article 1(7) and Article 2(2)(h), as well as in the Preamble and Article 1(4). Similarly, one finds a commitment to protection and promotion of human rights in Article 1(7) as well as Article 2(2)(i).

ARTICLE 1: PURPOSES

The Purposes of ASEAN are:

1. To maintain and enhance peace, security and stability and further strengthen peace-oriented values in the region;

Compare Article 1(1) of the Charter of the United Nations.

See also the Preamble of the ASEAN Charter: 'united by a common desire and collective will to live in a region of lasting peace, security and stability'.

'Peace-oriented values' is an example of the odd phraseology that results when non-English-speaking non-lawyers insist on drafting legal documents by committee. Some inkling of what it involves may

[1] Report of the Eminent Persons Group on the ASEAN Charter, paras 58 and 60.

perhaps be found in the Bali Declaration on ASEAN Community in a Global Community of Nations (Bali Concord III),[2] which commits ASEAN to promoting a 'culture of peace, which includes, *inter alia,* respect for diversity, promotion of tolerance, and understanding of faiths, religions and cultures'.

The 1967 ASEAN Declaration[3] is the instrument that brought ASEAN into being as an association for regional cooperation. The second aim of the organisation was 'to promote regional peace and stability through abiding respect for justice and the rule of law in the relationship among countries of the region and adherence to the principles of the United Nations Charter'. In 1971 the Zone of Peace, Freedom and Neutrality (ZOPFAN) Declaration,[4] was issued, declaring that Southeast Asia should be a 'zone of peace, freedom and neutrality, free from any form of interference by outside powers'. Practically all subsequent ASEAN declarations repeat the aim of fostering peace, security and stability in what was once a very unstable part of the globe.

To a large extent, ASEAN has succeeded in this aim over the last half century. Despite disputes over delimitation of land and maritime frontiers, there have been no incidents of armed conflict among the ASEAN-6 since the organisation's founding. The newer ASEAN member states are another matter. There was an exchange of fire between Cambodian and Thai forces in the vicinity of the temple of Preah Vihear as recently as 2011. A ceasefire was achieved through the mediation of the ASEAN Chair at the time, Indonesia (*see* the commentary to Articles 23 and 28). This is a positive precedent for the role that ASEAN can play in maintaining peace in Southeast Asia.

The latest declaration of the commitment to peace is in the ASEAN Human Rights Declaration[5] (AHRD), which contains a right to 'enjoy peace within an ASEAN framework of security and stability, neutrality and freedom': *see* Article 38 of the AHRD.

---

2 Signed by the Heads of State/Government at the Nineteenth ASEAN Summit in Bali, Indonesia, on 17 Nov. 2011. Measure A.1.D.

3 Signed in Bangkok on 8 Aug. 1967.

4 Signed in Kuala Lumpur on 27 Nov. 1971 by the Foreign Ministers of Indonesia (Mr Adam Malik), Malaysia (Tun Abdul Razak, who was by then Prime Minister and Foreign Minister), the Philippines (Mr Carlos Romulo), Singapore (Mr S. Rajaratnam) and Thailand (Mr Thanat Khoman, then Special Envoy of the National Executive Council). For the background to this *see* Severino, *In Search of an ASEAN Community*, 166–7.

5 Adopted by the Heads of State/Government at the Twenty-first ASEAN Summit in Phnom Penh, Cambodia, on 18 Nov. 2012.

2. To enhance regional resilience by promoting greater political, security, economic and socio-cultural cooperation;

This was one of the major objects of the 1967 ASEAN Declaration. Regional cooperation was seen as a guarantee of independence and a bulwark against the advancing tide of Communism. Over the years (and especially since the end of the Vietnamese occupation of Cambodia), the economic dimension has taken on greater significance and now provides the main driving force behind ASEAN integration. Though the ASEAN Declaration expressed the ideal that there would be cooperation in the social and cultural fields, this area has lagged somewhat behind political cooperation (especially among the ASEAN-6 after the fall of South Vietnam) and economic integration. The Bali Concord II[6] declared that an ASEAN Community would be created, comprising three pillars: the ASEAN Political-Security Community (APSC),[7] the ASEAN Socio-Cultural Community (ASCC) and the ASEAN Economic Community (AEC). Each of these now has its own Community Council: *see* Article 9.

3. To preserve Southeast Asia as a Nuclear Weapon-Free Zone and free of all other weapons of mass destruction;

The Treaty on the Southeast Asia Nuclear Weapon-Free Zone (SEANWFZ) was signed by the ASEAN Heads of State/Government on 15 December 1995 at the Fifth ASEAN Summit in Bangkok. It came into force on 27 March 1997.

4. To ensure that the peoples and Member States of ASEAN live in peace with the world at large in a just, democratic and harmonious environment;

There are several references to democracy repeated throughout the Charter: *see* the Preamble, Article 1(7) and Article 2(2)(h). The term 'harmonious' was used to make clear that it is not just tolerance amongst peoples but harmony that is the aim of ASEAN.

---

[6] Officially, the Declaration of ASEAN Concord II, signed in Bali at the Ninth ASEAN Summit (Oct. 2003) by the Heads of State/Government.

[7] This is referred in Bali Concord II as the ASEAN Security Community, abbreviated ASC. It was later realised that the acronym ASC had already been used for the ASEAN Standing Community. When drafting the Charter the ASEAN Security Community was re-designated as the ASEAN Political-Security Community or APSC to avoid confusion.

5. To create a single market and production base which is stable, prosperous, highly competitive and economically integrated with effective facilitation for trade and investment in which there is free flow of goods, services and investment; facilitated movement of business persons, professionals, talents and labour; and freer flow of capital;

This is a reference to the ASEAN Economic Community (AEC). The original formulation appears in ASEAN Vision 2020, issued at the Second Informal ASEAN Summit in Kuala Lumpur on 15 December 1997, and repeated in the Hanoi Plan of Action[8] and the Bali Concord II.[9] Some delegations pushed for a free flow of labour. This was not acceptable to all, and the compromise was to use the term 'facilitated flow'. The input of the ASEAN Economic Ministers Meeting (AEM) was significant in the drafting of this paragraph, though their reference to 'skilled labour' was deleted and 'professionals' substituted. The ASEAN Economic Community Blueprint was adopted at the Thirteenth ASEAN Summit in Singapore on 20 November 2007. This Blueprint (together with the ASEAN Political-Security Community Blueprint, the ASEAN Socio-Cultural Community Blueprint and the Initiative for ASEAN Integration Workplan 2) forms the Roadmap for an ASEAN Community (2009–15).[10]

6. To alleviate poverty and narrow the development gap within ASEAN through mutual assistance and cooperation;

The elimination of poverty was an objective of the 1976 Declaration of ASEAN Concord (Bali Concord).[11] Poverty alleviation is one of the elements

---

[8] Signed in Hanoi by the Heads of State/Government at the Sixth ASEAN Summit on 15 Dec. 1998.

[9] The Declaration of ASEAN Concord II, signed in Bali at the Ninth ASEAN Summit (Oct. 2003) by the Heads of State/Government; *see* paras 1 and 3 under the section ASEAN Economic Community.

[10] See the Cha-Am Hua Hin Declaration on the Roadmap for the ASEAN Community (2009–15), adopted by the Heads of State/Government at the Fourteenth ASEAN Summit in Cha-Am, Thailand, on 1 Mar. 2009. Private sector businessmen have expressed scepticism about the realisation of this grand design; *see* for example Razeen Sally, 'The ASEAN Charter and the ASEAN Economic Community: A Watershed for Regional Economic Integration?', E. Pedrosa, 'Implications of an Uncerain Global Economy on Integration Initiatives', and M. Hutagalung, 'ASEAN: An Integrated Market?', in Tiwari, ed., *Life After the Charter*, chapters 7–9 . Although these articles were written in 2010, shortly after the entry into force of the Charter, similar doubts have repeatedly been expressed to the author by business leaders in the years leading up to the realisation of the ASEAN Economic Community. The private sector is not optimistic.

[11] Adopted by the Heads of State/Government at the First ASEAN Summit in Bali on 24

of the ASEAN Socio-Cultural Community Blueprint.[12] A meeting of ASEAN Ministers on Rural Development and Poverty Eradication (AMRDPE) had been established as early as 1997. Regular framework action plans on rural development and poverty eradication are issued.

With the accession of the CLMV countries to ASEAN[13] it became clear that there was a gap in economic development between the ASEAN-6 and the new members. World Bank figures for 2013 show the per capita GDP of ASEAN member states as follows:[14] Singapore US$55,182; Brunei US$38,563; Malaysia US$10,514; Thailand US$5,779; Indonesia US$3,475; Philippines US$2,765; Vietnam US$1,911; Laos US$1,646; Cambodia US$1,008.[15]

Narrowing the development gap is a major aim of ASEAN. At the Fourth ASEAN Informal Summit in Singapore (November 2000) the Initiative for ASEAN Integration (IAI) was launched by the Heads of State/Government. The objective was to accelerate the economic integration of the CLMV countries and narrow the development gap. Measures to do so are to be found in the ASEAN Economic Community Blueprint[16] and the Initiative for ASEAN Integration Workplan 2, both of which form part of the Roadmap for an ASEAN Community (2009–15).[17]

The ASEAN Human Rights Declaration[18] (AHRD) commits member states to adopt 'meaningful people-oriented and gender responsive development programmes aimed at poverty alleviation': *see* Article 36 of the AHRD.

Feb. 1976.

[12] This was adopted by the Heads of State/Government at the Fourteenth ASEAN Summit in Cha-Am, Thailand, on 1 Mar. 2009 as an annex to the Cha-Am Hua Hin Declaration on the Roadmap for the ASEAN Community (2009–15).

[13] Vietnam joined ASEAN in 1995, followed by Laos and Myanmar in 1997. Cambodia became part of the organisation in 1999.

[14] 'Countries and Economies,' *World Bank*, online: data.worldbank.org/country. No GDP figures are given for Myanmar.

[15] The last potential candidate for membership, Timor-Leste, has a per capita GDP of US$1,371.

[16] Adopted by the Heads of State/Government at the Thirteenth ASEAN Summit in Singapore on 20 Nov. 2007.

[17] Annexed to the Cha-Am Hua Hin Declaration on the Roadmap for the ASEAN Community (2009–15), adopted by the Heads of State/Government at the Fourteenth ASEAN Summit in Cha-Am, Thailand, on 1 Mar. 2009.

[18] Adopted by the Heads of State/Government at the Twenty-first ASEAN Summit in Phnom Penh, Cambodia, on 18 Nov. 2012.

7. To strengthen democracy, enhance good governance and the rule of law, and to promote and protect human rights and fundamental freedoms, with due regard to the rights and responsibilities of the Member States of ASEAN;

Democracy, good governance and the rule of law

The commitment to democracy, rule of law and good governance is repeated constantly in the Charter: *see* the Preamble. In the next Article on Principles, one again finds reference to 'adherence to the rule of law, good governance, the principles of democracy and constitutional government' in Article 2(2)(h). It was a conscious decision on the part of the HLTF to retain these repetitions to emphasise the importance of democracy, good governance and the rule of law. Despite the fact that many member states fall short (as do so many other countries in the world), these aspirational statements allow peer pressure to be brought on members if there is any backsliding. The ASEAN Human Rights Declaration (AHRD)[19] now contains the right to participate in the government of one's country, either directly or through democratically elected representatives, and the right to vote in periodic and genuine elections: *see* AHRD Article 25.

Fundamental freedoms and human rights

Article 2(2)(i) sets out 'respect for fundamental freedoms, the promotion and protection of human rights and the promotion of social justice' as one of the principles guiding ASEAN. Human rights was one of the most contentious issues during the process of drafting the Charter. Several delegations were extremely uncomfortable with having this enshrined in the Charter while others were arguing forcefully in favour of a robust Human Rights mechanism. Even the title of the mechanism proved contentious, some members pushing for a Commission, others stoutly resisting. Article 14 on the ASEAN Human Rights Body was the carefully-balanced, laboriously crafted compromise that resulted from the long (and sometimes heated) discussions.

The Terms of Reference (TOR) of the Human Rights Body had not been finalised when the Charter was signed in November 2007. These were to be negotiated by a High Level Panel (HLP) for drafting the TOR, established by the Foreign Ministers at their Retreat in Singapore on 20

[19] Adopted by the ASEAN leaders at the Twenty-first ASEAN Summit in Phnom Penh, Cambodia, on 18 Nov. 2012.

February 2008.[20] The HLP commenced work in July 2008 and settled the draft of the TOR on 14 February 2009 after eight meetings.[21] Meanwhile, the ASEAN Political-Security Community Blueprint[22] specifically committed ASEAN to establish a human rights body.[23] The finalised TOR[24] was endorsed by the Forty-second ASEAN Foreign Ministers' Meeting held in Phuket, Thailand, on 20 July 2009. It was agreed that the body would be named the ASEAN Intergovernmental Commission on Human Rights (AICHR).[25] The AICHR was finally established in October 2009 at the Fifteenth ASEAN Summit.[26] It held its first meeting at the ASEAN Secretariat in from 28 March–1 April 2010. One of its major tasks was to develop an ASEAN Human Rights Declaration (AHRD).[27] The AHRD was adopted by the ASEAN leaders at the Twenty-first ASEAN Summit in Phnom Penh, Cambodia, on 18 November 2012.

The ASEAN Human Rights Declaration (AHRD) affirms all the rights in the Universal Declaration of Human Rights: *see* the Preamble, Articles 10 and 26 of the AHRD. In addition, it explicitly sets out the following fundamental rights and freedoms:

- The right to life: AHRD Article 11.
- The right to personal liberty and security: AHRD Article 12.
- Freedom from servitude and slavery: AHRD Article 13.
- Freedom from torture and cruel, inhuman or degrading treatment or punishment: AHRD Article 14.
- Freedom of movement and residence within the borders of each state, and the right to leave and return to one's own country: AHRD Article 15.
- The right to seek and receive asylum: AHRD Article 16. Note that this is qualified by the laws of the receiving state.

---

20 The Terms of Reference for the High Level Panel were approved by the Forty-first ASEAN Ministerial Meeting, 21 July 2008 in Singapore.

21 'Press Release by the Chair of the High Level Panel on an ASEAN Human Rights Body at the Conclusion of the Eighth Meeting of the HLP on AHRB,' issued on 14 Feb. 2009 at Luang Prabang, Laos.

22 Adopted by the Heads of State/Government at the Fourteenth ASEAN Summit in Cha-Am, Thailand, on 1 Mar. 2009 as an annex to the Cha-Am Hua Hin Declaration on the Roadmap for an ASEAN Community (2009-15).

23 *See* para A.1.5(i) of the APSC Blueprint.

24 This is to be found at http://aichr.org/?dl_name=TOR-of-AICHR.pdf.

25 Joint Communiqué of the Forty-second ASEAN Foreign Ministers' Meeting, para 8.

26 Cha-Am Hua Hin Declaration on the Intergovernmental Commission on Human Rights, issued by the ASEAN leaders at the Fifteenth ASEAN Summit, 23 Oct. 2009.

27 Terms of Reference of the ASEAN Intergovernmental Commission on Human Rights, para 4.2.

- The right to property: AHRD Article 17.
- The right to nationality: AHRD Article 18. This right is also qualified by national law.
- The right to marry, found a family and divorce: AHRD Article 19. This right is confined to 'men and women of full age' and is subject to national law.
- The right to the presumption of innocence: AHRD Article 20(1).
- Protection against retroactive criminal laws: AHRD Article 20(2).
- Protection against double jeopardy: AHRD Article 20(3).
- Freedom from arbitrary interference with a person's privacy, family, home or correspondence (including personal data) and from attacks on his honour and reputation: AHRD Article 21.
- Freedom of thought, conscience and religion: AHRD Article 22.
- Freedom of opinion and expression: AHRD Article 23.
- The right of peaceful assembly: AHRD Article 24.
- The right to participate in the government of one's country, either directly or through democratically-elected representatives: AHRD Article 25(1).
- The right to vote in periodic and genuine elections: AHRD Article 25(2).
- The right to work: AHRD Article 27(1).
- The right to form and join trade unions: AHRD Article 27(2).
- Freedom from economic and social exploitation for children and young persons: AHRD Article 27(3).
- The right to an adequate standard of living: AHRD Article 28.
- The right of access to health care and medical services: AHRD Article 29(1).
- The right to social security: AHRD Article 30(1).
- The right to education: AHRD Article 31(1).
- The right to take part in cultural life and enjoy the arts and benefits of scientific progress: AHRD Article 32.
- The right to enjoy peace: AHRD Article 38.

It is explicitly stated in AHRD Article 6 that 'the enjoyment of human rights and fundamental freedoms must be balanced with the performance of corresponding duties as every person has responsibilities to all other individuals, the community and the society where one lives'. Article 7 of the AHRD provides a caveat that 'the realisation of human rights must be considered in the regional and national context bearing in mind different political, economic, legal, social, cultural, historical and religious backgrounds'. Furthermore, AHRD Article 8 provides that 'the human rights and fundamental freedoms of every person shall be exercised with due regard to the human rights and fundamental freedoms of others'.

Critics will of course carp at the fact that there is no supervisory or enforcement mechanism. Translation of the grand declarations of principle into concrete action is left to each individual member state. However, considering the heated controversy that human rights provoked during the the Charter-drafting process, it is an achievement to have gotten so far. The AHRD, like the Charter itself, may not be perfect but it is a good basis on which to continue the evolution of ASEAN as a people-oriented, law-abiding, rules-based community.

See also Article 14 on the ASEAN Human Rights Body (now known as the ASEAN Intergovernmental Commission on Human Rights).

8. To respond effectively, in accordance with the principle of comprehensive security, to all forms of threats, transnational crimes and transboundary challenges;

Comprehensive security

ASEAN is not and never has been a security organisation. Of the founding members, Indonesia was non-aligned and deeply suspicious of foreign bases in the region. Thailand and the Philippines were allies of the United States, while Singapore and Malaysia had strong defence links with Great Britain and the Commonwealth. Removal of foreign bases was an implicit aim of the ASEAN Declaration in 1967.[28] In 1971 the Zone of Peace, Freedom and Neutrality (ZOPFAN) Declaration[29] was issued, declaring that Southeast Asia should be a 'zone of peace, freedom and neutrality, free from any form of interference by outside powers'.

The end of the Cold War changed the climate. Security in Southeast Asia and the wider region are now discussed in the ASEAN Regional Forum (ARF), which was established after the Twenty-sixth ASEAN Ministerial Meeting and Post-Ministerial Conference, held in Singapore on 23–24

[28] The ASEAN Declaration, adopted in Bangkok, Thailand on 8 Aug. 1967. *See* preamble.

[29] Signed in Kuala Lumpur on 27 Nov. 1971 by the Foreign Ministers of Indonesia (Mr Adam Malik), Malaysia (Tun Abdul Razak, who was by then Prime Minister and Foreign Minister), the Philippines (Mr Carlos Romulo), Singapore (Mr S. Rajaratnam) and Thailand (Mr Thanat Khoman, then Special Envoy of the National Executive Council). For the background to this *see* Severino, *In Search of an ASEAN Community*, 166–67.

July 1993.[30] The first ARF was held in Bangkok on 25 July 1994. An annual ASEAN Defence Ministers Meeting (ADMM) was inaugurated in 2006. The ADMM has been broadened into the ADMM Plus[31] to discuss five areas of practical cooperation, viz, maritime security, counter-terrorism, humanitarian assistance and disaster relief, peacekeeping operations and military medicine. The inaugural meeting took place in Hanoi on 12 October 2010.

The ASEAN Political-Security Blueprint[32] sets out the elements of the shared responsibility for comprehensive security thus:[33]

- Conflict prevention and confidence building measures.
- Conflict resolution and pacific settlement of disputes. Reliance on peaceful settlement of disputes is a fundamental principle of ASEAN: *see* Article 2(2)(d). This has been so since the conclusion of the Treaty of Amity and Cooperation (TAC).[34] For further discussion, *see* the commentary to Chapter VIII on Settlement of Disputes.
- Post-conflict peace building, which includes *inter alia* strengthening ASEAN humanitarian assistance.
- Dealing with non-traditional security issues (e.g., transnational crimes and terrorism).
- Strengthening cooperation on disaster management and emergency response.[35]
- Ensuring an effective response to urgent issues or crises affecting ASEAN.

---

30 A paper setting out the aims of the ARF was adopted at the Second ASEAN Regional Forum in Bandar Seri Begawan on 1 Aug. 1995: *see* the ASEAN Regional Forum: A Concept Paper. The current participants besides the ASEAN member states are Australia, Bangladesh, Canada, China, North Korea, the European Union, India, Japan, Mongolia, New Zealand, Pakistan, Papua New Guinea, South Korea, Russia, Sri Lanka, Timor-Leste and the United States of America.

31 This includes eight other countries: Australia, China, India, Japan, New Zealand, South Korea, Russia and the United States.

32 This was adopted by the Heads of State/Government at the Fourteenth ASEAN Summit in Cha-am, Thailand, on 1 Mar. 2009 as an annex to the Cha-Am Hua Hin Declaration on the Roadmap for an ASEAN Community (2009–15).

33 *See* section B: A Cohesive, Peaceful and Resilient Region with Shared Responsibility for Comprehensive Security.

34 Signed on 24 Feb. 1976 at the First ASEAN Summit in Denpasar, Bali by the Heads of State/Government of the original five members. Accession to the TAC has become a prerequisite for membership of ASEAN.

35 An ASEAN Agreement on Disaster Management and Emergency Response (AADMER) was signed by the Foreign Ministers at the Thirty-eighth ASEAN Ministerial Meeting in Vientiane, Laos, on 26 July 2005. It came into force on 24 Dec. 2009.

Transnational crimes and transboundary challenges

An ASEAN Ministerial Meeting on Transnational Crime (AMMTC) was established in 1997, meeting biennially. The ASEAN Declaration on Transnational Crime was issued after the first meeting in Manila on 20 December 1997. This identified terrorism, drug trafficking,[36] arms smuggling, money-laundering, trafficking in persons and piracy as threats to regional stability.[37] The ASEAN Political-Security Blueprint[38] adds illegal fishing, trade in small arms and light weapons, cybercrimes, hijacking and forgery of identification and travel documents to the list of transnational crimes to be dealt with. Since the inauguration of the AMMTC, meetings with China, South Korea and Japan (AMMTC+3) have also been established, the first such being held in Bangkok on 10 January 2004. A separate meeting with China has been held since 2009 as well.

Cooperation in this field has seen the conclusion of the Treaty on Mutual Legal Assistance in Criminal Matters[39] and the ASEAN Convention on Counter-Terrorism.[40] Meanwhile, work on an ASEAN Extradition Treaty, which was envisaged as far back as 1967 in the ASEAN Declaration, progresses at glacial pace.

---

[36] The ASEAN Senior Officials on Drug Matters (ASOD) has been meeting annually since 1976: *see* commentary to Article 1(12) below.

[37] To implement the 1997 ASEAN Declaration on Transnational Crime, in 1998 ASEAN established a high-level ad hoc Experts Group to draft the ASEAN Plan of Action on Transnational Crime, which was later adopted in 1999. In 2002, ASEAN adopted the Work Programme to Implement the Plan of Action to Combat Transnational Crime.

[38] Adopted by the Heads of State/Government at the Fourteenth ASEAN Summit in Cha-Am, Thailand, on 1 Mar. 2009 as an annex to the Cha-Am Hua Hin Declaration on the Roadmap for an ASEAN Community (2009-15). *See* B.4.1 of the Blueprint.

[39] This does not have the status of an ASEAN treaty. Elevating it to the status of an ASEAN treaty is part of the ASEAN Political-Security Blueprint: *see* B.4.1(iii). It was adopted by the Ministers of Law/Attorneys-General in Kuala Lumpur, Malaysia, on 29 Nov. 2004. At the time of writing nine ASEAN member states have ratified the Treaty, viz, namely Brunei, Cambodia, Indonesia, Laos, Malaysia, Myanmar, the Philippines, Singapore and Vietnam. Thailand has signed but not ratified. *See* Robert Beckman and J. Ashley Roach, eds., 'Piracy and International Maritime Crimes in ASEAN: Prospect for Cooperation', Appendix, (NUS Centre for International Law and Edward Elgar, 2012), 242.

[40] This was signed by the Heads of State/Government at the Twelfth ASEAN Summit in Cebu, the Philippines, on 13 Jan. 2007 and entered into force on 27 May 2011. It has now been ratified by all ASEAN member states. *See* 'ASEAN Convention on Counter-Terrorism Completes Ratification Process', available at http://www.asean.org/news/asean-secretariat-news/item/asean-convention-on-counter-terrorism-completes-ratification-process.

9. To promote sustainable development so as to ensure the protection of the region's environment, the sustainability of its natural resources, the preservation of its cultural heritage and the high quality of life of its peoples;

Protection of the Environment

Environmental sustainability falls under the purview of the ASEAN Socio-Cultural Community. There is a regular ASEAN Ministerial Meeting on the Environment (AMME). The environmental ministers met for the first AMME in Manila in 1981 to issue an ASEAN Declaration on the Environment. The ASEAN Socio-Cultural Community Blueprint[41] sets out the elements of the plan to promote sustainable development and environmental protection.

The one concrete measure set out is managing and preventing transboundary environmental pollution.[42] An ASEAN Agreement on Transboundary Haze Pollution was signed in Kuala Lumpur on 10 July 2002.[43] The fate of this treaty is symptomatic of the ASEAN problem of lack of full implementation. The primary cause of the pollution is the regular burning of peatland vegetation, which creates a pall of smoke over the neighbouring countries. Curbing this annual nuisance would be a tangible symbol of ASEAN cooperation. All the ASEAN countries have ratified the Treaty except Indonesia, from which most of the haze originates. While numerous ASEAN meetings, bodies and subsidiary arrangements were implemented following the 2002 agreement, these were not able to effectively enforce bans on burning or in sufficiently improving fire-fighting capabilities at a national level.[44] At the time of writing it is reported that Indonesia is still considering ratification of the Agreement.

Other elements of the Blueprint regarding environmental protection include promoting sustainable management of forests (which would also partly deal with the haze problem), biodiversity, water resources and other natural resources as well as sustainable use of the coastal and marine

---

[41] Adopted by the Heads of State/Government at the Fourteenth ASEAN Summit in Cha-Am, Thailand, on 1 Mar. 2009 as an annex to the Cha-am Hua Hin Declaration on the Roadmap for an ASEAN Community (2009–15).

[42] ASEAN Socio-Cultural Blueprint: D.2.

[43] It entered into force on 25 Nov. 2003: *see* the table of ASEAN Legal Instruments at http://agreement.asean.org.

[44] Under the Agreement, the ASEAN Co-ordinating Centre for Transboundary Haze Pollution was set up. The Conference of the Parties is held annually. There is also a Secretariat to the Agreement. The ASEAN Transboundary Haze Pollution Control Fund was also established.

environments. Dealing with illegal, unreported and unregulated fishing comes under transboundary challenges to be dealt with by the ASEAN Political-Security Community; *see* commentary to Article 1(8) above.

Cultural heritage

Preservation and promotion of the ASEAN cultural heritage is also part of the ASEAN Socio-Cultural Community Blueprint.[45] *See* the commentary to Article 1(14) below. In the context of this particular paragraph, preservation of ASEAN's cultural heritage deals principally with the physical protection of heritage sites and the promotion of traditional and classical art forms through the activities of the ASEAN Committee on Culture and Information (COCI) since 1978 and the ASEAN Ministerial Meeting on Culture (AMCA) since 2003.

10. To develop human resources through closer cooperation in education and life-long learning, and in science and technology, for the empowerment of the peoples of ASEAN and for the strengthening of the ASEAN Community;

A Southeast Asian Ministers of Education Organization (SEAMEO) has existed since 1965.[46] This is not an ASEAN organ, though all ten ASEAN states are members, together with Timor-Leste. The promotion of Southeast Asian studies is one of the objectives listed in the founding Bangkok Declaration and Bali Concord I.[47]

The ASEAN Education Ministers (ASED) have been meeting annually since 2006, when the first such meeting was held in Singapore. The education agenda comes under the ASEAN Socio-Cultural Community, as does the development of human resources.[48] Advancement of education in ASEAN takes place in collaboration with SEAMEO and the ASEAN University Network (AUN).[49] SEAMEO has twenty regional centres that

---

45 Adopted by the Heads of State/Government at the Fourteenth ASEAN Summit in Cha-am, Thailand, on 1 Mar. 2009 as an annex to the Cha-Am Hua Hin Declaration on the Roadmap for the ASEAN Community (2009–15). *See* section E.2 of the Blueprint.

46 It has its own webpage, www.seameo.org. SEAMEO was established in Bangkok on 30 Nov. 1965 (before the foundation of ASEAN), with Laos, Malaysia, Singapore, Thailand and South Vietnam as the founding members.

47 *See* the ASEAN Declaration (Bangkok, Aug. 1967), Article 2(6) and Declaration of ASEAN Concord ('Bali Concord I') (Bali, Feb. 1976).

48 *See* the ASEAN Socio-Cultural Community Blueprint, adopted in Cha-Am, Thailand at the Fourteenth ASEAN Summit by the Heads of State/Government. A.1 and A.2.

49 *See* the ASEAN Socio-Cultural Community Blueprint, A.1(11)(v).

undertake training and research in the fields of education, science and culture.[50] Cooperation in higher education is coordinated by the AUN.[51] This was established in November 1995 pursuant to a decision of the Fourth ASEAN Summit.[52] The AUN Secretariat is based at Chulalongkorn University in Bangkok.

Article 31 of the ASEAN Human Rights Declaration (AHRD) sets out the right to education. Primary education is to be compulsory and free to all. Secondary, technical and vocational education are to be made generally available. Higher education is to be accessible on the basis of merit.

11. To enhance the well-being and livelihood of the peoples of ASEAN by providing them with equitable access to opportunities for human development, social welfare and justice;

In the ASEAN Socio-Cultural Community Blueprint,[53] human development is to be promoted *inter alia* in the following ways:

- Advancing and prioritising education. *See* also the commentary to Article 1(10) above.
- Investing in human resource development. This includes *inter alia* the promotion of English as an international business language in the workplace. *See* also Article 34, which states that English shall be the working language of ASEAN.
- Promoting information and communication technology.
- Facilitating access to applied science and technology.
- Strengthening entrepreneurship skills for women, youth, the elderly and persons with disabilities.
- Building civil service capacity.

---

[50] A list is available on the SEAMEO website, www.seameo.org.

[51] The AUN is among the officially recognised ASEAN Bodies listed in the ASEAN Socio-Cultural Community Section of Annex 2 to the Charter. A list of member universities is to be found at www.aunsec.org.

[52] Held in Singapore from 27–29 Jan. 1992. Para 7 of the Singapore Declaration issued by the Summit recorded the leaders' Decision to strengthen the network of universities in the region with a view to ultimately establishing an ASEAN University.

[53] Adopted by the Heads of State/Government at the Fourteenth ASEAN Summit in Cha-Am, Thailand, on 1 Mar. 2009 as an annex to the Cha-am Hua Hin Declaration on the Roadmap for an ASEAN Community (2009–15). *See* section A.2 of the Blueprint.

In 2011, ASEAN issued a Framework for Equitable Economic Development (AFEED),[54] taking cognisance of equitable development issues related to the ASEAN economic integration agenda.

12. To strengthen cooperation in building a safe, secure and drug-free environment for the peoples of ASEAN;

The 1976 Declaration of ASEAN Concord (Bali Concord)[55] called for cooperation among ASEAN states to eradicate drug abuse. This led to the First Meeting of ASEAN Drug Experts in Singapore that same year. The drug experts have been meeting annually since then. In 1984 the meeting was redesignated as the ASEAN Senior Officials on Drug Matters (ASOD). They work in collaboration with the UN Office on Drugs and Crime (UNODC). ASEAN Vision 2020[56] envisaged a Southeast Asia free from the production, trafficking and use of illicit drugs. The following year, the Foreign Ministers signed the Joint Declaration for a Drug-free ASEAN by 2020 at the Thirty-first ASEAN Ministerial Meeting in July 1998. The target date was advanced to 2015 at the Thirty-third ASEAN Ministerial Meeting in July 2000. The ASEAN leaders reaffirmed the commitment to a drug-free ASEAN Community by 2015 in the ASEAN Leaders' Declaration on Drug-free ASEAN.[57]

Combating the trafficking of illicit drugs falls under the purview of the ASEAN Ministerial Meeting on Transnational Crime (AMMTC); *see* commentary to Article 1(8) above. This is an issue that cuts across the ASEAN Political-Security and ASEAN Socio-Cultural Communities.[58]

---

[54] Noted by the Heads of State/Government at the Nineteenth ASEAN Summit (Bali, 14–19 Nov. 2011).

[55] Signed on 24 Feb. 1976 in Denpasar, Bali, at the First ASEAN Summit. *See* C.4 on eradication of drug abuse.

[56] Issued at the Second ASEAN Informal Summit in Kuala Lumpur, Malaysia, on 15 Dec. 1997. *See* section on 'A Community of Caring Societies'.

[57] Issued in Phnom Penh, Cambodia, on 4 Apr. 2012 at the Twentieth ASEAN Summit. For further information on ASEAN cooperation against drugs and narcotics, *see* http://www.asean.org/communities/asean-political-security-community/item/cooperation-on-drugs-and-narcotics-overview.

[58] *See* the ASEAN Political-Security Blueprint and ASEAN Socio-Cultural Community Blueprint, both of which form part of the Roadmap for the ASEAN Community (2009–15), adopted by the Heads of State/Government at the Fourteenth ASEAN Summit in Cha-Am, Thailand, on 1 Mar. 2009. *See* section B6 of the ASCC Blueprint and B4.1(vii) of the ASPC Blueprint.

13. To promote a people-oriented ASEAN in which all sectors of society are encouraged to participate in, and benefit from, the process of ASEAN integration and community building;

Since its inception, ASEAN has been a somewhat distant and aloof entity for most of the people of the member states. ASEAN does not impinge on the average citizen; there is no common currency or open borders. Creation of a people-oriented ASEAN falls primarily within the purview of the ASEAN Socio-Cultural Community. According to Thai HLTF member Khun Pradap Pibulsonggram, 'people must feel a sense of ownership and belonging to the ASEAN Community, and must be the direct beneficiary [sic] of and have their voices heard in the community-building process'.[59] Steps to be taken include greater engagement with civil society and ASEAN-affiliated NGOs.[60]

14. To promote an ASEAN identity through the fostering of greater awareness of the diverse culture and heritage of the region; and

ASEAN is one of the most culturally diverse regions of the world. Indochina is where the civilisations of China and the Indian subcontinent intersect.[61] Buddhism is the dominant religion in Myanmar, Laos, Cambodia, Vietnam and Thailand. Islam holds sway in Indonesia, Malaysia and Brunei. The Philippines is a Roman Catholic-majority country. The ASEAN region is also home to UNESCO world heritage sites like Angkor Wat (Cambodia) and Borobudur (Indonesia). The 1967 ASEAN Declaration listed promotion of Southeast Asian studies as an aim of the organisation from the outset.[62]

Article 35 states that 'ASEAN shall promote its common ASEAN identity and a sense of belonging among its peoples in order to achieve its shared destiny, goals and values'. The ASEAN Socio-Cultural Community Blueprint lists several measures to build an ASEAN identity, none of really great potential impact. The challenge is to create an identity common to such a disparate group of countries. Note however Article 2(2)(l), which states the guiding principle of 'respect for the different cultures, languages

---

59 *See* Pibulsonggram, 'The Thai Perspective', in Koh, Manalo and Woon, eds., *Making of the ASEAN Charter*, chapter 7, 85.

60 *See* the ASEAN Socio-Cultural Community Blueprint, section E4 para 46.

61 For an anthropological summary of the origins of the peoples of Southeast Asia, *see* Nicholas Tarling, *Southeast Asia: A Modern History* (Australia, Oxford University Press, 2001), 3–10.

62 The ASEAN Declaration, adopted in Bangkok, Thailand on 8 Aug. 1967. *See* Article 2(6).

and religions of the peoples of ASEAN, while emphasising their common values in the spirit of unity in diversity'.

Cultural cooperation was one of the earliest and most active fields to be established in ASEAN, with the creation of the Committee on Culture and Information in 1978. The Committee and its subcommittees on Information and culture meet annually, and disburse the ASEAN Cultural Fund that was established in the same year. The ASEAN Ministers Responsible for Culture and the Arts (AMCA) have been meeting irregularly since their inaugural meeting in Kuala Lumpur in 2003.

ASEAN now has its own anthem, 'The ASEAN Way', composed by Kittikhun Sodprasert, Sampow Triudom and Payom Valaipatchra: *see* Article 40 below. ASEAN day is 8 August, the day the ASEAN Declaration was signed in 1967: *see* Article 39. An ASEAN flag was adopted by the Foreign Ministers at the Twenty-seventh ASEAN Ministerial Meeting in Bangkok in July 1994: *see* Article 37. The flag, together with the ASEAN emblem, are probably the most recognisable ASEAN symbols. Nonetheless, not even the most optimistic of ASEAN's supporters could realistically claim that there is anything like a pan-ASEAN identity, even in an embryonic form. There is no generally accepted word as yet to designate a citizen of ASEAN, as one might speak of a European or African or Latin American. People in ASEAN would no doubt be surprised to be called 'Aseanese' or even 'Southeast Asians'.

15. To maintain the centrality and proactive role of ASEAN as the primary driving force in its relations and cooperation with its external partners in a regional architecture that is open, transparent and inclusive.

In 1967 the great fear in Southeast Asia was of external meddling. This was one of the drivers that impelled the five original members to form the association. The idea was to keep foreign powers out of Southeast Asia. At the signing of the ASEAN Declaration[63] Indonesian Foreign Minister Adam Malik said that Indonesia's vision was of Southeast Asia as a 'region which can stand on its own two feet, strong enough to defend itself against any negative influence from outside the region'.[64] The Foreign Minister of Singapore, Mr S Rajaratnam, spoke in the same vein: 'we want to ensure a stable Southeast Asia, not a balkanized Southeast Asia.'

---

[63] At the Saranrom Palace in Bangkok on 8 Aug. 1967.

[64] Quoted in 'The Founding of ASEAN', the first chapter in Flores and Abad, *ASEAN at 30*.

In the roughly half-century since then, ASEAN members have found a voice in international relations. ASEAN is open to engagement with all countries and international organisations. The 1976 Treaty of Amity and Cooperation in Southeast Asia (TAC) is open to accession by any states, even ones far removed geographically from Southeast Asia.[65] The ASEAN Regional Forum brings together the major players in Asia to discuss security issues. Meetings with dialogue partners are a regular feature of ASEAN Summits and Foreign Ministers' Meetings. The principal objective of ASEAN diplomacy is to be friends with everyone: *see* Article 41(1) on Conduct of External Relations.

The 'centrality of ASEAN' and its associated concept of ASEAN as a 'primary driving force' or 'in the driver's seat' came into use in the 1990s as ASEAN expanded its role as a convenor in forums such as the ASEAN Regional Forum (ARF) (established in 1994) and the ASEAN Plus Three (established in 1997). What these terms entail was explained by Mr George Yeo, the Foreign Minister of Singapore, in a statement at the closing ceremony of the Forty-first ASEAN Ministerial Meeting when Singapore handed over the Chairmanship to Thailand:[66]

> With the rise of China and India changing the polarity of the world, we must make sure that the political, economic and security architecture of the region takes into account the interest of ASEAN. Over the years, ASEAN, in a peaceful non-threatening way, has helped to bring countries in the region together. We have been able to do this through

[65] The Protocol Amending the Treaty of Amity and Cooperation in Southeast Asia (TAC First Protocol) was signed in 15 Dec. 1987 and opened the TAC for accession by other states in Southeast Asia as well as states outside Southeast Asia with the consent of all states in the region. The Second Protocol signed on 25 July 1998 specified the list of Southeast Asian states whose consent was required. The Third Protocol signed on 23 July 2010 provided for accession by regional organizations (such as the EU). At the time of writing the following have acceded to the TAC (*see* the ASEAN Legal Instruments list at http://agreement.asean.org): Papua New Guinea (10 Aug. 1989); the People's Republic of China (8 Oct. 2003); India (8 Oct. 2003); Japan (2 July 2004); Pakistan (2 July 2004); Republic of Korea (27 Nov. 2004); the European Communities and European Union (28 May 2009); the Russian Federation (29 Nov. 2004); Australia (28 July 2005); Mongolia (28 July 2005); New Zealand (28 July 2005); France (13 Jan. 2007); Timor Leste (13 Jan. 2007); Bangladesh (1 Aug. 2007); Sri Lanka (1 Aug. 2007); the Democratic People's Republic of Korea (24 July 2008); the United States of America (22 July 2009); Canada (23 July 2010); Turkey (23 July 2010); the United Kingdom (3 July 2012); Brazil (17 Nov. 2012); Norway (1 July 2013). Serbia has also expressed interest in acceding to the TAC: *see* the Chairman's Statement of the Twenty-first ASEAN Summit (Phnom Penh, Nov. 2012).

[66] Issued in Singapore on 24 July 2008. Available on the ASEAN website under the Political-Security Community, Forty-first AMM: www.asean.org/communities/asean-political-security-community.

enlightened diplomacy and by offering our hand of friendship to all the major powers. We must never lose this position. We must take an active interest in regional and global affairs and play a role which is helpful to others. We ensure the centrality of ASEAN in the evolving regional architecture, not by force or assertion but by the openness and neutrality of our position and by our usefulness to others.

See also Article 2(2)(m) regarding the centrality of ASEAN as one of the fundamental principles of the organisation and Article 41(3) on Conduct of External Relations. It is part of the role of the member state holding the Chair to ensure the centrality of ASEAN: *see* Article 32(b).

Article 2. Principles

1. In pursuit of the Purposes stated in Article 1, ASEAN and its Member States reaffirm and adhere to the fundamental principles contained in the declarations, agreements, conventions, concords, treaties and other instruments of ASEAN.

The first ASEAN treaty to set out fundamental principles for member states' relations with each other was the Treaty of Amity and Cooperation in Southeast Asia (TAC).[67] The Charter is meant to be a restatement and consolidation of all the various principles.[68] Article 2 was only finalised at the third HLTF meeting in Manila, 28–29 March 2007 – a measure of how slow the going was at the beginning of the drafting process.

2. ASEAN and its Member States shall act in accordance with the following Principles:

(a) respect for the independence, sovereignty, equality, territorial integrity and national identity of all ASEAN Member States;

This comes word for word from Article 2(a) of the 1976 Treaty of Amity and Cooperation in Southeast Asia (TAC).

[67] Signed on 24 Feb. 1976 by the Heads of State/Government in Bali at the First ASEAN Summit.

[68] *See* para 4 of the Kuala Lumpur Declaration on the Establishment of the ASEAN Charter, adopted by the Heads of State/Government at the Eleventh ASEAN Summit in Kuala Lumpur, Malaysia on 12 Dec. 2005.

(b) shared commitment and collective responsibility in enhancing regional peace, security and prosperity;

The 1967 ASEAN Declaration states that one of the purposes of ASEAN is to promote regional peace and stability. In 1971 the Zone of Peace, Freedom and Neutrality (ZOPFAN) Declaration[69] was issued, declaring that Southeast Asia should be a 'zone of peace, freedom and neutrality, free from any form of interference by outside powers.' Practically all subsequent ASEAN declarations repeat the aim of fostering peace, security and stability in what was once a very unstable part of the globe.

(c) renunciation of aggression and of the threat or use of force or other actions in any manner inconsistent with international law;

Article 2(e) of the 1976 Treaty of Amity and Cooperation in Southeast Asia (TAC)[70] commits the parties to the renunciation of the threat or use of force. *See* also Article 2(4) of the Charter of the United Nations.

(d) reliance on peaceful settlement of disputes;

The 1976 Declaration of ASEAN Concord (Bali Concord)[71] declared that 'Member states, in the spirit of ASEAN solidarity, shall rely exclusively on peaceful processes in the settlement of intra-regional differences'. The member states renounced the use of force and committed themselves to settlement of differences or disputes by peaceful means in Article 2(d) of the 1976 Treaty of Amity and Cooperation in Southeast Asia (TAC). The Eminent Persons Group (EPG) on the ASEAN Charter was specifically asked to look into effective conflict resolution mechanisms.[72] In its report the EPG recommended the establishment of dispute settlement mechanisms in all fields of ASEAN cooperation, including monitoring and

---

69 Signed in Kuala Lumpur on 27 Nov. 1971 by the Foreign Ministers of Indonesia (Mr Adam Malik), Malaysia (Tun Abdul Razak, who was by then Prime Minister and Foreign Minister), the Philippines (Mr Carlos Romulo), Singapore (Mr S. Rajaratnam) and Thailand (Mr Thanat Khoman, then Special Envoy of the National Executive Council). For the background to this *see* Severino, *In Search of an ASEAN Community,* 166–7.

70 Signed on 24 Feb. 1976 by the Heads of State/Government in Bali at the First ASEAN Summit.

71 Signed on 24 Feb. 1976 in Denpasar, Bali, by the Heads of State/Government at the First ASEAN Summit, together with the Treaty of Amity and Cooperation in Southeast Asia.

72 Terms of Reference of the Eminent Persons Group on the ASEAN Charter, para 4.2(i).

enforcement mechanisms.[73] These are now to be found in Chapter VIII of the Charter.

(e) non-interference in the internal affairs of ASEAN Member States;

Compare with Article 2(7) of the Charter of the United Nations.

The fundamental principle of non-interference in the internal affairs of the member states appears for the first time in the 1971 Zone of Peace, Freedom and Neutrality (ZOPFAN) Declaration,[74] which was 'inspired by the worthy aims and objectives of the United Nations, in particular by the principles of respect for the sovereignty and territorial integrity of all states, abstention from threat or use of force, peaceful settlement of international disputes, equal rights and self-determination and non-interference in affairs of States,' according to its Preamble. It is repeated in the Declaration of ASEAN Concord (Bali Concord)[75] and in Article 2(c) of the 1976 Treaty of Amity and Cooperation in Southeast Asia (TAC). *See* also the Preamble of the Charter.

The principle of non-interference in an ASEAN context means that the member states do not resort to publicly lecturing one another (or other countries) about their domestic situation. It does not mean that matters of common concern are not raised *sub rosa* at the informal Foreign Ministers' and leaders' meetings. For instance, ASEAN managed to persuade Myanmar to allow aid to flow in after Cyclone Nargis. The devastation caused by the cyclone was beyond the ability of the government to deal with, but the Myanmars were suspicious of foreign meddling especially by former colonial powers and what were perceived to be hostile states. The ASEAN Foreign Ministers convinced Myanmar that it was essential to allow assistance from abroad. Peer pressure (or more precisely, forceful but friendly persuasion) is often applied behind the scenes. ASEAN's *raison d'être* is to create confidence among the member states. By and large, each member state considers the other member states as 'family' (occasional hiccups in bilateral relations notwithstanding). Advice from

73 Report of the Eminent Persons Group on the ASEAN Charter, Executive Summary, para 6.

74 Signed in Kuala Lumpur on 27 Nov. 1971 by the Foreign Ministers of the original five member states. For the background to this *see* Severino, *In Search of an ASEAN Community*, 166–7.

75 Signed on 24 Feb. 1976 in Denpasar, Bali, by the Heads of State/Government at the First ASEAN Summit, together with the Treaty of Amity and Cooperation in Southeast Asia.

family, even when the message is unwelcome, is more palatable than hectoring from outsiders.

The existence of the Charter now justifies this legally. The ASEAN member states have voluntarily signed up to the principles of good governance, democracy and rule of law. ASEAN cooperation extends practically to all fields. Note Article 2(2)(g) which commits the member states to 'enhanced consultation' in matters that seriously affect the common interest. This may plausibly cover domestic problems that spill over borders or imperil ASEAN cooperation with external partners. Thus, for instance, the riots in Rakhine State, Myanmar, between Buddhists and Muslims in 2012 were the subject of discussion among the Foreign Ministers.[76] No details of the discussion were given, but it is significant that it even took place. There were no words of condemnation; rather, the ministers expressed their readiness to extend humanitarian assistance if requested by Myanmar. Myanmar in return welcomed the Foreign Ministers' statement.

Of course, no ASEAN member state can be forced to discuss its domestic affairs. The principle of consensus also ensures that a subject may not be placed on a meeting agenda if any member state objects. However, while there are no overt sanctions for consistently ignoring the concerns of the other member states, a price will be paid in terms of diplomatic goodwill.

(f) respect for the right of every Member State to lead its national existence free from external interference, subversion and coercion;

This paragraph comes word for word from Article 2(b) of the 1976 Treaty of Amity and Cooperation in Southeast Asia (TAC).[77]

The 1967 ASEAN Declaration[78] was meant to keep the member states free of external interference in their affairs. Implicit in the Declaration was the desire for the removal of all foreign bases, which were stated to be temporary.

---

[76] *See* the Statement of the ASEAN Foreign Ministers on the Recent Developments in the Rakhine State, Myanmar, issued in Phnom Penh, Cambodia, on 17 Aug. 2012.

[77] Signed on 24 Feb. 1976 by the Heads of State/Government in Bali at the First ASEAN Summit.

[78] Signed by the Foreign Ministers of Indonesia, Malaysia, the Philippines, Singapore and Thailand on 8 Aug. 1967 in Bangkok.

Given the unhappy history of European colonisation in Southeast Asia,[79] this aversion to foreign interference is entirely understandable. Myanmar, Malaysia, Brunei and Singapore were all British colonies or protectorates. Myanmar fell under British rule after three imperialist wars.[80] Most of the Malay states of peninsular Malaya also progressively came within the British sphere of influence.[81] Malacca, the seat of a Malay empire from the fifteenth century, was conquered successively by the Portuguese, Dutch and British. What is now Indonesia was formerly the Dutch East Indies.[82] British and Indian troops were deployed to crush the Indonesian nationalists from September 1945, after the Japanese surrender, in order to restore Dutch rule. The Dutch had to be expelled by force. The same is true of Vietnam, Cambodia and Laos, all of which formed part of French Indochina.[83] Vietnam in particular had to fight the French and Americans for her independence, as well as beat off a Chinese incursion in early 1979. Thailand managed to remain free of the European colonial powers, but only at the cost of having parts of her territory lopped off by the French and British.[84]

ASEAN was conceived at the height of the Cold War, which had turned hot in Indochina. It was against this backdrop that the Zone of Peace, Freedom and Neutrality (ZOPFAN) Declaration[85] was issued in 1971, declaring that Southeast Asia should be a 'zone of peace, freedom and neutrality, free from any form of interference by outside powers.'[86]

---

[79] Tarling, *Southeast Asia,* 44–117, gives an overview of all Southeast Asian states. *See also* Nicholas Tarling ed., *The Cambridge History of Southeast Asia*, vol. 2 (Cambridge: Cambridge University Press, 1993).

[80] For a quick overview, *see* Britannica Online www.britannica.com under Myanmar – History.

[81] For a quick overview, *see* Britannica Online www.britannica.com under Malaysia – History.

[82] *See* Tarling, *Cambridge History of Southeast Asia*. Britannica Online provides a quick overview under 'Indonesia – History', www.britannica.com.

[83] *See* Tarling, *Cambridge History of Southeast Asia*. Britannica Online provides a quick overview under the respective histories of the three countries.

[84] For a quick overview, see 'Thailand – History', Britannica Online, www.britannica.com. The colonial legacy still creates border problems, as in the case of the Temple of Preah Vihear, discussed in more detail in the commentary to Chapter VIII: Settlement of Disputes.

[85] Signed in Kuala Lumpur on 27 Nov. 1971 by the Foreign Ministers of Indonesia (Mr Adam Malik), Malaysia (Tun Abdul Razak, who was by then Prime Minister and Foreign Minister), the Philippines (Mr Carlos Romulo), Singapore (Mr S. Rajaratnam) and Thailand (Mr Thanat Khoman, then Special Envoy of the National Executive Council). For the background to this *see* Severino, *In Search of an ASEAN Community,* 166–7.

[86] The vision of Mr Adam Malik (Indonesia's Foreign Minister and a signatory of the ASEAN Declaration in 1967) was of a Southeast Asia 'that can be on its own feet, strong enough to defend itself from any negative influence from outside the region'. *See* 'The

(g) enhanced consultations on matters seriously affecting the common interest of ASEAN;

The 2003 Declaration of ASEAN Concord II (Bali Concord II)[87] stated that ASEAN would nurture a habit of consultation on matters of common concern. The examples given in the Bali Concord II were environmental degradation, maritime security cooperation and defence cooperation. With reference to non-traditional security issues and transboundary challenges, the Eminent Persons Group Report on the ASEAN Charter also recommended the calibration of non-intervention 'in areas where the common interest dictates closer cooperation'.[88]

This paragraph goes further in requiring 'enhanced consultations', which implies a deeper and broader cooperation among the members.

(h) adherence to the rule of law, good governance, the principles of democracy and constitutional government;

Democracy, rule of law and good governance

The commitment to democracy, rule of law and good governance is repeated constantly in the Charter: *see* the Preamble. In the previous Article on Purposes, one finds that it is an aim of ASEAN to strengthen democracy and enhance the rule of law and good governance: *see* Article 1(7). It was a conscious decision on the part of the HLTF to retain these repetitions to emphasise the importance of democracy, good governance and the rule of law. Despite the fact that many member states fall short (as do so many other countries in the world), these aspirational statements allow peer pressure to be brought on members if there is any backsliding.

The ASEAN Human Rights Declaration (AHRD)[89] now contains the right to participate in the government of one's country, either directly or through democratically-elected representatives, and the right to vote in periodic and genuine elections: *see* AHRD Article 25.

Founding of ASEAN', the first chapter in Flores and Abad, *ASEAN at 30,* and Djani, 'A Long Journey', in Koh, Manalo and Woon, eds., *Making of the ASEAN Charter,* chapter 11, 137.

87 Signed in Bali on 7 Oct. 2003 by the Heads of State/Government at the Ninth ASEAN Summit. *See* para 4.

88 Report of the Eminent Persons Group on the ASEAN Charter, Executive Summary, para 3.

89 Adopted by the ASEAN leaders at the Twenty-first ASEAN Summit in Phnom Penh, Cambodia, on 18 Nov. 2012.

Constitutional government

Adherence to constitutional government provoked some disagreement during the drafting of the charter. The matter was a delicate one. Thailand had been rocked by a series of political crises in 2005–06, with mass protests culminating in a military coup that removed Prime Minister Thaksin Shinawatra. Indeed, the Charter was signed on behalf of Thailand by General Surayud Chulanont, who had been installed after a coup d'état.[90] In Myanmar, a series of mass protests known as the 'Saffron Revolution' were suppressed in 2007. It was against this backdrop that negotiations on this principle proceeded.

Some delegations wanted an explicit rejection of unconstitutional changes of government. This was opposed by certain other delegations. The Report of the Eminent Persons Group (EPG) on the ASEAN Charter[91] had stated that the rejection of unconstitutional and undemocratic changes of government should be one of the fundamental principles of ASEAN.[92] Indeed, as early as 2003 the ASEAN Security Community Plan of Action[93] issued after Bali Concord II[94] had declared that 'ASEAN member countries shall not condone unconstitutional and undemocratic changes of government'. The matter was put to the Foreign Ministers after the eighth meeting of the High Level Task Force for Drafting of the ASEAN Charter in Manila in July 2007. The instructions from the Foreign Ministers were to omit mention of unconstitutional and undemocratic changes of government, in deference to the sensitivities of some member states.

Nonetheless, if the principle of constitutional government is to have any real substance, it must mean in practice that member states cannot accept changes of government by force of arms or unconstitutional means. Any serious breach of the obligations of membership is to be referred to the ASEAN Summit for decision under Articles 5(3) and 20(4). A coup d'état[95] would by definition be a very serious breach of the

---

[90] BBC profile published on 1 Oct. 2006: http://news.bbc.co.uk/2/hi/asia-pacific/5392722.stm. History repeated itself during the writing of this book. At the present time, Thailand is again under a military government installed after a coup d'état. By a curious twist of history, Thai HLTF member Sihasak Puanketkeow is the current Permanent Secretary for Foreign Affairs of Thailand.

[91] Endorsed by the Heads of State/Government in the Cebu Declaration on the Blueprint of the ASEAN Charter, issued at the Twelfth ASEAN Summit in Cebu, the Philippines, on 13 Jan. 2007.

[92] EPG Report, para 3 of the Executive Summary and para 60.

[93] Available at www.asean.org/news/item/asean-security-community-plan-of-action.

[94] Officially, the Declaration of ASEAN Concord II, signed by the leaders in Bali at the Ninth ASEAN Summit on 7 Oct. 2003.

[95] What exactly amounts to a coup d'état may be controversial. The Royal Thai Army

principles of democracy, rule of law, good governance and constitutional government. Though the Charter contains no provisions for expulsion of a member state (which in any case would not improve matters), in theory there is nothing to prevent the ASEAN Summit refusing to accept the new regime as representing the member state.

The test of ASEAN's resolve in this matter came in May 2014. At the Twenty-Fourth ASEAN Summit the ASEAN Foreign Ministers' Meeting (AMM)[96] issued a statement on developments in Thailand in which they emphasised their 'full support for a peaceful resolution to the ongoing challenge in the country through dialogue and in [sic] full respect of democratic principles and rule of law.' Barely a fortnight after the Summit the Thai armed forces staged a coup d'état. Indonesian President Susilo Bambang Yudhoyono was the most direct when he declared that the ASEAN Charter made it obligatory for members to respect democratic values and human rights; he stated: 'Indonesia is concerned because a military coup is not democratic', although it was an internal affair of Thailand.[97] Other ASEAN countries were not as forthright.[98] It appears that *realpolitik* had taken precedence over principle. It is hard to see how ASEAN could have done otherwise in practical terms. Expulsion from the grouping was politically out of the question; it would have torn ASEAN apart. A boycott of the new regime would have done nothing to improve matters in Thailand, in the absence of any realistic alternative government. At the time of writing the ASEAN Summit has yet to meet and pronounce on this issue.

---

announced martial law on 20 May 2014, on the basis of a 1914 law that allows it to intervene in times of crisis: *see* 'Army Invokes Martial Law', *Bangkok Post*, 20 May 2014: available at www.bangkokpost.com/news/ under the rubric Thailand under Martial Law. It was said that this did not amount to a coup as the government was left in charge of all matters except security. Two days later the mask fell and the military took over: *see BBC News* 22 May 2014: http://www.bbc.com/news/world-asia-27519940.

[96] Held in Nay Pyi Taw, Myanmar on 10 May 2014.

[97] See the Antara News website 24 May 2014, http://www.antaranews.com/en/news/94188/asean-must-address-coup-in-thailand-yudhoyono.

[98] A Joint Statement was issued after the Twentieth EU-ASEAN Joint Ministerial Meeting in Brussels on 23 July 2014, available at http://www.eeas.europa.eu/statements/docs/2014/140723_03_en.pdf. Paragraph 6 blandly notes that the EU ministers expressed concern about recent political developments in Thailand; nothing was said about the ASEAN ministers' reaction. Those familiar with such meetings might conclude that ASEAN chose to close ranks, especially since Thai Acting-Minister for Foreign Affairs Sihasak Phuangketkeow was there to explain the situation from Thailand's point of view.

(i) respect for fundamental freedoms, the promotion and protection of human rights, and the promotion of social justice;

Human rights and fundamental freedoms

Human rights was one of the most contentious issues during the process of drafting the Charter. Several delegations were extremely uncomfortable with having this enshrined in the Charter while others argued forcefully in favour of a robust Human Rights mechanism. Even the name of the body proved contentious, some members pushing for a 'Commission', others stoutly resisting. Article 14 on the ASEAN Human Rights Body was the carefully balanced, laboriously crafted compromise that resulted from the long (and sometimes heated) discussions among the HLTF as well as among the ASEAN Foreign Ministers.

The Terms of Reference (TOR) of the Human Rights Body had not been finalised when the Charter was signed. These were to be negotiated by a High Level Panel (HLP) for drafting the TOR, established by the Foreign Ministers at their Retreat in Singapore on 20 February 2008. The HLP commenced work in July 2008 and settled the draft of the TOR on 14 February 2009 after eight meetings.[99] Meanwhile, the ASEAN Political-Security Community Blueprint[100] specifically committed ASEAN to establish a human rights body.[101] The finalised TOR[102] was endorsed by the Forty-second ASEAN Foreign Ministers' Meeting held in Phuket, Thailand, on 20 July 2009. It was agreed that the body would be named the ASEAN Intergovernmental Commission on Human Rights (AICHR).[103] The AICHR was finally established in October 2009 at the Fifteenth ASEAN Summit.[104] It held its first meeting at the ASEAN Secretariat in April 2010. One of its major tasks was to develop an ASEAN Human Rights Declaration (AHRD).[105] The AHRD was adopted by the ASEAN leaders at the Twenty-first ASEAN Summit in Phnom Penh, Cambodia, on 18 November 2012.

---

99 Press Release by the Chair of the HLP issued on 14 Feb. 2009 at Luang Prabang, Laos.

100 Adopted by the Heads of State/Government at the Fourteenth ASEAN Summit in Cha-am, Thailand, on 1 Mar. 2009 as an annex to the Cha-Am Hua Hin Declaration on the Roadmap for an ASEAN Community (2009–15).

101 *See* para A.1.5(i) of the 2009 ASEAN Political-Security Community Blueprint.

102 This is to be found at http://aichr.org/?dl_name=TOR-of-AICHR.pdf.

103 Joint Communiqué of the Forty-second ASEAN Foreign Ministers' Meeting, para 8.

104 Cha-Am Hua Hin Declaration on the Intergovernmental Commission on Human Rights, issued by the ASEAN leaders at the Fifteenth ASEAN Summit, 23 Oct. 2009.

105 Terms of Reference of the ASEAN Intergovernmental Commission on Human Rights, para 4.2.

The ASEAN Human Rights Declaration (AHRD) affirms all the rights in the Universal Declaration of Human Rights: *see* the Preamble, Articles 10 and 26 of the AHRD. In addition, it explicitly sets out the following fundamental rights and freedoms:

- The right to life: AHRD Article 11.
- The right to personal liberty and security: AHRD Article 12.
- Freedom from servitude and slavery: AHRD Article 13.
- Freedom from torture and cruel, inhuman or degrading treatment or punishment: AHRD Article 14.
- Freedom of movement and residence within the borders of each state, and the right to leave and return to one's own country: AHRD Article 15.
- The right to seek and receive asylum: AHRD Article 16. Note that this is qualified by the laws of the receiving state.
- The right to property: AHRD Article 17.
- The right to nationality: AHRD Article 18. This right is also qualified by national law.
- The right to marry, found a family and divorce: AHRD Article 19. This right is confined to 'men and women of full age' and is subject to national law.
- The right to the presumption of innocence: AHRD Article 20(1).
- Protection against retroactive criminal laws: AHRD Article 20(2).
- Protection against double jeopardy: AHRD Article 20(3).
- Freedom from arbitrary interference with a person's privacy, family, home or correspondence (including personal data) and from attacks on his honour and reputation: AHRD Article 21.
- Freedom of thought, conscience and religion: AHRD Article 22.
- Freedom of opinion and expression: AHRD Article 23.
- The right of peaceful assembly: AHRD Article 24.
- The right to participate in the government of one's country, either directly or through democratically-elected representatives: AHRD Article 25(1).
- The right to vote in periodic and genuine elections: AHRD Article 25(2).
- The right to work: AHRD Article 27(1).
- The right to form and join trade unions: AHRD Article 27(2).
- Freedom from economic and social exploitation for children and young persons: AHRD Article 27(3).
- The right to an adequate standard of living: AHRD Article 28.
- The right of access to health care and medical services: AHRD Article 29(1).

- The right to social security: AHRD Article 30(1).
- The right to education: AHRD Article 31(1).
- The right to take part in cultural life and enjoy the arts and benefits of scientific progress: AHRD Article 32.
- The right to enjoy peace: AHRD Article 38.

It is explicitly stated in AHRD Article 6 that 'the enjoyment of human rights and fundamental freedoms must be balanced with the performance of corresponding duties as every person has responsibilities to all other individuals, the community and the society where one lives'. Article 7 of the AHRD provides a caveat that 'the realisation of human rights must be considered in the regional and national context bearing in mind different political, economic, legal, social, cultural, historical and religious backgrounds'. Furthermore, AHRD Article 8 provides that 'the human rights and fundamental freedoms of every person shall be exercised with due regard to the human rights and fundamental freedoms of others'.

Critics will of course carp at the fact that there is no supervisory mechanism. It is left entirely to each individual member state to translate the grand declarations of principle into concrete measures. However, considering the controversy that human rights provoked even at the start of the Charter-drafting process, it is an achievement to have even gotten so far. The AHRD, like the Charter itself, may not be perfect but it is a good basis on which to continue the evolution of ASEAN as a people-oriented, law-abiding, rules-based community. At the very least, the AHRD provides a standard to which the ASEAN member states have voluntarily signed up. There can be no excuses that these are norms made by others and imposed upon an unwilling ASEAN. The standards contained in the AHRD are those by which the behaviour of ASEAN member states will be judged, both by the world and their own peoples.

See also Article 14 on the ASEAN Human Rights Body (now known as the ASEAN Intergovernmental Commission on Human Rights).

Social justice

Social justice is mentioned in the 1967 ASEAN Declaration as a 'cherished ideal'. The 1976 Declaration of ASEAN Concord[106] made it an aim of ASEAN to eliminate poverty, disease, hunger, disease and illiteracy through economic and social development with particular

[106] Signed by the Heads of State/Government of the five original members at the First ASEAN Summit in Bali, Indonesia, on 24 Feb. 1976.

emphasis on the promotion of social justice. ASEAN Vision 2020[107] envisioned a 'socially cohesive and caring ASEAN' by the year 2020 in which social justice and the rule of law would reign. Thus 'social justice' has been a theme of ASEAN declarations from the first, though it had not been defined. Promotion of social justice now falls under the purview of the ASEAN Socio-Cultural Community (ASCC).[108] Section C of the ASCC Blueprint sets out in detail what is involved in promoting social justice and rights, namely:

- Promotion and protection of the rights and welfare of women, children, the elderly and persons with disabilities.
- Promotion and protection of the rights of migrant workers.
- Promoting corporate social responsibility in order to contribute to sustainable socio-economic development in ASEAN member states.

These matters are also repeated in the Initiative for ASEAN Integration Work Plan 2 (2009–15),[109] which is designed to narrow the development gap between the CLMV countries and the ASEAN-6. There is also some overlap with the programmes under the purview of the sectoral bodies for social development and the ministerial meeting for rural development and poverty eradication.[110]

(j) upholding the United Nations Charter and international law, including international humanitarian law, subscribed to by ASEAN Member States;

The 1967 ASEAN Declaration states that one of the purposes of ASEAN is to promote regional peace and stability through 'abiding respect for justice and the rule of law ... and adherence to the principles of the UN Charter'. The Declaration of ASEAN Concord (Bali Concord)[111] reaffirmed this commitment to the UN Charter in its Preamble.

---

[107] Issued at the Second ASEAN Informal Summit in Kuala Lumpur, Malaysia, on 15 Dec. 1997.

[108] *See* para 6 of the ASEAN Socio-Cultural Community Blueprint, which forms part of the Roadmap for an ASEAN Community (2009–15) adopted by the Heads of State/ Government at the Fourteenth ASEAN Summit in Cha-Am, Thailand, on 1 Mar. 2009.

[109] This also forms part of the Roadmap for an ASEAN Community (2009–15).

[110] The senior officials-level Committee on Social Development was one of the earliest committees established in 1978, with the objective of addressing social risks to and raising the living standards of disadvantaged groups. In 1998, ASEAN established the ASEAN Ministerial Meeting on Rural Development and Poverty Eradication.

[111] Signed on 24 Feb. 1976 in Denpasar, Bali by the Heads of State/Government at the First ASEAN Summit, together with the Treaty of Amity and Cooperation in Southeast Asia.

The specific mention of international humanitarian law was a proposal originating from the Eminent Persons Group (EPG) Report,[112] following active lobbying of several EPG members by representatives of the International Committee of the Red Cross. The qualification of 'international humanitarian law' by the phrase 'subscribed to by ASEAN Member States' makes clear that not everything that is asserted by some parties to be international humanitarian law is accepted as such by individual ASEAN member states.

(k) abstention from participation in any policy or activity, including the use of its territory, pursued by any ASEAN Member State or non-ASEAN State or any non-State actor, which threatens the sovereignty, territorial integrity or political and economic stability of ASEAN Member States;

Article 10 of the 1976 Treaty of Amity and Cooperation in Southeast Asia (TAC)[113] commits the High Contracting Parties not to 'participate in any activity which shall constitute a threat to the political and economic stability, sovereignty or territorial integrity of another High Contracting Party'.

This paragraph is a compromise text going beyond the recommendations of the Eminent Persons Group (EPG) on the ASEAN Charter to take into account a wider spectrum of threats to the member states. In the view of Laotian HLTF member Bounkeut Sangsomak, 'adherence to this principle has significantly healed the historical wounds stemmed [sic] from proxy wars in Southeast Asia'.[114]

(l) respect for the different cultures, languages and religions of the peoples of ASEAN, while emphasising their common values in the spirit of unity in diversity;

ASEAN is one of the most culturally diverse regions of the world. Indochina is where the civilizations of China and the Indian subcontinent intersect.[115]

---

[112] Report of the Eminent Persons Group on the ASEAN Charter, paras 27 and 60.

[113] Signed on 24 Feb. 1976 by the Heads of State/Government in Bali at the First ASEAN Summit.

[114] Bounkeut Sangsomak, 'A New Turning Point in the Relations Among the Southeast Asian States', in T Koh, Manalo and Woon, eds., *Making of the ASEAN Charter*, chapter 13,164.

[115] For an anthropological summary of the origins of the peoples of Southeast Asia, *see* Tarling, *Southeast Asia*, 3–10.

Buddhism is the dominant religion in Myanmar, Laos, Cambodia, Vietnam and Thailand. Islam holds sway in Indonesia, Malaysia and Brunei. The Philippines is a Roman Catholic-majority country. Historically, there has been no culture or language common to all the ten ASEAN member states. Article 1(14) lists the creation of an ASEAN identity as one of the purposes of the organisation. Article 35 states that 'ASEAN shall promote its common ASEAN identity and a sense of belonging among its peoples in order to achieve its shared destiny, goals and values.' This identity however will not be a melding of the different cultures. Unity in diversity is the guiding principle.

The phrase 'unity in diversity' is a nod in the direction of Indonesia, being the translation of the Javanese phrase 'Bhinneka Tunggal Ika', the motto of the Republic of Indonesia inscribed on its coat of arms.

(m) the centrality of ASEAN in external political, economic, social and cultural relations while remaining actively engaged, outward-looking, inclusive and non-discriminatory; and

The 'centrality of ASEAN' and its associated concept of ASEAN as a 'primary driving force' or 'in the driver's seat' came into use in the 1990s as ASEAN expanded its role as a convenor in forums such as the ASEAN Regional Forum (ARF), established in 1994, and the ASEAN Plus Three (established in 1997). What these terms entail was explained by Mr George Yeo, the Foreign Minister of Singapore, in a statement at the closing ceremony of the Forty-first ASEAN Ministerial Meeting when Singapore handed over the Chairmanship to Thailand:[116]

> 'With the rise of China and India changing the polarity of the world, we must make sure that the political, economic and security architecture of the region takes into account the interest of ASEAN. Over the years, ASEAN, in a peaceful non-threatening way, has helped to bring countries in the region together. We have been able to do this through enlightened diplomacy and by offering our hand of friendship to all the major powers. We must never lose this position. We must take an active interest in regional and global affairs and play a role which is helpful to others. We ensure the centrality of ASEAN in the evolving

[116] Issued in Singapore on 24 July 2008. Available on the ASEAN website under the Political-Security Community, Forty-first AMM: www.asean.org/communities/asean-political-security-community.

regional architecture, not by force or assertion but by the openness and neutrality of our position and by our usefulness to others'.

ASEAN is open to engagement with all countries and international organisations. The ASEAN Regional Forum brings together the major players in Asia to discuss security issues. Meetings with dialogue partners are a regular feature of ASEAN Summits and Foreign Ministers' Meetings. The 1976 Treaty of Amity and Cooperation in Southeast Asia (TAC) is open to accession by any state or regional organisation, even ones far removed geographically from Southeast Asia.[117] The principal objective of ASEAN diplomacy is to be friends with everyone: *see* Article 41(1) on Conduct of External Relations.

See also Articles 1(15) and 41(3) regarding the centrality of ASEAN. It is part of the role of the member state holding the Chair to ensure the centrality of ASEAN: *see* Article 32(b).

(n) adherence to multilateral trade rules and ASEAN's rules-based regimes for effective implementation of economic commitments and progressive reduction towards elimination of all barriers to regional economic integration, in a market-driven economy.

Article 1(5) states that it is one of the purposes of ASEAN 'to create a single market and production base which is stable, prosperous, highly competitive and economically integrated with effective facilitation for trade and investment in which there is free flow of goods, services and investment; facilitated movement of business persons, professionals, talents and labour; and freer flow of capital'. The Fourth ASEAN Summit held in Singapore (27–29 January 1992) was the first one after the settlement of the Cambodian problem[118] and marked a shift in focus to

[117] At the time of writing the following have acceded to the TAC (*see* the ASEAN Legal Instruments list at http://agreement.asean.org): Papua New Guinea (10 Aug. 1989); the People's Republic of China (8 Oct. 2003); India (8 Oct. 2003); Japan (2 July 2004); Pakistan (2 July 2004); Republic of Korea (27 Nov. 2004); the Russian Federation (29 Nov. 2004); Australia (28 July 2005); Mongolia (28 July 2005); New Zealand (28 July 2005); France (13 Jan. 2007); Timor Leste (13 Jan. 2007); Bangladesh (1 Aug. 2007); Sri Lanka (1 Aug. 2007); the Democratic People's Republic of Korea (24 July 2008); the European Communities and European Union (28 May 2009); the United States of America (22 July 2009); Canada (23 July 2010); Turkey (23 July 2010); the United Kingdom (3 July 2012); Brazil (17 Nov. 2012); Norway (1 July 2013). Serbia has also expressed interest in acceding to the TAC: *see* the Chairman's Statement of the Twenty-first ASEAN Summit (Phnom Penh, Nov. 2012).

[118] This had occupied the attention of ASEAN diplomats from the Vietnamese invasion of Cambodia in Dec. 1978 to the withdrawal of Vietnamese troops and the election of a

economic matters. Two major economic agreements were signed: the Agreement on the Common Effective Preferential Tariff (CEPT) Scheme for the ASEAN Free Trade Area and the Framework Agreement on Enhancing ASEAN Economic Cooperation. In the Singapore Declaration issued on 28 January 1992, the leaders declared the intention that ASEAN move to a higher plane of political and economic cooperation. The Bali Concord II[119] declared that an ASEAN Economic Community (AEC) would be created. The AEC is now the most advanced of the three pillars of the ASEAN Community.[120] This paragraph complements the aim of creating the AEC and furthering ASEAN economic integration.

new Cambodian government in 1991.

[119] Officially, the Declaration of ASEAN Concord II, signed in Bali at the Ninth ASEAN Summit by the Heads of State/Government on 7 Oct. 2003.

[120] However, the private sector appears sceptical about the realisation of ASEAN's grand ambitions. *See* for example R. Sally, 'The ASEAN Charter and the ASEAN Economic Community: A Watershed for Regional Economic Integration?', E. Pedrosa, 'Implications of an Uncerain Global Economy on Integration Initiatives', and M. Hutagalung, 'ASEAN: An Integrated Market?', in Tiwari, ed., *Life After the Charter,* chapters 7–9. Although these articles were written in 2010, shortly after the entry into force of the Charter, similar doubts have repeatedly been expressed to the author by business leaders in the years leading up to deadline for the ASEAN Economic Community in 2015.

CHAPTER II.
LEGAL PERSONALITY

Article 3. Legal Personality of Asean

ASEAN, as an inter-governmental organisation, is hereby conferred legal personality.

Compare Article 47 of the Treaty on European Union, which provides simply, 'The Union shall have legal personality'. The Charter of the United Nations does not explicitly confer legal personality on the UN.

Legal personality in domestic law

Malaysia proposed to reform the institutional framework of ASEAN in a paper entitled 'Review of ASEAN Institutional Framework: Proposals for Change' circulated at the Foreign Ministers' retreat in Ha Long Bay, Vietnam, in March 2004. The ASEAN Secretariat put up a draft of a Charter, which was a review of the institutional framework and highlighted the need for a legal personality for the organisation. Several practical problems arose because ASEAN did not exist formally as an entity. For instance, external parties would donate money to ASEAN, which technically did not exist as a legal person; this meant that the donors could not claim tax credit in their home countries, since ASEAN was a 'non-entity'. Other donors expressed a wish to sign agreements with ASEAN, rather than with the individual member states. The pragmatic solution was for the ASEAN Secretariat (ASEC) to receive the funds and sign the agreements. The Eminent Persons Group (EPG) on the ASEAN Charter[1] recommended that ASEAN should 'be conferred legal personality and be able to engage

[1] *See* the Report of the Eminent Persons Group on the ASEAN Charter, Executive Summary para 7, and also paras 43 and 66.

in legal proceeding (sic)'. This was endorsed by the leaders in the Cebu Declaration on the Blueprint of the ASEAN Charter.[2] The focus was entirely on the legal personality of ASEAN according to the domestic law of the member states.

Indonesia had recognised ASEC's legal personality in the 1976 Agreement on the Establishment of the ASEAN Secretariat, the 1979 Agreement between the Government of Indonesia Relating to the Privileges and Immunities of the ASEAN Secretariat[3] and the 1981 Agreement on the Use and Maintenance of the Premises of the ASEAN Secretariat. The 1979 Agreement stated that ASEC (as opposed to ASEAN as an organisation) would have capacity to conclude contracts, acquire and dispose of immovable and movable properties and institute legal proceedings. The Charter was meant to ensure that ASEAN as an entity would similarly have a legal personality in all the member states. There was no discussion during the drafting process about theoretical issues of legal personality of international organisations. The High Level Task Force (HLTF) on Drafting the ASEAN Charter was concerned solely with the mundane problems of holding property, making contracts, suing and being sued. Thus, Article 55 vests the assets and funds of ASEAN in the organisation.

After the signing of the Charter, a High Level Legal Experts' Group (HLEG) on Follow-up to the ASEAN Charter was set up to look into the legal aspects of implementation.[4] The HLEG's instructions confined it mainly to the domestic aspects of ASEAN's legal personality in the member states.[5] The recommendation of the HLEG regarding the legal personality of ASEAN was endorsed by the Forty-second Foreign Ministers' Meeting held in Phuket, Thailand, on 20 July 2009.[6] The 2009 Agreement on the Privileges and Immunities of ASEAN[7] provides in Article 2(1) that ASEAN shall have the capacity under the domestic laws of the member states to enter into contracts, acquire and dispose of movable and immovable

---

2 Issued at the Twelfth ASEAN Summit in Cebu, the Philippines, on 13 Jan. 2007.

3 This has been superseded by a new agreement between Indonesia and ASEAN signed in Phnom Penh on 2 Apr. 2012.

4 Joint Communiqué of the Forty-first ASEAN Foreign Ministers' Meeting, para 11.

5 *See* Jeffrey Chan, 'ASEAN Legal Personality under its New Charter', in Tiwari, ed., *Life After the Charter*, chapter 1, 6–7. Mr Jeffrey Chan was Deputy Solicitor-General of Singapore and chaired the HLEG for part of its term of office.

6 Joint Communiqué of the Forty-second ASEAN Foreign Ministers' Meeting, para 9.

7 Adopted at the Fifteenth ASEAN Summit in Cha-Am Hua Hin, Thailand, on 25 Oct. 2009. This is not yet in force according to the ASEAN Legal Instruments list at http://agreement.asean.org.

property and institute and defend legal proceedings.[8] Thus, apart from contracting and owning property, ASEAN as an entity would be in a position to defend its intellectual property in the courts of member states. These include the ASEAN motto, the ASEAN flag, the ASEAN anthem and the ASEAN emblem, as well as the publications of the ASEAN Secretariat.[9] The problem lies in controlling the unauthorised use of these symbols by NGOs and other groups. It is left to the member states to ensure that this is translated into a legally binding form according to their domestic laws.

Rules of Authorisation for Legal Transactions under Domestic Laws were promulgated in 2010.[10] The 2012 Agreement Between the Government of the Republic of Indonesia and the Association of Southeast Asian Nations on Hosting and Granting Privileges and Immunities to the ASEAN Secretariat superseded the 1979 and 1981 agreements, and provided for privileges and immunities of ASEAN and its juridical capacity under Indonesian law: *see* commentary to Article 17(2).

Conclusion of international agreements

ASEAN may conclude agreements with countries or other international institutions: *see* Article 41(7). Rules of Procedure for this purpose were adopted by the Ninth ASEAN Coordinating Council in Bali on 17 November 2011.[11] A new Agreement on Hosting and Granting Privileges and Immunities was signed between ASEAN and Indonesia in Phnom Penh on 2 April 2012. The Agreement was executed by Dr Surin Pitsuwan, the Secretary-General, on behalf of ASEAN. This new agreement superseded a previous Agreement between Indonesia and ASEAN regarding the privileges and immunities of the ASEAN Secretariat (ASEC).[12] Interestingly, this old Agreement was purportedly signed on behalf of ASEAN by the 'Secretary-General of the ASEAN Secretariat', Datuk Ali bin Abdullah.

---

[8] Compare Article I of the 1946 Convention on the Privileges and Immunities of the United Nations.

[9] *See* Chalermpalanupap, 'Life in ASEAN after the Entry into Force of the ASEAN Charter', 59. Dr Termsak was a senior official of the ASEAN Secretariat for many years and served as Special Assistant to Secretary-General Ong Keng Yong. He served as resource person to both the Eminent Persons Group on the ASEAN Charter and High Level Task Force on the ASEAN Charter.

[10] Adopted by the ASEAN Foreign Ministers Meeting on 27 Oct. 2010. The text of this is available on the documents database of the Centre for International Law, National University of Singapore, cil.nus.edu.sg.

[11] The text of this is available on the documents database of the Centre for International Law, National University of Singapore, cil.nus.edu.sg.

[12] 1979 Agreement between the Government of Indonesia and ASEAN Relating to the Privileges and Immunities of the ASEAN Secretariat.

According to two former senior ASEAN officials, ASEC had been signing agreements and memoranda of understanding with external parties even before the conclusion of the Charter.[13]

International legal personality

This Article states that ASEAN has a legal personality. Whether ASEAN's international legal personality will be recognised by non-member states and other international organisations is quite another matter. However, ASEAN probably fulfils most of the criteria for international legal personality.[14] The fact that 79 ambassadors to ASEAN[15] have been accredited under Article 46 is also significant, implying as it does a recognition of ASEAN's international legal personality by a majority of states, including all five permanent members of the UN Security Council. ASEAN also has observer status at the United Nations, though without a permanent mission.[16]

The real question is not what status ASEAN has in international law but what it can do. Entering international agreements is specifically provided for in Article 41. Whether non-member states or international entities will choose to enter into agreements with ASEAN (as opposed to ASEAN member states individually or collectively) is quite another thing; this is a question of policy and not principle. In international law it is not theory but practice that counts.

Inter-governmental organisation

The phrase 'as an inter-governmental organisation' was inserted by the HLTF in order to make clear that there is no supranational element to ASEAN. It was clear from the very beginning of the Charter-drafting process that member states were not ready to share sovereignty in any way. This reluctance on the part of the member states to pool sovereignty makes them ambivalent about creating independent institutions in

---

13 Dr Termsak Chalermpalanupap (who was at one time Special Assistant to Secretary-General Ong Keng Yong) at a seminar on ASEAN's Legal Personality organised by the Centre for International Law, National University of Singapore on 16 Aug. 2010. This was confirmed by Mr Rodolfo Severino, a former Secretary-General of ASEAN, at the same seminar.

14 *See Reparations for Injuries Suffered in the Service of the United Nations* (1949) ICJ 174 16 ILR 318.

15 As of Aug. 2014. For a current list, *see* http://www.asean.org/news/item/ambassadors-to-asean.

16 *See* UN website www.un.org/en/members/intergovorg.shtml.

ASEAN. Former Secretary-General Ong Keng Yong has commented that national egos remain strong and bureaucratic agencies in member countries are 'reluctant to commit to region-wide initiatives for fear of losing their national independence of action.'[17]

Thus one finds that the Secretary-General is still kept on a very tight leash, despite the fact that he has ministerial rank and is supposed to speak for ASEAN as an organisation.[18] Similarly, the member states are reluctant to concede the ASEAN Secretariat any independent role.[19] ASEAN member states have yet to fully come to terms with the fact that they are supposed to have created an independent entity called ASEAN, which is meant to be more than the sum of its constituent members. For the ASEAN member states, the legal personality of ASEAN does not imply that the organisation has any independent right of action. All decisions, even mundane ones like human resource management, are subject to the oversight of the member states.[20]

---

17 *See* 'At Close Quarters with the Drafting of the ASEAN Charter', in Koh, Manalo and Woon, eds., *Making of the ASEAN Charter* , chapter 10, 108.

18 *See* commentary to Article 11. Confirmed in conversation with two former Secretaries-General.

19 For example, consider the way that the ASEAN Secretariat's role in interpreting the Charter has been severely circumscribed: *see* commentary to Article 51.

20 For example, the Committee of Permanent Representatives was intimately involved in approving the ASEAN Secretariat Staff Regulations. Officials of the Secretariat and even some of the Permanent Representatives themselves complained that the CPR was micro-managing; *see* commentary to Article 12.

CHAPTER III.

MEMBERSHIP

Article 4. Member States

The Member States of ASEAN are Brunei Darussalam, the Kingdom of Cambodia, the Republic of Indonesia, the Lao People's Democratic Republic, Malaysia, the Union of Myanmar, the Republic of the Philippines, the Republic of Singapore, the Kingdom of Thailand and the Socialist Republic of Viet Nam.

The Association of Southeast Asian Nations was founded on 8 August 1967 by means of the ASEAN Declaration, a modest document that did not even purport to be a treaty. It was signed in Bangkok by the Foreign Ministers of Indonesia (Mr Adam Malik), Malaysia (Tun Abdul Razak, who was Deputy Prime Minister rather than Foreign Minister), the Philippines (Mr Narciso Ramos), Singapore (Mr S. Rajaratnam) and Thailand (Mr Thanat Khoman). The original five were joined by Brunei in 1984.[1] Vietnam joined

[1] Declaration of the Admission of Brunei Darussalam into ASEAN, signed in Jakarta on 7 Jan. 1984. Brunei ratified the Treaty of Amity and Cooperation in Southeast Asia (TAC) on 6 June 1987.

ASEAN in 1995,[2] Laos[3] and Myanmar[4] in 1997. Cambodia finally became the tenth ASEAN member in 1999.[5]

Before the ASEAN Charter, ASEAN instruments used various terms to refer to ASEAN member states (e.g., ASEAN states, ASEAN members, ASEAN countries etc.). After the adoption of the ASEAN Charter, the term 'ASEAN member states' has been used more consistently in ASEAN instruments.

In 2008, the full official name of Myanmar was changed from the 'Union of Myanmar' to the 'Republic of the Union of Myanmar' under its new Constitution.

See Article 6 as to admission of new members.

Article 5. Rights and Obligations

1. Member States shall have equal rights and obligations under this Charter.

Equality has been recognised as a fundamental principle since the 1976 Treaty of Amity and Cooperation in Southeast Asia (TAC).[6] This principle is reiterated in Article 2(2)(a) of the Charter. All members have an equal voice and the organisation works by consensus. It is hard to see how it could function otherwise, as no country would join if it could be outvoted on matters that it considered to be vital to its national interest.

---

[2] Declaration of the Admission of the Socialist Republic of Viet Nam into the Association of Southeast Asian Nations, signed in Bandar Seri Begawan, Brunei Darussalam on 28 July 1995. Vietnam had acceded to the Treaty of Amity and Cooperation in Southeast Asia (TAC) on 22 July 1995, having ratified it on 30 May.

[3] Declaration on the Admission of the Lao People's Democratic Republic into the Association of Southeast Asian Nations, signed in Subang Jaya, Malaysia on 23 July 1997. Laos had acceded to the Treaty of Amity and Cooperation in Southeast Asia (TAC) on 29 June 1992 and ratified it on 17 July 1996.

[4] Declaration on the Admission of the Union of Myanmar into the Association of Southeast Asian Nations, signed in Subang Jaya, Malaysia on 23 July 1997. Myanmar ratified the Treaty of Amity and Cooperation in Southeast Asia (TAC) on 10 July 1996, having acceded to it on 27 July 1995.

[5] Declaration on the Admission of the Kingdom of Cambodia into the Association of Southeast Asian Nations, signed in Hanoi, Vietnam, on 30 Apr. 1999. Cambodia ratified the Treaty of Amity and Cooperation in Southeast Asia (TAC) on 25 July 1995, having acceded on 25 Jan. 1995.

[6] Signed at the First ASEAN Summit in Bali on 24 Feb. 1976 by the Heads of State/Government of the original five member states. Accession to the TAC was a necessary step in order to join ASEAN before the Charter came into force. *See* commentary to Article 5.4.

2. Member States shall take all necessary measures, including the enactment of appropriate domestic legislation, to effectively implement the provisions of this Charter and to comply with all obligations of membership.

This commitment to implementation was reiterated by the leaders in the Singapore Declaration on the ASEAN Charter, issued on 20 November 2007, the same day that the Charter was signed.

3. In the case of a serious breach of the Charter or non-compliance, the matter shall be referred to Article 20.

The Eminent Persons Group suggested that there should be provisions for the ASEAN Summit to impose measures including suspension of membership in cases of a serious breach of ASEAN obligations.[7] Some HLTF delegations wanted a more robust statement regarding the consequences of a breach, but no consensus could be reached. At their Retreat in Siem Reap (1–2 March 2007) most of the Foreign Ministers were against expulsion even if there were to be an egregious breach of the Charter. It would be a problem to find a consensus for expulsion. In any case, it was felt that a provision for expulsion would be contrary to the family spirit of ASEAN. The Foreign Ministers consequently instructed that there should be no mention of suspension, expulsion or withdrawal in the Charter. Contrast Articles 5 and 6 of the Charter of the United Nations, which provide for the suspension or expulsion of UN members.

The present wording of Article 5(3) was the bare-minimum text that could be agreed upon. Again, the drafting looks odd to the legal practitioner. This particular provision was settled at the twelfth HLTF meeting in Bandar Seri Begawan, Brunei (3–5 October 2007), by which date there was little time left to quibble about the wording, the reservations of the lawyers notwithstanding. What it means is that if there is non-compliance with any of the provisions of the Charter, the matter shall be referred to the ASEAN Summit for decision. The Charter is silent on who may refer an instance of non-compliance to the ASEAN Summit. Clearly any member state should be able to do so; otherwise the commitment

---

[7] The EPG proposals further specified that such measures must be taken by unanimity without the participation of the member state to which the measure may be applied, and also proposed that there should be no recourse to expulsion unless Decided by the ASEAN Leaders in exceptional circumstances. *See* Report of the Eminent Persons Group on the ASEAN Charter, para 61.

in Article 5(2) to comply with the Charter would be meaningless. It is an open question whether the Secretary-General may also do so as part of his duty to monitor the implementation of ASEAN agreements and decisions under Article 11(2)(b). The HLTF did not consider this matter at all. However, the Eminent Persons Group recommended that the Secretary-General should be entrusted with the role of reporting non-compliance to the Summit.[8]

Article 6. Admission of New Members

1. The procedure for application and admission to ASEAN shall be prescribed by the ASEAN Coordinating Council.

The ASEAN Coordinating Council (ACC) comprises the Foreign Ministers of ASEAN. *See* Article 8.

2. Admission shall be based on the following criteria:

(a) location in the recognised geographical region of Southeast Asia;
(b) recognition by all ASEAN Member States;
(c) agreement to be bound and to abide by the Charter; and
(d) ability and willingness to carry out the obligations of Membership.

The 1967 ASEAN Declaration[9] stated that 'the Association is open for participation to all states in the Southeast Asian Region' subscribing to the aims, principles and purposes set out in the Declaration. The geographical limits of the Southeast Asian Region were not defined. There are only two non-ASEAN countries in the broader geographical area of Southeast Asia: Papua New Guinea and Timor-Leste. Both of these share islands with Indonesia, respectively New Guinea and Timor.

The island of New Guinea might perhaps be considered to be only peripherally linked to Southeast Asia. In ecological terms it lies across Wallace's Line separating Australasia from Asia. Culturally, it is quite

[8] See the Report of the Eminent Persons Group on the ASEAN Charter, para 62, 'Secretary-General of ASEAN'.

[9] Signed on 8 Aug. 1967 in Bangkok by the Foreign Ministers of Indonesia, Malaysia, the Philippines, Singapore and Thailand.

distinct. Nonetheless, Papua New Guinea was accorded the status of special observer in 1976 and acceded to the Treaty of Amity and Cooperation in Southeast Asia (TAC) on 10 August 1989, the first non-ASEAN state to have done so. A delegation from Papua New Guinea first attended the ASEAN Ministerial Meeting in 1976 as a guest of the Philippine government.[10]

Timor-Leste (or East Timor) was a former Portuguese colony that was absorbed into Indonesia in 1976.[11] It was returned to the status of a territory under UN supervision after a referendum in August 1999 (which was accompanied by a paroxysm of violence) and finally achieved independence in 2002. Timor-Leste applied formally to join ASEAN in 2011, having acceded to the TAC on 13 January 2007.[12]

3. Admission shall be decided by consensus by the ASEAN Summit, upon the recommendation of the ASEAN Coordinating Council.

Timor-Leste's application

At the Eighteenth ASEAN Summit in Jakarta (May 2011) the leaders decided that Timor-Leste's formal application to join ASEAN needed further consideration. The Foreign Ministers were tasked with looking into this issue in their capacity as the ASEAN Coordinating Council.[13] An ASEAN Coordinating Council Working Group (ACCWG) was set up later that year to discuss Timor-Leste's application and its implications for ASEAN.[14] The ACCWG is to make its recommendations based on whether Timor-Leste is able to meet all the obligations of ASEAN membership. Among the major concerns were the number of meetings that needed to be supported and the commitment of government resources that joining ASEAN would entail. Capacity-building was vital. The ACCWG got off to a slow start. By the time of the Twentieth ASEAN Summit in Phnom Penh in April 2012 it had not yet held its first meeting.[15] In September 2013 the ACCWG made a visit to Timor-Leste to assess its ability to fulfil the obligations of ASEAN membership. The Chairman's Statement of

---

10 *See* the Joint Communiqué of the Ninth ASEAN Ministerial Meeting, Manila, para 3.

11 *See* Britannica Online: www.britannica.com/EBchecked/596313/East-Timor.

12 ASEAN Legal Instruments list, available at http://agreement.asean.org.

13 *See* the Chairman's Statement of the Eighteenth ASEAN Summit (Jakarta, May 2011), para 138.

14 *See* the Chairman's Statement of the Nineteenth ASEAN Summit (Bali, Nov. 2011), para 146.

15 *See* the Chairman's Statement of the Twentieth ASEAN Summit (Phnom Penh, Apr. 2012), para 82.

the Twenty-third ASEAN Summit blandly welcomed the progress made by the ACCWG in their deliberations on Timor-Leste's application.[16] An almost-identical statement was made at the end of the Twenty-fourth ASEAN Summit the following year.[17] The application was still pending at the time of writing and no timeline for a decision has been set by ASEAN.

4. An applicant State shall be admitted to ASEAN upon signing an Instrument of Accession to the Charter.

Before the Charter came into force, an applicant state would accede to the Treaty of Amity and Cooperation in Southeast Asia 1976 as a preliminary step and subsequently sign a Declaration of Admission, followed by separate accession instruments to the key ASEAN agreements (in the case of Brunei and Vietnam), or a Protocol of accession (in the case of Laos, Myanmar and Cambodia) to all the ASEAN treaties.[18] Candidates for accession were often also invited to observe ASEAN Summits and Ministerial Meetings as guests of the Chair. The last state to join ASEAN was Cambodia, on 30 April 1999. There was a special ceremony in Hanoi to mark the occasion, at which the Declaration on the Admission of the Kingdom of Cambodia into the Association of Southeast Asian Nations was signed.

---

16 *See* the Chairman's Statement of the Twenty-second ASEAN Summit (Bandar Seri Begawan, Oct. 2013), para 54.

17 *See* Chairman's statement of the Twenty-fourth ASEAN Summit (Nay Pyi Taw, May 2014), para 78.

18 *See* for example the Protocol for the Accession of the Kingdom of Cambodia to ASEAN Agreements, signed on 30 Apr. 1999 in Hanoi. Cambodia ratified the Treaty of Amity and Cooperation in Southeast Asia (TAC) on 25 July 1995, having acceded on 25 Jan. 1995. For a more comprehensive set of examples of accession documents, please visit the CIL Documents Database at http://cil.nus.edu.sg/2009/cil-documents-database/ and the 'ASEAN Accession' category.

CHAPTER IV.

ORGANS

Former Secretary-General Rodolfo Severino has made the point that in ASEAN, the institutions follow the substance.[1] *The process starts first, and the institutions develop later in support. The evolution of the ASEAN Summit and the ASEAN Ministerial Meeting are cases in point: see the commentary to Articles 7 and 10. As one senior Thai diplomat put it to the author, ASEAN solves problems by improvisation. To change the paradigm, the Eminent Persons Group (EPG) for drafting of the ASEAN Charter recommended a rationalisation of the institutions, from the top down. The EPG Report contained a detailed list of organs,*[2] *which the High Level Task Force (HLTF) was supposed to flesh out. That process proved difficult. It was necessary to balance theory against practicality. Many of the suggested organs were completely new (e.g., the ASEAN Coordinating Council, the three Community Councils and the Committee of Permanent Representatives). There was no experience to draw on. It will take time to rub down the rough edges of the interface among these institutions.*

ARTICLE 7: ASEAN SUMMIT

History of the ASEAN Summit

The founders of ASEAN did not initially envisage a summit meeting of the leaders of the member states. Indeed, the ASEAN Declaration merely

[1] Severino, *In Search of an ASEAN Community*, 23–4.

[2] Report of the Eminent Persons Group on the ASEAN Charter, para 62. This comprises nine pages of the Report, but does not go into detail regarding the exact function of the listed organs.

provided for an annual meeting of Foreign Ministers, known as the ASEAN Ministerial Meeting (AMM).[3] The Heads of State/Government did not get involved in any formal way. That changed after the fall of South Vietnam. The First ASEAN Summit was held in Bali only in February 1976, nearly nine years after the ASEAN Declaration. One of the main results of the First ASEAN Summit was the Declaration of ASEAN Concord ('Bali Concord'), which provided for meetings of heads of government 'as and when necessary'. All the members of ASEAN agreed to sign the Treaty of Amity and Cooperation in Southeast Asia (TAC),[4] which committed the parties to the peaceful settlement of disputes. A second summit was held in Kuala Lumpur the following year, at which the ASEAN Economic Ministers' Meeting (AEM) was formalised. After that there was a ten-year hiatus until the Third ASEAN Summit in Manila in 1987.[5] The major diplomatic result was the amendment of the TAC to allow for the accession of states outside Southeast Asia.[6]

Thereafter, summit meetings continued to be held at irregular intervals, the fourth taking place in Singapore in January 1992. The Fourth Summit was the first one after the settlement of the Cambodian problem and marked a shift in focus to economic matters. Two major economic agreements were signed: the Agreement on the Common Effective Preferential Tariff (CEPT) Scheme for the ASEAN Free Trade Area and the Framework Agreement on Enhancing ASEAN Economic Cooperation. In the Singapore Declaration issued on 28 January 1992, the leaders declared the intention that ASEAN move to a higher plane of political and economic cooperation. It was announced that an ASEAN Free Trade

---

[3] The very first AMM was the one at which the ASEAN Declaration was adopted on 8 Aug. 1967.

[4] Accession to the TAC eventually became an essential step towards membership of ASEAN.

[5] The hiatus is said to have been due to ASEAN member states' reluctance to convene a summit in the Philippines (next state in the alphabetical rotation) under the government of Ferdinand Marcos. *See* Severino, *In Search of an ASEAN Community*, 18–19.

[6] At the time of writing the following have acceded to the TAC (*see* the ASEAN Legal Instruments list at http://agreement.asean.org): Papua New Guinea (10 Aug. 1989); the People's Republic of China (8 Oct. 2003); India (8 Oct. 2003); Japan (2 July 2004); Pakistan (2 July 2004); Republic of Korea (27 Nov. 2004); the Russian Federation (29 Nov. 2004); Australia (28 July 2005); Mongolia (28 July 2005); New Zealand (28 July 2005); France (13 Jan. 2007); Timor Leste (13 Jan. 2007); Bangladesh (1 Aug. 2007); Sri Lanka (1 Aug. 2007); the Democratic People's Republic of Korea (24 July 2008); the European Communities and European Union (28 May 2009); the United States of America (22 July 2009); Canada (23 July 2010); Turkey (23 July 2010); the United Kingdom (3 July 2012); Brazil (17 Nov. 2012); Norway (1 July 2013). Serbia has also expressed interest in acceding to the TAC: *see* the Chairman's Statement of the Twenty-first ASEAN Summit (Phnom Penh, Nov. 2012).

Area (AFTA) would be established using the CEPT scheme. This was the embryo of the ASEAN Economic Community. It was decided that formal summit meetings would be held every three years, with informal summits in the intervening period.

The Fifth Summit was held in Bangkok in December 1995. Vietnam had just become a member of ASEAN and the vision of bringing all Southeast Asian countries within the fold was progressing nicely.[7] The Treaty on the Southeast Asia Nuclear Weapon-Free Zone (SEANWFZ) was signed. The Fifth Summit was followed by the first and second informal ASEAN Summits, which were held in Jakarta (30 November 1996) and Kuala Lumpur (14–16 December 1997).[8] The 1997 Summit was declared to be a commemorative summit, marking the thirtieth Anniversary of the founding of ASEAN. ASEAN Vision 2020 was adopted by the leaders as a programme to bring ASEAN into the twenty-first century.

The Sixth ASEAN Summit took place in Hanoi in December 1998, followed by two more informal summits in Manila (27–28 November 1999) and Singapore (22–25 November 2000). Thereafter, the pace of summitry picked up, with annual formal summits from 2001 onwards.

The Ninth ASEAN Summit in Bali (October 2003) saw the adoption of the Declaration of ASEAN Concord II (Bali Concord II). This was a significant gesture, referring back to the original Bali Concord issued at the First ASEAN Summit twenty-seven years previously. The Bali Concord II was a re-imagining of the ASEAN idea. In it the leaders of the member states declared their intention to establish an ASEAN Community consisting of three pillars: political and security cooperation, economic cooperation and socio-cultural cooperation. The first pillar was the longest-established, political dialogue having been driven by the Foreign Ministers since the foundation of ASEAN. The second pillar, economic cooperation, had its own ministerial body and progressed in parallel with the first ever since the First ASEAN Summit in 1976. The third pillar was new, sweeping together other activities that did not belong under the first two pillars. The Joint Ministerial Meeting (JMM)[9] was revived, comprising the AMM, AEM, AFMM and the Secretary-General. The Bali Concord II

---

[7] Laos and Cambodia attended as observers. They joined ASEAN in 1997 and 1999 respectively.

[8] In order to coordinate between the AMM and AEM, a Joint Ministerial Meeting (JMM) had been created at the Third Summit (Manila, 1987). However, continued rivalry between the AMM and AEM made it difficult in practice to convene the JMM. It was decided that the solution lay in holding more frequent meetings of the leaders, which led to the convening of the informal annual summits in the gap between the official ones.

[9] This had been established at the Third Summit (Manila, 1987).

paved the way for the eventual adoption of the ASEAN Charter at the Thirteenth Summit in Singapore in November 2007.[10]

By the first decade of the twenty-first century, the ASEAN Summit had become the major event in the life of the organisation. ASEAN had broadened out its reach to engage dialogue partners like Japan, China, the Republic of Korea (which collectively came to be known as ASEAN+3), India, Australia, New Zealand, Russia, Canada, the European Union and the United States. Meetings with external partners were held back-to-back with the Summits. Framework agreements for closer economic cooperation were concluded with major dialogue partners.[11] The logic of economic integration led to a spate of ASEAN economic agreements. The pace and intensity of the meetings made it necessary to double the number of summits per year, as recognised by the Eminent Persons Group in its report.

There were no summits in 2008.[12] Since the Charter came into force in December 2008 two summits have been held every year. The first under the new Charter provisions was the Fourteenth ASEAN Summit, held in Cha-Am, Thailand from 26 February to 1 March 2009.[13] This saw the adoption of the Cha-Am Hua Hin Declaration on the Roadmap for the ASEAN Community (2009–15), which incorporated the Blueprints for the ASEAN Political-Security Community (APSC), the ASEAN Economic

---

[10] There were actually two summits in 2007: in Cebu, the Philippines, from 9–15 Jan. and in Singapore from 18–22 Nov. 2007. The Cebu summit was postponed from Dec. 2006 on account of a typhoon threat.

[11] Such an agreement had already been concluded with China in 2002: *see* the Framework Agreement on Comprehensive Economic Cooperation between ASEAN and China. At the Ninth Summit in 2003, agreements were signed with India and Japan: *see* the Framework Agreement on Comprehensive Economic Cooperation between India and ASEAN and the Framework Agreement for Comprehensive Economic Partnership between Japan and ASEAN. The Eleventh Summit in Kuala Lumpur saw the conclusion of the Framework Agreement on Comprehensive Economic Cooperation among the Governments of Member Countries of ASEAN and the Republic of Korea (2005).

[12] The Dec. 2008 Summit that was to have taken place in Cha-Am Hua Hin, Thailand was postponed due to a political crisis in Thailand and protests at the summit venue. Ostensibly, according to Secretary-General Surin Pitsuwan (a Thai himself and a former Foreign Minister of Thailand), the reason was the Thais' 'fear of complicating ASEAN progress on works already laid out [sic] due to the entry into force of the Charter': *see* ASEAN Secretariat Press Release dated 30 Nov. 2008. The Summit was eventually held from 26 Feb. to 1 Mar. 2009, as the first meeting of the bi-annual summit cycle.

[13] The subsequent ASEAN+1, ASEAN+3 and East Asia Summits were scheduled to be held in Apr. 2009 instead of back-to-back with the ASEAN Summit as was usually the practice. These were abandoned when protests got out of hand in Pattaya. *See* BBC news, 11 Apr. 2009, available on the website of the BBC: news.bbc.co.uk. They were finally held in conjunction with the Fifteenth ASEAN Summit in Cha-Am Hua Hin, Thailand, in Oct. 2009.

Community (AEC) and the ASEAN Socio-Cultural Community (ASCC). At the Fifteenth ASEAN Summit[14] the ASEAN Intergovernmental Commission on Human Rights (AICHR) was inaugurated. The Sixteenth Summit in Hanoi (8–9 April 2010) saw the signing of the Protocol to the ASEAN Charter on Dispute Settlement Mechanisms.[15] The Nineteenth ASEAN Summit was held in Bali from 14–19 November 2011. Bali seems to have become a kind of spiritual home for ASEAN, having been the place where the Treaty of Amity and Cooperation in Southeast Asia 1976 was signed and where the Bali Concord and Bali Concord II were issued. The Bali Declaration on ASEAN Community in a Global Community of Nations (Bali Concord III) was signed by the Heads of State/Government at the Nineteenth ASEAN Summit.[16] This adopted a common platform on global issues, to be realised by 2022.[17] The Twenty-first ASEAN Summit in Phnom Penh (18 November 2012) adopted the ASEAN Human Rights Declaration (AHRD).[18] Thereafter, Summits have been held in Brunei[19] and Myanmar.[20]

1. The ASEAN Summit shall comprise the Heads of State or Government of the Member States.

The Eminent Persons Group on the ASEAN Charter recommended that the ASEAN Summit be redesignated the ASEAN Council and that it should meet twice a year.[21] The High Level Task Force (HLTF) drafting the Charter came to the conclusion that there were too many councils in the EPG proposal (viz, the ASEAN Council and three Community Councils). It was decided after a short discussion that there was no reason to re-name the ASEAN Summit. The terminology had been used for four decades and was familiar to all. The Foreign Ministers agreed with the HLTF at their Retreat in Siem Reap (February 2007) that the name could be kept.

---

[14] Held in Cha-Am Hua Hin, Thailand, 23–25 Oct. 2009.

[15] Which at the time of writing is still not in force.

[16] Held in Bali, Indonesia, 14–19 Nov. 2011.

[17] A Bali Concord III Plan of Action 2013-17 was adopted at the Twenty-first ASEAN Summit in Phnom Penh, Cambodia, on 18 Nov. 2012.

[18] *See* commentary to Articles 1(7) and 14.

[19] The Twenty-second Summit from 24–25 Apr. 2013 and the Twenty-third from 9–10 Oct. 2013.

[20] The Twenty-fourth Summit was held in Nay Pyi Taw from 10–11 May 2014.

[21] Report of the Eminent Persons Group on the ASEAN Charter, Executive Summary para 4 and para 24 of the main text.

As a matter of practice only executive heads of state attend the ASEAN Summit.[22] Ceremonial heads of state may grace the occasion but do not participate. The Secretary-General also participates in the meetings of the ASEAN Summit: *see* Article 11(2)(c).

2. The ASEAN Summit shall:

(a) be the supreme policy-making body of ASEAN;

The 1967 Bangkok Declaration made no provision for a supreme policy-making body. The ASEAN Ministerial Meeting (AMM) comprising the Foreign Ministers took on the role of coordinating activities at ASEAN level. It was only after the Fourth ASEAN Summit in 1992[23] that the Heads of State/Government began to meet on a regular basis. They naturally took over the role of supreme ASEAN policy-making body from the Foreign Ministers.

(b) deliberate, provide policy guidance and take decisions on key issues pertaining to the realisation of the objectives of ASEAN, important matters of interest to Member States and all issues referred to it by the ASEAN Coordinating Council, the ASEAN Community Councils and ASEAN Sectoral Ministerial Bodies;

As to the ASEAN Coordinating Council, *see* Article 8; the ASEAN Community Councils, *see* Article 9; ASEAN Sectoral Ministerial Bodies, *see* Article 10.

(c) instruct the relevant Ministers in each of the Councils concerned to hold ad hoc inter-Ministerial meetings, and address important issues concerning ASEAN that cut across the Community Councils. Rules of procedure for such meetings shall be adopted by the ASEAN Coordinating Council;

(d) address emergency situations affecting ASEAN by taking appropriate actions;

---

[22] Viz, the Sultan of Brunei, the President of Indonesia, the President of Myanmar and the President of the Philippines.

[23] Singapore, 27–29 Jan. 1992.

See also Article 7(3)(b) on convening of special or ad hoc Summit meetings.

(e) decide on matters referred to it under Chapters VII and VIII;

This refers to decisions when consensus cannot be achieved under Article 20(2), serious breaches of the Charter under Article 20(4) and unresolved disputes between member states under Article 26.

(f) authorise the establishment and the dissolution of Sectoral Ministerial Bodies and other ASEAN institutions; and

As to Sectoral Ministerial Bodies *see* Article 10. These are listed in Annex 1 to the Charter. There are six such bodies under the ASEAN Political-Security Community (APSC), 14 under the ASEAN Economic Community (AEC) and 17 under the ASEAN Socio-Cultural Community (ASCC). Prior to the ASEAN Charter, there was no specific procedure for the establishment of sectoral ministerial bodies or ASEAN institutions. The ASEAN Ministerial Meeting (AMM) was established by the 1967 Bangkok Declaration, which was signed by the Foreign Ministers of the five founding members. The ASEAN Economic Ministers Meeting (AEM) came into being as a result of an Indonesian initiative[24] and was formalized in the Bali Concord signed at the First ASEAN Summit.[25] Thereafter, ministerial meetings were established whenever a need was felt in a particular sector.[26] The proliferation of ASEAN sectoral bodies both at senior officials' as well as ministerial level led to concerns about resource commitments for Member States as well as the ASEAN Secretariat.

(g) appoint the Secretary-General of ASEAN, with the rank and status of Minister, who will serve with the confidence and at the pleasure of the Heads of State or Government upon the recommendation of the ASEAN Foreign Ministers Meeting.

---

24 Severino, *In Search of an ASEAN Community*, 214.

25 Declaration of ASEAN Concord (Bali Concord), para B5.

26 *See* commentary to Article 10(2) for examples.

The Secretary-General

As to the appointment of the Secretary-General *see* Article 11(1). Secretaries-General serve a non-renewable term of five years. They are nominated by the member states in alphabetical rotation.

The ASEAN Foreign Ministers Meeting

The ASEAN Declaration provided for an annual meeting of Foreign Ministers, known as the ASEAN Ministerial Meeting (AMM).[27] After coming into force of the Charter the AMM was redesignated the ASEAN Foreign Ministers Meeting. Thus, the meeting in Singapore in July 2008 was the last ASEAN Ministerial Meeting.[28] From the next meeting in Thailand in July 2009 the name was changed to the Foreign Ministers Meeting.[29] The sequence was not broken however, and this meeting is still referred to as the Forty-second AMM on the website of the ASEAN Secretariat. *See* the commentary to Article 10.

3. ASEAN Summit Meetings shall be:

(a) held twice annually, and be hosted by the Member State holding the ASEAN Chairmanship; and

This came from the Report of the Eminent Persons Group on the ASEAN Charter.[30] The rationale was that with events moving faster, the leaders had to meet more often to give greater political impetus to ASEAN's efforts to build an ASEAN Community. As to the ASEAN Chairmanship, *see* Article 31.

At the Informal ASEAN Ministerial Meeting on 27 September 2007, the Foreign Ministers reached an understanding that with the increase to two summits a year, one summit would continue the existing model as meeting among ASEAN Member States followed by summit meetings with dialogue partners from other countries, while the other summit would be reserved for discussion of ASEAN integration and would benefit from an informal retreat setting. However, it was agreed by the

---

[27] The very first AMM was the one at which the ASEAN Declaration was adopted on 8 Aug. 1967.

[28] Forty-first ASEAN Ministerial Meeting, Singapore, 17–24 July 2008.

[29] Forty-second ASEAN Foreign Ministers Meeting, Phuket, Thailand, 17–23 July 2009.

[30] *See* Executive Summary para 4 and para 24 of the main text.

Foreign Ministers that the agenda and format of the Summits need not be prescribed in the Charter.

(b) convened, whenever necessary, as special or ad hoc meetings to be chaired by the Member State holding the ASEAN Chairmanship, at venues to be agreed upon by ASEAN Member States.

This provision covers the convening of special or ad hoc summit meetings outside the fixed schedule of formal summits, to make a high-profile demonstration of unity and launch emergency measures or campaigns. Examples of such meetings are the Special ASEAN Leaders Meeting on Severe Acute Respiratory Syndrome (SARS) on 29 April 2003 and the Special ASEAN Leaders Meeting on the Aftermath of Earthquake and Tsunami held in Jakarta on 6 January 2005. Similar meetings have been convened among the ASEAN Foreign Ministers and ASEAN Economic Ministers. *See* also Article 7(2)(d) on the ASEAN Summit actions to address emergency situations.

Article 8. Asean Coordinating Council

1. The ASEAN Coordinating Council shall comprise the ASEAN Foreign Ministers and meet at least twice a year.

This was initially called the ASEAN Executive Board in earlier drafts of the ASEAN Charter. After their Retreat in Manila on 30 July 2007, the Foreign Ministers instructed that it should be called the ASEAN Coordinating Council (ACC). The main task of the ACC is to prepare for and coordinate the ASEAN Summits. The twice-yearly frequency follows the pre-charter practice of one ASEAN Ministerial Meeting (held annually in July since 1988) and an Informal ASEAN Ministerial Meeting on the sidelines of the United Nations General Assembly in September. The inaugural meeting of the ACC was held on 15 December 2008 in Jakarta, after the Special ASEAN Foreign Ministers' Meeting to mark the entry into force of the ASEAN Charter.[31]

The ACC takes over the administrative functions of the ASEAN Ministerial Meeting (AMM) provided for in the Bangkok Declaration as

31 *See* the ASEAN Annual Report 2008–09, 4.

an annual meeting of Foreign Ministers.[32] The Foreign Ministers are to continue to discuss policy and strategic issues and external relations at the ASEAN Foreign Ministers Meeting. Currently, the Foreign Ministers also meet annually as the ASEAN Political-Security Community Council and SEANWFZ Commission. As to the ASEAN Foreign Ministers Meeting, *see* Article 10.

The Secretary-General also participates in the meetings of the ACC: *see* Article 11(2)(c).

2. The ASEAN Coordinating Council shall:

(a) prepare the meetings of the ASEAN Summit;

As to meetings of the ASEAN Summit, *see* Article 7(3).

(b) coordinate the implementation of agreements and decisions of the ASEAN Summit;

(c) coordinate with the ASEAN Community Councils to enhance policy coherence, efficiency and cooperation among them;

As to the ASEAN Community Councils, *see* Article 9.

(d) coordinate the reports of the ASEAN Community Councils to the ASEAN Summit;

As to reports of the ASEAN Community Councils to the ASEAN Summit, *see* Article 9(4)(c). The ASEAN Economic Ministers Meeting was not too happy about having the Foreign Ministers in charge and wanted to be named as the body responsible for reporting to the Summit on the ASEAN Economic Community. The compromise reached was that ACC would 'coordinate', (i.e., transmit but not interfere with the reports of the other Community Councils, while highlighting cross-cutting issues for the attention of the ASEAN Summit).

(e) consider the annual report of the Secretary-General on the work of ASEAN;

---

[32] The very first AMM was the one at which the ASEAN Declaration was adopted on 8 Aug. 1967.

As to the Secretary-General's report, *see* Article 11(2)(b). The Committee of Permanent Representatives is to assist in considering this report.[33]

(f) consider the report of the Secretary-General on the functions and operations of the ASEAN Secretariat and other relevant bodies;

The ACC here takes over the role of the ASEAN Ministerial Meeting; according to the 1992 revision to the Agreement on the Establishment of the ASEAN Secretariat, the Secretary-General submitted his annual report to the ASEAN Ministerial Meeting.[34] The Committee of Permanent Representatives is to assist in considering this report.[35]

(g) approve the appointment and termination of the Deputy Secretaries-General upon the recommendation of the Secretary-General; and

As to the recommendation of the Secretary-General regarding appointment and termination of the Deputy Secretaries-General, *see* Article 11(2)(e).

(h) undertake other tasks provided for in this Charter or such other functions as may be assigned by the ASEAN Summit.

For instance, the ACC has been given the task of setting up a working group to consider the application of Timor-Leste to join ASEAN.[36] The ACC also plays a key role in the settlement of disputes under the 2010 Protocol to the ASEAN Charter on Dispute Settlement Mechanisms[37] and approval of the ASEAN Secretariat's operating budget.[38] The ACC also

---

[33] Para 4(f) of the Terms of Reference of the Committee of Permanent Representatives to ASEAN, approved by the Forty-first ASEAN Ministerial Meeting in Singapore on 21 July 2008.

[34] 1992 Protocol Amending the Agreement on the Establishment of the ASEAN Secretariat.

[35] Para 4(g) of the Terms of Reference of the Committee of Permanent Representatives to ASEAN, approved by the Forty-first ASEAN Ministerial Meeting in Singapore on 21 July 2008.

[36] *See* the Chairman's Statement of the Nineteenth ASEAN Summit (Bali, Nov. 2011), para 146.

[37] *See* the commentary to Articles 25, 26 and 27.

[38] Article 30(3).

recommended to the Summit the nomination of Mr Le Luong Minh of Vietnam as Secretary-General at its eleventh meeting.[39]

3. The ASEAN Coordinating Council shall be supported by the relevant senior officials.

The senior officials referred to are primarily the Committee of Permanent Representatives (CPR).[40] Before the adoption of the Charter, the ASEAN Ministerial Meeting was supported by the Senior Officials Meeting (SOM) and the ASEAN Standing Committee (ASC). The ASC is now defunct, having been replaced by the Committee of Permanent Representatives (CPR).[41] The relationship between the SOM and the CPR is still evolving.

Article 9. ASEAN Community Councils

1. The ASEAN Community Councils shall comprise the ASEAN Political-Security Community Council, ASEAN Economic Community Council, and ASEAN Socio-Cultural Community Council.

The three Community Councils are new organs created by the ASEAN Charter. The Report of the Eminent Persons' Group proposed these new institutions to oversee the three communities and to ensure inter-sectoral coordination.[42] There was initial scepticism on the part of a few ASEAN members that these bodies could be effective, not least because of the concern that they would hinder ongoing attempts to streamline the operations of ASEAN and reduce the administrative burden that the proliferation of ASEAN meetings places on the member states and the Secretariat. Nonetheless, the HLTF was instructed to make provision in the Charter for the Community Councils.

Each ASEAN Community Council prescribes its own procedure: Article 21(1). In theory, the ASEAN Coordinating Council (comprising the Foreign Ministers) is supposed to coordinate with the Community Councils to 'enhance policy coherence, efficiency and cooperation among them':

---

39 Held in Phnom Penh, Cambodia on 17 Nov. 2012. *See* the ASEAN Annual Report 2012–13, 17.

40 *See* the ASEAN Annual Reports, the latest being 2012–13, 17.

41 R. G. Manalo, 'Drafting ASEAN's Tomorrow: The Eminent Persons Group and the ASEAN Charter', in Koh, Manalo and Woon, eds., *Making of the ASEAN Charter*, chapter 4, 44. Ambassador Rosario Manalo was assistant to Philippine EPG member President Fidel Ramos, as well as the Filipino member of the HLTF, which she chaired for the first half of the process.

42 Report of the Eminent Persons Group on the ASEAN Charter, para 24.

Article 8(2)(c). In practice this has proven to be problematic. For instance, the ASEAN Economic Ministers Meeting was not too happy about having the Foreign Ministers in charge and wanted to be named as the body responsible for reporting to the Summit on the ASEAN Economic Community. The compromise reached was that ACC would 'coordinate', (i.e., transmit but not interfere with the reports of the other Community Councils, while highlighting cross-cutting issues for the attention of the ASEAN Summit).

The first meetings of the ASEAN Community Councils were convened in April 2009 in Pattaya, Thailand. The Community Councils have continued to meet annually but have functioned with a limited agenda covering pro-forma adoption of sectoral meetings' reports and review of key initiatives currently in progress under their purview.

2. Each ASEAN Community Council shall have under its purview the relevant ASEAN Sectoral Ministerial Bodies.

As to Sectoral Ministerial Bodies, *see* Article 10. These are listed in Annex 1 to the Charter. There are six such bodies under the ASEAN Political-Security Community (APSC), 14 under the ASEAN Economic Community (AEC) and 17 under the ASEAN Socio-Cultural Community (ASCC).

3. Each Member State shall designate its national representation for each ASEAN Community Council meeting.

The composition of the Community Councils was extensively discussed by the High Level Task Force. Mr Ong Keng Yong, the Secretary-General, warned against what he termed a 'jamboree', where all the sectoral ministers from the ten member states would be present. This could lead to meetings with over a hundred ministers in attendance, an organisational nightmare. Several proposals were considered, including (a) agenda-based representation with one representative from each ASEAN member state; (b) Foreign or Economic Ministers of the ASEAN member states (depending on the community) joined by the chairs of all the sectoral bodies in that community pillar; and (c) ten country representatives determined by the respective Member States, joined by the chairs of all of the sectoral bodies in that community pillar. The HLTF finally settled on the suggestion of ASEAN Secretariat that the representatives would be determined by the respective ASEAN Member States according to their own procedures, and either be pre-designated or appointed ad hoc according to the agenda.

Thus, for example, the ASEAN Political-Security Community (APSC) Council consists mainly of the Foreign Ministers. The ASEAN Economic Community (AEC) Council is more of mixed bag, comprising ministers of trade, commerce, economics and even finance. The 2007 ASEAN Economic Community Blueprint specifies that the existing ASEAN Economic Ministers Meeting (AEM) will continue to be the ministers in charge of the ASEAN Economic Community. The AEM are the de facto members of the ASEAN Economic Community (AEC) Council, which is scheduled back-to-back with the ASEAN Economic Ministers Meeting and ASEAN Free Trade Area Council (also attended by the economic ministers). The most miscellaneous is the ASEAN Socio-Cultural Community (ASCC) Council, where one finds a mix of ministers of culture, social affairs, labour etc. The current composition of the Councils is to be found on the website of the ASEAN Secretariat.[43]

4. In order to realise the objectives of each of the three pillars of the ASEAN Community, each ASEAN Community Council shall:

(a) ensure the implementation of the relevant decisions of the ASEAN Summit;

As to the Summit, *see* Article 7.

(b) coordinate the work of the different sectors under its purview, and on issues which cut across the other Community Councils; and

The main challenge to the smooth functioning of the Community Council structures is the reluctance of certain powerful ministers to accept the authority of a member of the Community Council who might be of equal status or even junior to them. The most prominent examples are the ASEAN Finance Ministers Meeting (AFMM) in the AEC, and the ASEAN Defence Ministers Meeting (ADMM) in the APSC. Both the AFMM and ADMM were established with direct reporting lines to the ASEAN Summit before the adoption of the Charter, which they have been reluctant to relinquish. The verb 'coordinate' was selected very carefully to imply that the Community Council would neither take on the role of directing sectoral meetings, nor

---

43 *See* www.asean.org/asean/asean-structure under Community Councils.

become the body to which sectoral meetings under its purview reported. The operationalisation of these provisions in the Charter has proceeded cautiously and the *modus vivendi* is still evolving. *See also* Articles 8(2)(d) and 10(1)(d).

(c) submit reports and recommendations to the ASEAN Summit on matters under its purview.

Reports to the ASEAN Summit are submitted through the ASEAN Coordinating Council (ACC); *see* Article 8(2)(d). The ACC will transmit but not interfere with the reports of the other Community Councils.

5. Each ASEAN Community Council shall meet at least twice a year and shall be chaired by the appropriate Minister from the Member State holding the ASEAN Chairmanship.

The Chairmanship rotates among the member countries in alphabetical order (with the occasional exception): *see* Article 31(1). The Secretary-General also participates in the meetings of the ASEAN Community Councils: *see* Article 11(2)(c).

6. Each ASEAN Community Council shall be supported by the relevant senior officials.

The Coordinating Conference for the ASEAN Political Security Community (ASCCO),[44] attended by senior officials from the foreign ministries of the member states, does the preparation for the ASEAN Political-Security Community Council. For the ASEAN Socio-Cultural Community Council, that function is fulfilled by the Senior Officials Committee on the ASEAN Social Cultural Community (SOCA), attended by officials from the designated coordinating ministries (representatives vary for each member state). The ASEAN Economic Ministers meeting as the ASEAN Economic Community Council continue to be supported by the existing Senior Economic Officials Meeting (SEOM).

---

[44] Originally established in Sept. 2006 to coordinate among the different sectors in order to implement the Vientiane Action Programme. *See* the ASEAN Annual Report 2006-07, 13.

Article 10. ASEAN Sectoral Ministerial Bodies

Prior to the ASEAN Charter, the formats for sectoral cooperation were not standardised. Early sectoral cooperation began with officials-level committees, with the first permanent committees established by the ASEAN Ministerial Meeting of 1968.[45] The numerous sectoral bodies established subsequently varied in the level of representation (ministerial, senior officials, officials) and frequency of meetings. Prior to the Charter, there was no formal procedure for the establishment of sectoral bodies; *see* Article 7(2)(f).

1. ASEAN Sectoral Ministerial Bodies shall:

(a) function in accordance with their respective established mandates;

Few of the existing sectoral ministerial bodies of ASEAN operate with a formally approved mandate or terms of reference. The first to be established, the ASEAN Ministerial Meeting (comprising Foreign Ministers), had no elaboration of its functions except that it should 'carry out these aims and purposes' of ASEAN, along with the ASEAN Standing Committee. It was simply understood to be the main executive body of ASEAN up to the regular convening of the ASEAN Summit after 1992. Some notable exceptions are the ASEAN Economic Ministers Meeting (AEM), ASEAN Regional Forum (ARF) and the ASEAN Defence Ministers Meeting (ADMM). The AEM was formalised and its functions briefly described in the Joint Communiqué of the First ASEAN Summit[46] and the Bali Concord.[47] Both the ARF and ADMM adopted concept papers detailing their own objectives and institutions in 1995 and 2006 respectively.[48]

---

[45] Joint Communiqué of the Second ASEAN Ministerial Meeting, Jakarta, 6–7 Aug. 1968.

[46] Joint Communiqué, the First ASEAN Heads of Government Meeting, Bali, 23–24 Feb. 1976, para 9–10.

[47] 1976 Declaration of ASEAN Concord, para B5. Signed in Bali on 24 Feb. 1976 by the Heads of State/Government.

[48] The ASEAN Regional Forum: A Concept Paper, adopted by the Second ASEAN Regional Forum in Bandar Seri Begawan, Brunei on 1 Aug. 1995. The Concept Paper for the Establishment of an ADMM was adopted at the inaugural ASEAN Defence Ministers Meeting in Kuala Lumpur, Malaysia on 9 May 2006.

(b) implement the agreements and decisions of the ASEAN Summit under their respective purview;

The ASEAN Summit is the supreme policy-making body of ASEAN: Article 7(2)(a).

(c) strengthen cooperation in their respective fields in support of ASEAN integration and community building; and

(d) submit reports and recommendations to their respective Community Councils.

As to the ASEAN Community Councils, *see* Article 8. Annex 1 sets out which sectoral ministerial bodies belong under which Community Council.

2. Each ASEAN Sectoral Ministerial Body may have under its purview the relevant senior officials and subsidiary bodies to undertake its functions as contained in Annex 1. The Annex may be updated by the Secretary-General of ASEAN upon the recommendation of the Committee of Permanent Representatives without recourse to the provision on Amendments under this Charter.

Annex 1 to the ASEAN Charter was compiled by the ASEAN Secretariat. There are six such bodies listed under the ASEAN Political-Security Community (APSC), 14 under the ASEAN Economic Community (AEC) and 17 under the ASEAN Socio-Cultural Community (ASCC). Some of the bodies listed are not in fact ministerial meetings. The list includes the officials-level meetings (e.g., the ASEAN University Network and various ASEAN Specialised Centres including the ASEAN Centre for Energy, ASEAN-Japan Centre in Tokyo, and ASEAN Specialised Meteorological Centre).[49] The assignment of pre-existing sectoral bodies to the three communities was challenging as certain bodies had been dealing with cross-cutting issues involving more than one community. The categorisation also imposed a new reporting system for each sectoral body to a specific Community Council.

---

[49] A full list of ASEAN Centres and Facilities can be found at http://www.asean.org/asean/entities-associated-with-asean/asean-centres-facilites.

The ASEAN Foreign Ministers Meeting

The 1967 ASEAN Declaration provided for an annual meeting of Foreign Ministers, known as the ASEAN Ministerial Meeting (AMM).[50] To support the work of the Foreign Ministers, a standing committee (the ASEAN Standing Committee or ASC) was also created, under the chairmanship of the country hosting the AMM.[51] Initially, this comprised the Foreign Minister of the host country as chair, and ambassadors to the host of the next AMM. In 1992 this was changed to directors-general in charge of ASEAN at the respective foreign ministries, together with the Secretary-General.[52] In 1971 senior officials from the ministries of foreign affairs began meeting regularly at the ASEAN Senior Officials' Meeting (ASEAN SOM), a body which was not specifically created by any agreement but which evolved naturally. SOM was established to discuss political issues, especially sensitive ones, before submission to the AMM. The SOM leader was generally the permanent secretary (or his equivalent in countries that did not adopt the British nomenclature) of the ministry. The SOM has now been regularised by inclusion in the list of Sectoral Ministerial Bodies in Annex 1. The same officials in the SOM have stepped into the role of the senior officials supporting the ASEAN Coordinating Council, *see* Article 8(3).

From the start ASEAN was driven by the foreign ministries of the member states, the other ministries being kept on the sidelines for the most part. After the First ASEAN Summit (Bali, February 1976) it was clarified that the AMM was the principal organ for the coordination of overall policy direction for ASEAN.[53] The ASEAN Standing Committee was charged with conduct of ASEAN external relations. This function has now been taken over by the Committee of Permanent Representatives.[54]

The AMM is the most durable of the ASEAN institutions and continues to play a significant role in the steering of the organisation. There have been annual meetings of the Foreign Ministers since 1967.[55] After coming into force of the Charter the AMM was redesignated the ASEAN Foreign Ministers Meeting for the purposes of discussion of strategic issues and

---

50 The very first AMM was the one at which the ASEAN Declaration was adopted on 8 Aug. 1967.

51 The ASEAN Declaration, adopted on 8 Aug. 1967 in Bangkok, Thailand, Article 3(b).

52 Severino, *In Search of an ASEAN Community*, 22.

53 This was proclaimed in the Joint Communiqué of the Ninth AMM (Manila, June 1976), para 22.

54 *See* commentary to Article 12.

55 Except for 1970, when the Philippines was host. The meeting was postponed due to disagreements between the Philippines and Malaysia over Sabah. The ASEAN Ministerial Meeting was convened again only in Mar. 1971.

external relations, while the function of coordination and preparation for the ASEAN Summit was transferred to the new ASEAN Coordinating Council (*see* commentary to Article 8(1)). Thus, the meeting in Singapore in July 2008 was the last ASEAN Ministerial Meeting.[56] From the next meeting in meeting in Thailand in July 2009 the name was changed to the Foreign Ministers Meeting.[57] The sequence was not broken however, and this meeting is still referred to as the Forty-second AMM on the website of the ASEAN Secretariat.

In addition to the formal meetings, the Foreign Ministers held special meetings when necessary.[58] The AMM evolved into an occasion for engaging the dialogue partners,[59] in the Post-Ministerial Conferences (PMC). In 1999 the ASEAN Foreign Ministers' Retreat was inaugurated to enable frank and open discussion of issues of common interest in an informal setting away from the formal proceedings of the AMM.[60] Initially, the Retreats were held in conjunction with the AMM but from 2001 separate retreats were hosted by member states other than the AMM host.[61] From its rather modest beginnings the AMM evolved into one of the main motors of ASEAN. The Foreign Ministers' agenda grew steadily over the years, judging by the length and substance of the communiqués issued after each AMM. Article 41(6) now provides that the ASEAN Foreign Ministers Meeting 'shall ensure consistency and coherence in the conduct of ASEAN's external relations.'

Far from being marginalised by the ASEAN Charter, the Foreign Ministers now play an enhanced role. In addition to their own sectoral ministerial meeting (still referred to as the AMM despite the change of official nomenclature), the Foreign Ministers also comprise the ASEAN Coordinating Council,[62] are the main driving force behind the ASEAN Political-Security Committee Council,[63] supervise the Committee

---

[56] Forty-first ASEAN Ministerial Meeting, Singapore, 17–24 July 2008.
[57] Held in Phuket, Thailand, 17–23 July 2009.
[58] For instance, in 1997 to discuss the situation in Cambodia. It was Dec.ided to postpone Cambodia's accession to ASEAN because of the fighting between political factions in the country.
[59] At the time of writing the dialogue partners are: Australia, Canada, China, the European Union, India, Japan, New Zealand, the Republic of Korea, the Russian Federation and the USA.
[60] Joint Communiqué of the Thirty-second ASEAN Ministerial Meeting (Singapore, July 1999), para 5.
[61] Joint Communiqué of the Thirty-fourth ASEAN Ministerial Meeting (Hanoi, July 2001), para 8.
[62] *See* commentary to Article 8.
[63] *See* commentary to Article 9.

of Permanent Representatives[64] (and, through the CPR, the ASEAN Secretariat) as well as oversee ASEAN's external relations.[65]

The ASEAN Economic Ministers' Meeting

For much of the first two decades of ASEAN's life the focus had been on economic cooperation as opposed to integration. ASEAN Economic Ministers had first met in November 1975 at the behest of Indonesia.[66] At the First ASEAN Summit in Bali the following year the leaders agreed that the economic ministers would meet 'to consider measures to be taken to implement the decisions of the [ASEAN Summit] on matters of economic cooperation'.[67] This was formalised in the Bali Concord signed at that Summit.[68] ASEAN Economic Ministers' Meetings (AEM)[69] took place annually, preceded by a Senior Economic Officials' Meeting (SEOM). The AEM and SEOM did not report to the Foreign Ministers but rather progressed on their own path independently.[70] For better coordination, a Joint Ministerial Meeting of Foreign and Economic Ministers (JMM) was established by the Third ASEAN Summit in 1987.[71] The Fourth ASEAN Summit in Singapore in 1992 gave a push for greater economic integration of ASEAN. SEOM was tasked with handling all aspects of ASEAN economic cooperation. Oversight would be provided by the economic ministers.[72] This economic pillar took a life of its own separate from the diplomatic track that hitherto had dominated ASEAN. From the founding of ASEAN in 1967, it was the foreign ministries who had been

---

64 *See* commentary to Article 12.

65 *See* commentary to Article 41.

66 Severino, *In Search of an ASEAN Community*, 214.

67 Joint Communiqué of the First ASEAN Summit, para 9.

68 Declaration of ASEAN Concord (Bali Concord), para B5.

69 This nomenclature was adopted at the second economic ministers' meeting in Kuala Lumpur (Mar. 1976). It was institutionalised by the Second ASEAN Summit that year.

70 Though the Foreign Ministers took the opportunity in their ASEAN Ministerial Meeting (AMM) joint communiqués to 'commend' or express appreciation for the work of their economic colleagues in fostering ASEAN economic cooperation. The AMM also 'noted' agreements entered into by the economic ministers.

71 The Joint Communiqué of the Twenty-third AMM (Jakarta, July 1990) announced the convening of the inaugural ASEAN Joint Ministerial Meeting of Foreign and Economic Ministers. In practice, it proved difficult to convene the JMM regularly due to the competition between the foreign and economic ministers. The JMM was expanded to include the Finance Ministers and the Secretary-General by the Ninth ASEAN Summit (Bali, Oct. 2003): *see* the Joint Communiqué of the Thirty-seventh AMM (Jakarta, June 2004), para 66.

72 Singapore Declaration 1992 (Singapore, Jan. 1992), para 8.

in the driver's seat steering the organisation. The creation of an ASEAN Free Trade Area necessitated a much closer involvement of the various economic ministries in ASEAN affairs.

Over the years the AEM and SEOM acquired a whole host of supervisory and monitoring functions in order to realise the vision of creating an integrated economic area. These functions were conferred by various agreements entered into by the ASEAN member states. The first two were the Agreement on the Common Effective Preferential Tariff (CEPT) Scheme for the ASEAN Free Trade Area and the Framework Agreement on Enhancing ASEAN Economic Cooperation, both signed in 1992 at the Fourth ASEAN Summit in Singapore. The AEM was tasked with reviewing the progress of implementation of the latter agreement.[73] At the Fifth ASEAN Summit in 1995 a Framework Agreement on Services was signed, the aim of which was to liberalise trade in services beyond the commitments undertaken under GATS and to substantially eliminate restrictions to trade in services.[74] SEOM was charged with facilitation, supervision and review of the agreement.[75] In 1998 SEOM was tasked with monitoring the implementation of the ASEAN Framework Agreement on Mutual Recognition Arrangements, reporting to the AFTA Council.[76] That same year saw the conclusion of the Framework Agreement on the ASEAN Investment Area. The AEM was to create an AIA Council comprising ministers in charge of investment.[77] The AIA Council in turn established a Coordinating Committee on Investment (CCI) consisting of senior officials from ministries and government agencies responsible for investment. The CCI reported to the AIA Council through SEOM.[78] A further monitoring role for SEOM was given in the e-ASEAN Framework Agreement 2000, with reports going to the AEM.[79] In 2004 a Framework Agreement for Integration of Priority Sectors was signed in Vientiane; again SEOM was tasked with assisting the economic ministers with oversight, monitoring and coordination.[80] SEOM was also given a key

[73] 1992 Framework Agreement on Enhancing ASEAN Economic Cooperation, Article 8.

[74] 1995 ASEAN Framework Agreement on Services, Article I.

[75] Ibid., Article XI.

[76] ASEAN Framework Agreement on Mutual Recognition Arrangements, Article 13.

[77] Framework Agreement on the ASEAN Investment Area, Article 16. The membership of the AIA Council overlaps with that of the AEM but is not identical.

[78] Ibid., Article 16(5).

[79] e-ASEAN Framework Agreement, Article 13. This was signed at the Fourth Informal Summit (Singapore, Nov. 2000).

[80] 2004 ASEAN Framework Agreement for Integration of Priority Sectors, Article 19.

role in the settlement of economic disputes by the Protocol on Enhanced Dispute Settlement Mechanism.[81]

The High Level Task Force on ASEAN Economic Integration recommended the re-affirmation of the AEM's role as coordinator for all ASEAN economic integration and cooperation issues. Technical issues were to be resolved by SEOM, while issues of a policy nature were to be resolved by the AEM, AFTA Council and AIA Council. These recommendations were adopted in Bali Concord II.[82]

The AEM took place back-to-back with meetings of the AFTA Council and later the AIA Council which was set up under the Framework Agreement on the ASEAN Investment Area.[83] Both these Councils were overseen by the AEM. The first decade of the new millennium also saw increasing economic engagement with dialogue partners outside ASEAN. The ultimate aim was to create a free trade area between ASEAN and the respective partners. Framework agreements for the creation of closer economic ties were entered into with China, Japan, India and the Republic of Korea.[84] In 2011 a Framework for Regional Comprehensive Economic Partnership (RCEP) was adopted at the Nineteenth ASEAN Summit.[85] The AEM, supported by SEOM, played a coordinating role in negotiations for deepening economic cooperation under these framework agreements[86] and the proposed RCEP.[87]

---

[81] Signed by the economic ministers at the Tenth ASEAN Summit in Vientiane, 29 Nov. 2004.

[82] *See* para 14 of the HLTF-EI's recommendations, which were annexed to the Declaration of ASEAN Concord II, signed by the leaders in Bali at the Ninth ASEAN Summit on 7 Oct. 2003.

[83] Framework Agreement on the ASEAN Investment Area (1998), Article 16.

[84] For the sake of completeness, it should be mentioned that an Agreement Establishing the Australia New Zealand ASEAN Free Trade Area was concluded in 2009, after the entry into force of the ASEAN Charter.

[85] Held in Bali, Indonesia, 14–19 Nov. 2011. The RCEP is to be a free trade area encompassing ASEAN and Australia, China, India, Japan, Korea and New Zealand.

[86] *See* for example the Framework Agreement on Comprehensive Economic Cooperation between India and ASEAN and China, Article 12; Framework Agreement on Comprehensive Economic Cooperation between India and ASEAN (2004), Article 12; Framework Agreement on Comprehensive Economic Cooperation among the Governments of Member Countries of ASEAN and the Republic of Korea (2005), Article 5.3; Agreement Establishing the Australia New Zealand ASEAN Free Trade Area (2009), Chapter 16 Article 1(6). A Framework Agreement for Comprehensive Economic Partnership between Japan and ASEAN was also signed in 2003. Untypically, no specific mention was made of the role of the AEM. Nonetheless, the ASEAN-Japan Committee on Comprehensive Economic Partnership reported to the AEM.

[87] *See* the ASEAN Framework for Regional Comprehensive Economic Partnership, adopted at the Nineteenth ASEAN Summit in Bali, 14–19 Nov. 2011. A Joint Declaration on the Launch of the Regional Comprehensive Economic Partnership was issued at the Twenty-first ASEAN Summit in Phnom Penh, Cambodia, 20 Nov. 2012.

The AEM is the major organ steering the economic integration of ASEAN and has come to play a role of equal importance to the ASEAN Ministerial Meeting in the creation of the ASEAN community. The foregoing list of functions is far from exhaustive, and it is to be expected that the AEM and SEOM will play an ever-increasing role in the integration of ASEAN.

Nonetheless, they have been often sidelined. Even during the Charter-drafting process, the HLTF members from some countries were not sympathetic to requests from their economic colleagues.[88] Brunei HLTF member Pengiran Dato Paduka Osman Patra wryly noted that, to their dismay, the economic ministers had been unintentionally overlooked and left out of the photo sessions with the ASEAN leaders during the signing of the Charter at the Thirteenth ASEAN Summit.[89]

Other ministerial bodies

Apart from the ASEAN Ministerial Meeting and the ASEAN Economic Ministers Meeting, other ministries began meeting on a regular basis under the ASEAN umbrella. This has led to a veritable alphabet soup of acronyms. The first meeting of ASEAN labour ministers (ALMM) took place in Jakarta in April 1975, continuing roughly on a biennial basis thereafter. A meeting of the ASEAN Education Ministers (ASED) was first held in 1977 in Manila; however, ASED only met intermittently thereafter. In 1979, the first Meeting of the ASEAN Ministers of Agriculture and Forestry (AMAF) took place in Manila to issue the ASEAN Food Security Reserve Agreement.[90] ASEAN Ministers of Health at their First Meeting (AHMM) held in July 1980 in Manila adopted the Declaration on Collaboration in Health to strengthen and coordinate regional cooperation in health among ASEAN countries.[91] In October the same year the first ASEAN Ministerial Meeting on Science and Technology (AMMST) took place in Pattaya, Thailand. Also in 1980, the ASEAN Ministers on Energy Meeting (AMEM) was held for the first time in Bali. The environmental ministers met for the first ASEAN Ministerial Meeting on the Environment (AMME)

---

88 *See* Koh, 'The Negotiating Process', in Koh, Manalo and Woon, eds., *Making of the ASEAN Charter*, chapter 5, 56, 65–66. Ambassador Koh speculated that 'this could have been due to the fact that in some ASEAN countries, coordination between them [viz, the foreign ministries and the economic ministries] is not optimal and there is also considerable rivalry between them'.

89 *See* Pengiran Dato Paduka Osman Patra, 'Heart Labour' in Koh, Manalo and Woon, eds., *Making of the ASEAN Charter*, 10.

90 Thereafter, the meetings have taken place annually.

91 This meets every two years.

in Manila in 1981 to issue an ASEAN Declaration on the Environment. The ASEAN Law Ministers Meeting (ALAWMM) was established in 1986, to be held every 36 months thereafter with senior law officials meetings (ASLOM) in between. In 1989 a Conference of Ministers Responsible for Information (AMRI) was inaugurated, meeting irregularly thereafter.

The last decade of the twentieth century saw the establishment of more ASEAN ministerial meetings. The ASEAN Transport Ministers Meeting (ATM) was held for the first time in 1996, and annually thereafter. The finance ministers started meeting in 1997 (ASEAN Finance Ministers Meeting) after the leaders had directed that there should be greater economic integration; they have met annually since then. In December 1997 the ministers of the interior or home affairs of the ASEAN member states issued the ASEAN Declaration on Transnational Crime at the first ASEAN Conference on Transnational Crime in Manila. This was a result of the Twenty-ninth ASEAN Ministerial Meeting the previous year, which called for greater cooperation in combating transnational crime like the drug trade, money laundering and illegal migration, and the subsequent First Informal ASEAN Summit in Jakarta. The Declaration established the ASEAN Ministerial Meeting on Transnational Crime (AMMTC)[92] to coordinate the activities of ASEAN bodies like the ASEAN Senior Officials on Drug Matters (ASOD) and the meeting of ASEAN Chiefs of National Police (ASEANAPOL). The following year saw the formal establishment of the ASEAN Tourism Ministers Meeting (M-ATM).[93] The M-ATM supervises the ASEAN Tourism Agreement of 2002.[94] 1998 also saw an informal meeting of ASEAN Ministers on Rural Development and Poverty Eradication (AMRDPE) against the backdrop of the financial crisis. Thereafter, the ministers have met on an irregular basis to discuss poverty eradication.

To round up, in the new millennium the following meetings were established: the ASEAN Telecommunications and IT Ministers Meeting (TELMIN) in 2001;[95] the meeting of ASEAN Ministers Responsible for Culture and the Arts (AMCA) in 2003;[96] the ASEAN Ministerial Meeting on Minerals (AMMin) in 2005;[97] and the ASEAN Defence Ministers

92 The AMMTC meets every two years.

93 Tourism is one of the priority sectors for ASEAN integration.

94 Article 9 of the ASEAN Tourism Agreement 2002, signed in Phnom Penh at the Eighth ASEAN Summit.

95 This meets annually.

96 Meetings have not been regular.

97 This is supposed to meet at least once in three years.

Meeting (ADMM) in 2006.[98] Since the Charter came into force, one new ministerial body has been established, viz, the ASEAN Ministerial Meeting on Sports (AMMS).[99]

The foregoing list is not exhaustive, even regarding ministerial-level meetings; there are hundreds of other meetings, both formal as well as informal, at all levels. The pressing need for some sort of coordination mechanism led to the creation of the ASEAN Community Councils.

Updating Annex 1

As to the Secretary General of ASEAN *see* Article 11; Committee of Permanent Representatives, *see* Article 12. The list of sectoral ministerial bodies is not closed. New bodies are constantly being created (e.g., the ASEAN Connectivity Coordinating Committee, established in 2011). ASEAN may also consider amending the classification of sectoral bodies whose mandates span more than one community. It would be unnecessarily cumbersome to invoke the Charter amendment mechanism in Article 48 to add to or subtract from the list.

Article 11. Secretary-General of ASEAN and ASEAN Secretariat

The ASEAN Secretariat

The idea of establishing a secretariat for ASEAN was first expressed by Malaysia at the third ASEAN Ministerial Meeting (AMM) in 1969.[100] At the Sixth ASEAN Ministerial Meeting (AMM) in Pattaya, Thailand (April 1973), the Foreign Ministers decided that the time had come to do so. Indonesia volunteered to play host.[101] There was a competing offer from the Philippines to site the secretariat in Manila, but after negotiation this was withdrawn 'in the interest of regional unity and harmony'.[102] However, it was only in 1976 that the member states finally established the ASEAN Secretariat (ASEC) by means of an agreement signed by the

---

98 This meets annually. Since then it has adopted two three-year work programmes focusing *inter alia* on enhancing existing practical cooperation and developing possible cooperation in defence and security.

99 First held in Yogyakarta, Indonesia on 14 Dec. 2011.

100 Severino, *In Search of an ASEAN Community*, 19.

101 Joint Communiqué of the Sixth ASEAN Ministerial Meeting, para 8.

102 Joint Communiqué of the Seventh ASEAN Ministerial Meeting (Jakarta, May 1974), para 8.

Foreign Ministers.[103] An Agreement relating to Privileges and Immunities of the ASEAN Secretariat was executed by Indonesia on 20 January 1979, giving juridical personality to ASEC under Indonesian law and granting diplomatic privileges to the Secretary-General and officers of ASEC.[104]

The Secretary-General of the ASEAN Secretariat

The Secretary-General of the ASEAN Secretariat (as he was then known) was appointed by the ASEAN Foreign Ministers on a rotational basis for a two-year term.[105] The first Secretary-General was Hartono Rekso Dharsono of Indonesia,[106] a former general and diplomat. He was replaced in 1978 by Umarjadi Njotowijono, who served out the remainder of his predecessor's term. Mr Umarjadi was followed by Ali bin Abdullah (Malaysia), Narciso Reyes (Philippines), Chan Kai Yau (Singapore) and Phan Wanannamethee (Thailand). In 1985 the term of office of the Secretary-General was extended to three years.[107] At the following Nineteenth ASEAN Ministerial Meeting in Manila (June 1986), the Foreign Ministers appointed Roderick Yong Yin Fatt of Brunei as Secretary-General for three years, commencing on 16 July 1986. He was followed by one other, viz, Rusli Noor of Indonesia, before the enhancement of the Secretary-General's position under the 1992 Protocol Amending the Agreement on Establishment of the ASEAN Secretariat. In that Protocol the post was re-designated as Secretary-General of ASEAN and accorded ministerial status. His tenure was extended to five years, renewable by the Heads of Government on the recommendation of the ASEAN Ministerial Meeting.[108]

---

[103] Agreement on Establishment of the ASEAN Secretariat, signed in Bali on 24 Feb. 1976.

[104] This has been superseded by a new agreement between Indonesia and ASEAN signed in Phnom Penh on 2 Apr. 2012.

[105] 1976 Agreement on Establishment of the ASEAN Secretariat, Article 3.

[106] His appointment was confirmed at the Ninth ASEAN Ministerial Meeting (Manila, June 1976).

[107] 1985 Protocol Amending the Agreement on Establishment of the ASEAN Secretariat, adopted by the Foreign Ministers at the Eighteenth ASEAN Ministerial Meeting in Kuala Lumpur on 9 July 1985. *See* Article 1.

[108] 1992 Protocol Amending the Agreement on Establishment of the ASEAN Secretariat, Article 2

1. The Secretary-General of ASEAN shall be appointed by the ASEAN Summit for a non-renewable term of office of five years, selected from among nationals of the ASEAN Member States based on alphabetical rotation, with due consideration to integrity, capability and professional experience, and gender equality.

Appointment of the Secretary-General

The 1992 Protocol Amending the Agreement on Establishment of the ASEAN Secretariat[109] enhanced the position of the Secretary-General, giving him an enlarged mandate that included planning and monitoring functions, as well as acting as spokesperson and representative of ASEAN. His term of office was extended to five years, renewable by the Heads of Government on the recommendation of the ASEAN Ministerial Meeting.[110] The post was re-designated as Secretary-General of ASEAN and accorded ministerial status.[111]

The first Secretary-General appointed to the enhanced post was Ajit Singh (Malaysia). He was followed by Rodolfo Severino (Philippines) and Ong Keng Yong (Singapore). All were diplomats before their stints as ASEAN Secretary-General. The next Secretary-General was of a different character. Dr Surin Pitsuwan of Thailand was a politician and had been Foreign Minister of Thailand. As Secretary-General, Dr Surin was an active figure in ASEAN and attempted to fill the expanded role envisaged by the Eminent Persons Group[112] and described in the Charter. He exercised an unprecedented degree of autonomous leadership on various ASEAN initiatives and in representing ASEAN internationally. This may have contributed to the desire on the part of the member countries to keep the Secretary-General on a short leash lest they lose control of the organisation.[113] The appointment of the present incumbent, Le Luong

---

[109] Adopted by the Foreign Ministers at the Twenty-fifth ASEAN Ministerial Meeting in Manila on 22 July 1992. It came into force on 8 Aug. 1992.

[110] 1976 Agreement on Establishment of the ASEAN Secretariat, Article 3(1) as amended by the 1992 Protocol. *See* para 8 of the Singapore Dec.laration, issued after the Fourth ASEAN Summit on 28 Jan. 1992.

[111] 1976 Agreement on Establishment of the ASEAN Secretariat, Article 3(1) as amended by the 1992 Protocol.

[112] *See* the Report of the Eminent Persons Group on the ASEAN Charter, paras 36–7. The EPG clearly envisaged that the Secretary-General would be a personage of some importance who merited the status of a minister.

[113] It has also been suggested by a former Secretary-General in conversation with the author that member states keep a tight rein on the Secretary-General because they fear that a member state might use the post to gain a national advantage of some sort; hence the need for Article 11(9).

Minh of Vietnam, saw a return to the old pattern. He was a diplomat like all the earlier Secretaries-General.

See Article 7(2)(g) regarding the appointment of the Secretary-General by the ASEAN Summit. Despite the reference to gender equality there has never been a female Secretary-General. How the candidate is chosen is left to the nominating state.

Removal of the Secretary-General

Though there is no explicit provision on removal of the Secretary-General, it is made clear in Article 7(2)(g) that he serves at the pleasure of the Heads of State/Government. This means that he can be dismissed by them. The qualifying phrase 'upon the recommendation of the ASEAN Foreign Ministers Meeting' applies equally to removal as to appointment. Indeed, the recommendation of the Foreign Ministers Meeting is only meaningful in the context of removal, since the member states nominate the Secretary-General in turn for appointment by the ASEAN Summit.

Status

The Secretary-General ranks as a minister.[114] He enjoys diplomatic immunity.[115] The Eminent Persons Group recommended that the Secretary-General should be accorded 'ministerial rank and due recognition',[116] reflecting concerns that in practice the Secretary-General had not been accorded by officials the respect commensurate with his position and functions.

2. The Secretary-General shall:

(a) carry out the duties and responsibilities of this high office in accordance with the provisions of this Charter and relevant ASEAN instruments, protocols and established practices;

Apart from the functions listed in Article 11(2), the Secretary-General oversees the ASEAN Foundation: Article 15(2). He also has the important

[114] *See* Article 7(2)(g). This means a minister in the political sense, not a diplomatic rank. A minister in the diplomatic service ranks just below ambassador: *see* the 1961 Vienna Convention on Diplomatic Relations, Article 14(1). Political ministers clearly outrank ambassadors.

[115] *See* 2009 Agreement on the Privileges and Immunities of ASEAN, Article 4(4).

[116] *See* the Report of the Eminent Persons Group on the ASEAN Charter, para 36.

task of monitoring the results of any dispute settlement mechanism under Article 27(1). This does not exhaust the list of the Secretary-General's duties, as many other tasks have been laid on him by other ASEAN instruments. For instance, he was specifically charged with monitoring the Agreement on the Common Effective Tariff (CEPT) for the ASEAN Free Trade Area (AFTA) and was made a member of the AFTA Council.[117] Later on he also became a member of the ASEAN Investment Area Council.[118] The burdens on the Secretary-General can only grow heavier as ASEAN integration proceeds.

(b) facilitate and monitor progress in the implementation of ASEAN agreements and decisions, and submit an annual report on the work of ASEAN to the ASEAN Summit;

The Eminent Persons Group in its report stated baldly that: 'ASEAN must establish a culture of honouring and implementing its decisions and agreements, and carrying them out on time ... It is clear ... that ASEAN's problem is not one of lack of vision, ideas and action plans. The real problem is one of ensuring compliance and effective implementation of decisions.'[119] The EPG went on to recommend that the Secretary-General should be entrusted with the role of monitoring and reporting cases of non-compliance. Other sectoral ministerial bodies were uncomfortable with dominance of the Foreign Ministers, and thus preferred the Secretary-General to undertake this function. The Secretary-General's Report is nonetheless submitted to the ASEAN Summit through the ASEAN Community Council (ACC), which comprises the Foreign Ministers wearing a different hat: *see* Article 8(2)(e). This is a continuation of the pre-Charter practice of the Secretary-General submitting his annual report to the ASEAN Ministerial Meeting rather than directly to the ASEAN Summit.[120]

(c) participate in meetings of the ASEAN Summit, the ASEAN Community Councils, the ASEAN Coordinating Council, and ASEAN Sectoral Ministerial Bodies and other relevant ASEAN meetings;

---

[117] 1976 Agreement on Establishment of the ASEAN Secretariat, Article 3(1)(6)(h) as amended by the 1992 Protocol and the 1992 Agreement on the Common Effective Preferential Tariff (CEPT) Scheme for the ASEAN Free Trade Area, Article 7.

[118] 1998 Framework Agreement on the ASEAN Investment Area, Article 16.

[119] *See* the Report of the Eminent Persons Group on the ASEAN Charter, para 44.

[120] *See* the 1976 Agreement on the Establishment of the ASEAN Secretariat, Article 3(2)(14) as amended by the 1992 Protocol.

Given the number of ASEAN meetings, it is not uncommon for the Secretary-General to delegate this function to the relevant Deputy Secretary-General for certain Coordinating Council and Sectoral Meetings.

As to the ASEAN Summit, *see* Article 7; the ASEAN Community Councils, *see* Article 9; the ASEAN Coordinating Council, *see* Article 8; the ASEAN Sectoral Ministerial Bodies, *see* Article 10.

(d) present the views of ASEAN and participate in meetings with external parties in accordance with approved policy guidelines and mandate given to the Secretary-General; and

As to the external relations of ASEAN, *see* Article 41. The mandate is presumably to be given by the ASEAN Summit on the recommendation of the ASEAN Foreign Ministers Meeting, as provided in Article 41(5). The Secretary-General of ASEAN is supposed to be ASEAN's public face, in his capacity as spokesman and representative of the organisation.[121]

(e) recommend the appointment and termination of the Deputy Secretaries-General to the ASEAN Coordinating Council for approval.

When the post of Deputy Secretary-General (DSG) was introduced in 1989[122] appointment was made by the Foreign Ministers.[123] Subsequently, in a bid to professionalise the ASEAN Secretariat, the DSG was appointed by the Secretary-General after open recruitment and consideration by a panel.[124] In a retrograde step politically appointed DSGs were re-introduced in 1997, appointed by the member states in alphabetical rotation.[125]

See Article 8(2)(g) regarding the ASEAN Coordinating Council's role in the appointment and termination of DSGs.

---

[121] 1976 Agreement on Establishment of the ASEAN Secretariat, Article 3(1)(5)(a) as amended by the 1992 Protocol.

[122] 1989 Protocol Amending the Agreement on Establishment of the ASEAN Secretariat, adopted at the Twenty-second ASEAN Ministerial Meeting in Bandar Seri Begawan, Brunei (4 July 1989).

[123] *See* the 1976 Agreement on the Establishment of the ASEAN Secretariat, Article 4(2) as amended by the 1989 Protocol.

[124] *See* the 1976 Agreement on the Establishment of the ASEAN Secretariat, Article 4(2) as amended by the 1992 Protocol.

[125] *See* the 1976 Agreement on the Establishment of the ASEAN Secretariat, Article 4(2) as amended by the 1997 Protocol.

3. The Secretary-General shall also be the Chief Administrative Officer of ASEAN.

The Role of the Secretary-General

Originally, the function of the Secretary-General of the ASEAN Secretariat (as he was then known) was to take charge of the ASEAN Secretariat (ASEC). He was personally to attend all meetings of the ASEAN Ministerial Meeting (AMM) as secretary.[126] He was also to attend meetings of the ASEAN Standing Committee (ASC)[127] and other ASEAN committees or similar bodies in order to keep himself informed of their activities. Where necessary, he was to explain the directives of the ASC to the other committees or bodies. In short, the Secretary-General was meant as a conduit between the AMM/ASC and the other ASEAN bodies. He was also given a limited executive function, viz, to 'initiate plans and programmes of activities for ASEAN regional cooperation in accordance with approved policy guidelines'.[128] It is clear that at the start the Secretary-General was seen as 'more secretary than general'.[129] His status was below that of the ministers who comprised the AMM. Since he was a civil servant nominated by the member states, he would often also be junior in rank to the members of the ASC.

The role of the Secretary-General was enhanced by the 1992 Protocol Amending the Agreement on Establishment of the ASEAN Secretariat, when the post was accorded ministerial status.[130] He was, *inter alia*, to 'initiate, advise [sic], co-ordinate and implement ASEAN activities'[131] and to 'offer assessments and recommendations on ASEAN's external relations' to the AMM.[132] He was specifically charged with monitoring the Agreement on the Common Effective Tariff (CEPT) for the ASEAN Free Trade Area (AFTA) and was made a member of the AFTA Council.[133] Later

---

126 1976 Agreement on Establishment of the ASEAN Secretariat, Article 3(2)(iii)(a).

127 This had been set up under the 1967 ASEAN Declaration, originally to carry on the work of the Association between meetings of the Foreign Ministers. This role has now been taken over by the Committee of Permanent Representatives: *see* Article 12.

128 1976 Agreement on Establishment of the ASEAN Secretariat, Article 3(2)(viii).

129 A wry self-description by former Secretary-General Ong Keng Yong, quoted in Donald Emmerson, *Hard Choices: Security, Regionalism and Democracy in Southeast Asia* (Singapore: ISEAS Publishing, 2009), 48.

130 1976 Agreement on Establishment of the ASEAN Secretariat, Article 3(1) as amended by the 1992 Protocol. This has been reaffirmed by Article 7(2)(g).

131 1976 Agreement on Establishment of the ASEAN Secretariat, Article 3(1)(4) as amended by the 1992 Protocol.

132 1976 Agreement on Establishment of the ASEAN Secretariat, Article 3(1)(6)(c) as amended by the 1992 Protocol.

133 1976 Agreement on Establishment of the ASEAN Secretariat, Article 3(1)(6)(h) as

on he also became a member of the ASEAN Investment Area Council.[134] It was clear that there was a desire that the Secretary-General should play a bigger role in ASEAN as an organisation and not just function as the head of the secretariat. The Secretary-General of ASEAN was supposed to be ASEAN's public face, in his capacity as spokesman and representative of ASEAN.[135] Since he attended all the Summits, the AMM and the AEM as well as other meetings, he would be the one person who had a general overview of all the increasingly multifarious activities of ASEAN.

At least one former incumbent had reported to the Eminent Persons Group (EPG) on the ASEAN Charter that the Secretary-General was not respected by leaders of the Senior Officials Meeting[136] or the Senior Economic Officials Meeting.[137] The EPG envisaged that the Secretary-General was to be a personage of some significance and take on a greater role, being empowered to sign 'non-sensitive' agreements on behalf of the member states and representing ASEAN at the United Nations and other regional and international forums.[138] There has however been a significant degree of ambivalence among the member states regarding the position of the Secretary-General. Though he has the rank and status of a minister according to Article 7(2)(g),[139] and therefore is theoretically on par with the Foreign Ministers, in practice there has been a reluctance to let the Secretary-General have an independent role.

In negotiating the Charter, it was clear that the member states intended to keep full control of the ASEAN Secretariat and not allow it to evolve into anything resembling the European Commission. Any hint of supranationality was anathema. The expanded role of the Secretary-

---

amended by the 1992 Protocol and the 1992 Agreement on the Common Effective Preferential Tariff (CEPT) Scheme for the ASEAN Free Trade Area, Article 7.

134 1998 Framework Agreement on the ASEAN Investment Area, Article 16.

135 1976 Agreement on Establishment of the ASEAN Secretariat, Article 3(1)(5)(a) as amended by the 1992 Protocol.

136 In 1971 senior officials from the ministries of foreign affairs began meeting regularly at the ASEAN Senior Officials' Meeting (ASEAN SOM), a body which was not specifically created by any agreement but which evolved naturally. SOM was established to discuss political issues, especially sensitive ones, before submission to the AMM. The SOM leader was generally the permanent secretary (or his equivalent in countries that did not adopt the British nomenclature) of the ministry.

137 These precede the annual ASEAN Economic Ministers' Meetings (AEM) and are the equivalent of the Senior Officials Meeting of the foreign ministries.

138 Report of the Eminent Persons Group on the ASEAN Charter, para 37.

139 This status had already been accorded to the Secretary-General under the 1976 Agreement on Establishment of the ASEAN Secretariat, Article 3(1) as amended by the 1992 Protocol.

General envisaged by the EPG was not incorporated into the Charter.[140] Hence, it is explicitly provided that the Secretary-General is the Chief Administrative Officer of ASEAN rather than the Chief Executive Officer.[141] The implication is that the Secretary-General merely oversees the administration of ASEAN and has no independent executive power

This is abundantly clear when one examines the blueprints for the three communities. The Secretary-General of ASEAN is to report the progress of the ASEAN Economic Community (AEC)[142] and the ASEAN Socio-Cultural Community (ASCC)[143] to the relevant ministerial meetings and the Summit. The progress of the ASEAN Political-Security Community (APSC) Blueprint is to be reported to the Summit annually.[144] Under the Roadmap for an ASEAN Community (2009–15), the Secretary-General is also tasked with mobilising resources from the member states, dialogue and sectoral partners, development partners and other external parties.[145] The Secretary-General, along with the relevant ASEAN sectoral ministerial bodies, is responsible for implementation of the Roadmap.[146] Nowhere is the Secretary-General given an independent right of action, not even when offering good offices, conciliation and mediation in the settlement of disputes: *see* Article 23(2).

During the term of the previous incumbent, Dr Surin Pitsuwan of Thailand, it appeared that the member states were concerned with keeping the Secretary-General on a short leash. For instance, under the 2010 Protocol to the ASEAN Charter on Dispute Settlement Mechanisms[147] disputants must concur on a third arbitrator, failing which the appointment will be made by the Chair of the ASEAN Coordinating Council on the recommendation of the Secretary-General. The Secretary-General

---

[140] *See* R. G. Manalo, 'Drafting ASEAN's Tomorrow: The Eminent Persons Group and the ASEAN Charter', in Koh, Manalo and Woon, eds., *Making of the ASEAN Charter*, chapter 4, 44. Ambassador Rosario Manalo was assistant to Philippine EPG member President Fidel Ramos, as well as the Filipino member of the HLTF, which she chaired for the first half of the process.

[141] This reflects Article 97 of the United Nations Charter, where it is provided that the Secretary-General is the Chief Administrative Officer of the Organisation. The Eminent Persons Group specifically stated that the Secretary-General should be the Chief Administrative Officer of ASEAN: *see* the Report of the Eminent Persons Group on the ASEAN Charter, 36.

[142] ASEAN Economic Community Blueprint, para 71.

[143] ASEAN Socio-Cultural Community Blueprint, para III.A.4.

[144] ASEAN Political-Security Community Blueprint, para 32.

[145] Declaration on the Roadmap for the ASEAN Community (2009–15), para 4.

[146] Ibid., para 3.

[147] Signed by the Foreign Ministers at the Sixteenth ASEAN Summit held in Hanoi, 8–9 Apr. 2010.

however has to consult the Committee of Permanent Representatives before making his recommendation.[148] Another example: under the Rules of Authorisation for Legal Transactions under Domestic Laws[149] the Secretary-General must submit a list of persons authorised to enter into transactions to the Committee of Permanent Representatives, which has a power of veto. Similar constraints can be found in the 2010 ASEAN Secretariat Financial Rules and Procedures (AFRP) and 2011 Rules of Procedure for the Conclusion of International Agreements by ASEAN. Considering that the Permanent Representatives rank as ambassadors while the Secretary-General has ministerial status, this is incongruous to say the least.

However, the role of the Secretary-General has evolved from just administering the organisation. He is expected to engage with external parties as the face of ASEAN, as well as with the ASEAN public to create a people-centred ASEAN community. ASEAN now participates in G20 meetings and receives invitations to cooperate with organisations like the World Bank, Organisation for Security and Cooperation in Europe and the International Monetary Fund. A proactive high-profile Secretary-General may be good for ASEAN's image on the world stage, but his frequent absences from Jakarta mean that he cannot devote sufficient attention to the running of the Secretariat. It is vital that the member states decide exactly what role they expect the Secretary-General to play in the creation of the ASEAN community – is he to be just a glorified administrator or something more significant?

Role of the Secretary-General in the resolution of disputes

Article 23(2) explicitly states that the parties to a dispute may request the Secretary-General to provide good offices, mediation and conciliation. There was concern among some HLTF delegations that the Secretary-General should not be allowed to be too activist and independent of the member states. Nonetheless, nothing in the Charter actually prohibits the Secretary-General from offering his good offices, etc. A comparison with the equivalent provision in the 2004 Protocol on Enhanced Dispute Settlement Mechanism (Vientiane Protocol), which predates the Charter,

---

148 Protocol to the ASEAN Charter on Dispute Settlement Mechanisms 2010, rule 1(4)(b) of Annex 4.

149 Made pursuant to Article 2 of the 2009 Agreement on Privileges and Immunities of ASEAN and adopted by the Foreign Ministers at the Seventeenth ASEAN Summit (Hanoi, Oct. 2010).

is instructive. The Vientiane Protocol allows the Secretary-General to volunteer his services to the disputants without waiting to be asked.[150] It would be perfectly consistent with the spirit of the Charter to allow the Secretary-General to take the initiative to assist in settlement where there is a dispute between member states.

Potentially, the Secretary-General can play a pivotal role in the settlement of disputes within ASEAN. A Secretary-General who is perceived to be impartial and not beholden to his country of origin could have considerable influence in bringing disputing parties together. So much depends on the personalities involved, however. The Preah Vihear case[151] demonstrates graphically the limitations under which a politically-appointed Secretary-General works. The incumbent Secretary-General, Dr Surin Pitsuwan, had been Foreign Minister of Thailand in the past and was a member of the ruling Democrat Party. He clearly could not be a neutral interlocutor in a case between his country and Cambodia.[152] However, this was a problem not with the office of the Secretary-General as such but rather with the incumbent.

4. The Secretary-General shall be assisted by four Deputy Secretaries-General with the rank and status of Deputy Ministers. The Deputy Secretaries-General shall be accountable to the Secretary-General in carrying out their functions.

When the ASEAN Secretariat (ASEC) was first established in 1976[153] there was no provision for a deputy to the Secretary-General. In 1989 ASEC was reorganised and the post of Deputy Secretary-General (DSG) introduced.[154] Like the Secretary-General, the DSG's post was rotated among the member states in alphabetical order. To provide continuity, the DSG's appointment would overlap with the incoming and outgoing

---

150 2004 Protocol on Enhanced Dispute Settlement Mechanism, Article 4.

151 This dispute between Cambodia and Thailand over the Temple of Preah Vihear is discussed in more detail in the commentary to Article 28.

152 When asked how he might assist in resolving the dispute, Dr Surin reportedly quipped, 'This is a dispute between two Buddhist countries over a Hindu temple. What can I, a Muslim, do?'

153 *See* the Agreement on Establishment of the ASEAN Secretariat, signed in Bali on 24 Feb. 1976.

154 1989 Protocol Amending the Agreement on Establishment of the ASEAN Secretariat, adopted at the Twenty-second ASEAN Ministerial Meeting in Bandar Seri Begawan, Brunei (4 July 1989). Dr Chng Meng Kng of Singapore was appointed by the Twenty-third ASEAN Ministerial Meeting in July 1990.

Secretaries-General. It was explicitly provided that the DSG should be from the public service of the nominating member state. In diplomatic terms he ranked as minister[155] or minister-counsellor. The function of the DSG was, *inter alia*, to coordinate the research activities of ASEC and handle matters pertaining to ASEAN-affiliated NGOs.[156] In a bid to professionalize ASEC, it was provided in 1992 that the DSG should be openly recruited instead of politically appointed.[157]

A further expansion of the Secretariat was authorised in 1997, with the creation of a second DSG post.[158] In a retrograde step, the 1997 Protocol provided that the two DSGs should be nominated by member states instead of being openly recruited.[159] The DSG posts were rotated in alphabetical order just like the Secretary-General, so that at any one time three member states would have nominees at the apex of ASEC. The Charter increases the number of DSGs to four, two of whom are political appointees while the other two are openly recruited. Though there has been much talk over the years about strengthening and professionalising ASEC, this provision clearly demonstrates that some member states continue to hold the view that it is essential to have one of their nationals hold a key leadership position in ASEC.

There is now one DSG in charge of each of the three Communities, as recommended by the Eminent Persons Group.[160] The fourth is the DSG for Community and Corporate Affairs, who is responsible for providing strategic direction and guidance on research, public affairs and outreach programmes for the ASEAN Community. He is also in charge of corporate support functions.[161]

---

155 The diplomatic rank of minister is just below that of ambassador: *see* the 1961 Vienna Convention on Diplomatic Relations, Article 14(1). This diplomatic rank should not be confused with ministers in the political sense, who are politicians and generally (though not invariably) head a government ministry. In some countries the title deputy minister denotes the most senior civil service appointment in a ministry.

156 Article 5 of the 1976 Agreement on Establishment of the ASEAN Secretariat as amended by the 1989 Protocol.

157 Article 4(1) of the 1976 Agreement on Establishment of the ASEAN Secretariat as amended by the 1992 Protocol Amending the Agreement on Establishment of the ASEAN Secretariat, adopted by the Foreign Ministers at the Twenty-fifth AMM in Manila on 22 July 1992.

158 Article 4(1) of the 1976 Agreement on Establishment of the ASEAN Secretariat as amended by the 1997 Protocol Amending the Agreement on Establishment of the ASEAN Secretariat, adopted by the Foreign Ministers at the Thirtieth AMM in Subang Jaya, Malaysia on 23 July 1997.

159 1976 Agreement on Establishment of the ASEAN Secretariat, Article 4(2) as amended by the 1997 Protocol.

160 Report of the Eminent Persons Group on the ASEAN Charter, para 37.

161 For further information on ASEAN Deputy Secretaries-General and their portfolios, *see* www.asean.org/asean/asean-secretariat/deputy-secretaries-general-of-asean.

Like the Secretary-General, the DSGs enjoy diplomatic immunity.[162] It was the undertanding of the High Level Task Force that the status of Deputy Minister was equivalent to the most senior official in the respective foreign ministries (the Senior Officials Meeting leader) for protocol purposes. They rank above ambassadors. This is another source of potential friction with the Committee of Permanent Representatives, who have ambassadorial rank but oversee the operations of the Secretariat.

As to appointment of DSGs, *see* Article 8(2)(g) and 11(2)(e).

5. The four Deputy Secretaries-General shall be of different nationalities from the Secretary-General and shall come from four different ASEAN Member States.

Two of the four DSGs will be political appointees, appointed by the member states in alphabetical rotation: Article 11(6)(a). The other two will be openly recruited professionals. The effect of this clause is that at any one time five of the member states will be represented by someone at the apex of the Secretariat. In an unfortunate coincidence of circumstances, in the course of 2012 all four DSGs retired, as well as the Secretary-General. ASEAN thus began 2013 with a completely new group at the helm.

6. The four Deputy Secretaries-General shall comprise:

(a) two Deputy Secretaries-General who will serve a non-renewable term of three years, selected from among nationals of the ASEAN Member States based on alphabetical rotation, with due consideration to integrity, qualifications, competence, experience and gender equality; and

One former Secretary-General had represented to the Eminent Persons Group (EPG) on the ASEAN Charter that having political DSGs was not practical. It compromises the professionalism of the Secretariat. A cynic might conclude that the unspoken motive for some member states insisting on such arrangements is to protect their national interests. Given that a politically appointed DSG usually must return to his home service at the end of his limited tenure, one may be permitted to doubt whether such an appointee can really be independent. Recognising this, the EPG

---

162 *See* 2009 Agreement on the Privileges and Immunities of ASEAN, Article 4(4).

Report proposed that all four DSGs should be appointed on merit rather than by rotation, for a renewable term of four years.[163] However, despite the recommendation of the EPG, Article 11(6)(a) was inserted to meet the insistence of some HLTF delegations that each member state should have a chance to appoint a DSG. Indeed, one delegation even suggested that all the DSGs be politically appointed. The compromise was to have two political appointees and two professionals. The view of Secretariat officials expressed to this author is that it would have been better to have all four DSGs openly recruited. One senior ASEAN official went so far as to say that the political appointees have a national agenda and a career to consider when they return to their home countries. This makes it difficult for the Secretary-General to manage them, since he has no influence over their advancement. In a valedictory report to the ASEAN Coordinating Council in 2011, the outgoing Secretary-General also recommended that the DSGs should be openly recruited.

(b) two Deputy Secretaries-General who will serve a term of three years, which may be renewed for another three years. These two Deputy Secretaries-General shall be openly recruited based on merit.

In practice, the six-year limit on the term of service of the professional DSGs means that it is impossible to have a long-term career in ASEAN. A person who works his way up the ranks to the position of DSG has no assurance that he will be reappointed after his first three years are up. The six-year limit inevitably means that ASEAN will lose its most experienced staff if they opt to accept appointment as a DSG. This creates perverse incentives, since a competent director[164] who still has many years before retirement may balk at applying for promotion to DSG since that would mean the end of his career in ASEAN after three or six years. Moreover, when it comes to appointment or extension of employment, a DSG-candidate or incumbent DSG will become subject to objections by the member states through the ASEAN Coordinating Council on grounds that have nothing to do with his or her comptence or suitability. Under the circumstances it should be no surprise that it is a challenge to tempt good

[163] Report of the Eminent Persons Group on the ASEAN Charter, para 37.

[164] The Director rank in the ASEAN Secretariat is the head of a department, for example overseeing the staff coordinating one of the community pillars.

people to give up their careers in order to apply for the post of an openly recruited DSG in ASEAN.

On appointment of DSGs, *see* Article 8(2)(g) and 11(2)(e).

7. The ASEAN Secretariat shall comprise the Secretary-General and such staff as may be required.

The ASEAN Secretariat (ASEC)

The initial organisation of the Secretariat was very modest: three bureau directors, a foreign trade and economic relations officer, an administrative officer, a public relations officer and an assistant to the Secretary-General.[165] All of these personnel were to be nominated by the member states and appointed by the ASEAN Standing Committee (ASC) for a term of three years, which could be renewed. In terms of diplomatic rank the bureau directors rated as counsellors while the others were to be of at least first secretary level. It was envisaged that these officers would be seconded from the diplomatic service of a member state, as it was explicitly provided that secondment would not affect seniority or promotional prospects in the Home Service. Locally recruited staff would fill clerical and other junior posts.[166] ASEC's budget and the salaries of the political appointees were to be approved by the ASEAN Ministerial Meeting.[167]

In 1989 ASEC was reorganised and nine assistant directors were provided for in addition to the three bureau directors. It was explicitly stated that the bureau directors and assistant directors should be from the public service of the nominating state.[168] The 1992 reorganisation of ASEC added another bureau director, two more assistant directors and eight senior officers, a recognition of the increased demands on the secretariat. Hitherto, the DSG, bureau directors and assistant directors

---

[165] 1976 Agreement on Establishment of the ASEAN Secretariat, Article 4(1). In 1983 provision was made for more political appointees, as determined by the ASC; *see* the 1983 Protocol Amending the Agreement on Establishment of the ASEAN Secretariat.

[166] 1976 Agreement on Establishment of the ASEAN Secretariat, Article 6.

[167] 1976 Agreement on Establishment of the ASEAN Secretariat, Articles 7 and 9. Effectively, the ASC would have had oversight since they would prepare the recommendations for the AMM.

[168] Article 4 of the 1976 Agreement on Establishment of the ASEAN Secretariat as amended by the 1989 Protocol.

had been politically appointed.[169] They were now designated as openly-recruited staff in an attempt to professionalise the secretariat.[170] Although the professional staff were supposed to be openly recruited on the basis of merit, there was to be a quota system to ensure representation of all member countries in ASEC.[171] Informal secondment arrangements still continue to be practised, whereby the four newest member states may nominate two staff per country for an initial appointment of three years.

In practice, it is difficult to attract staff from the more developed member countries to work in ASEC, in large part because of income disparities between member states and the existence of more attractive career options elsewhere. There is a constant problem of staff turnover as well, as experienced officials leave for better-paid private sector work. Ironically, the setting up of new missions to ASEAN by non-member countries led to greater competition for staff, to the detriment of ASEC.

The ASEAN Secretariat is precisely that: a secretariat and not an independent institution capable of political action. When drafting the Charter it was clear that the member states would not accept a supranational institution.[172] However, ASEC has been increasingly entrusted with the role of monitoring compliance with ASEAN agreements, especially the economic ones. Under the Framework Agreement on Enhancing ASEAN Economic Cooperation 1992 ASEC was given the task of monitoring the progress of any arrangements arising from the agreement.[173] Similarly, under the Agreement on the Common Effective Preferential Tariff (CEPT) Scheme for the ASEAN Free Trade Area 1992 ASEC was to monitor the implementation of the agreement, reporting to SEOM.[174] The ASEAN Framework Agreement on Goods in Transit 1998 created a Transit Transport Coordinating Board including a representative of ASEC.[175] ASEC was to submit evaluation reports to the Board for further action. Under the 2004 ASEAN Framework Agreement for Integration of Priority Sectors ASEC was again required to submit reports to SEOM on

---

169 1976 Agreement on Establishment of the ASEAN Secretariat, Article 4. The subsequent amending Protocols did not change this system of political appointments.

170 1976 Agreement on Establishment of the ASEAN Secretariat, Article 4 as amended by the 1992 Protocol.

171 Para 8 of the Singapore Declaration (Jan. 1992).

172 There have been numerous proposals to strengthen the Secretariat over the years. *See* Severino, *In Search of an ASEAN Community*, 23 and Dewi Fortuna Anwar, *Indonesia in ASEAN: Foreign Policy and Regionalism* (Singapore: ISEAS Publishing, 1994), 85–8.

173 1992 Framework Agreement on Enhancing ASEAN Economic Cooperation, Article 7.

174 Agreement on the Common Effective Preferential Tariff (CEPT) Scheme for the ASEAN Free Trade Area, Article 7(3).

175 1998 Framework Agreement on Facilitation of Goods in Transit, Article 29.

the implementation of the agreement.[176] ASEC was also given the role of providing secretarial support to the many bodies that were formed pursuant to ASEAN agreements, not only amongst the member states but also with external partners.[177]

The demands on ASEC have expanded exponentially since its creation in 1976. ASEC not only provided secretarial support for ASEAN meetings, it was tasked with a host of monitoring functions under the many agreements entered in by ASEAN member states as well as assisting the Secretary-General in his facilitation and monitoring role provided for in Article 11(2)(b). In addition, ASEC is tasked in Article 52 to interpret the Charter upon the request of an ASEAN Member State. Under the Protocol on Enhanced Dispute Settlement Mechanisms and the Protocol to the ASEAN Charter on Dispute Settlement Mechanisms, ASEC's duty is not merely technical or administrative, it also has the responsibility to assist in the substantive legal, historical and procedural aspects of the disputes. It was estimated by the Secretary-General that ASEC was expected to service more than 1,100 ASEAN meetings in 2012. Despite repeated calls for the strengthening of ASEC,[178] not much has been done to give it more resources. In particular, ASEC lacks the legal experts who are vital if ASEAN is to realise its ambition to be an organisation based on the rule of law.[179]

Member states have shown a great deal of ambivalence regarding the role of ASEC. There has been a noticeable reluctance to empower ASEC to act on its own initiative. A glaring example is seen in question of interpretation of the Charter under Article 51. When drafting the Charter, the High Level Task Force (HLTF) came to the conclusion that setting up a new Legal Committee was not practical. The HLTF decided that interpretation of the Charter could be entrusted to a proper legal unit

---

[176] 2004 ASEAN Framework Agreement for Integration of Priority Sectors, Article 19.

[177] *See* for example the Framework Agreement on Comprehensive Economic Cooperation between India and ASEAN and China (2002), Article 12; Framework Agreement on Comprehensive Economic Cooperation between India and ASEAN (2003), Article 12; Framework Agreement for Comprehensive Economic Partnership between Japan and ASEAN (2003), Article 11; Framework Agreement on Comprehensive Economic Cooperation among the Governments of Member Countries of ASEAN and the Republic of Korea (2005), Article 5.4.

[178] A High Level Task Force on Strengthening the ASEAN Secretariat and Reviewing the ASEAN Organs has been established: *see* para 81 the Chairman's Statement of the Twenty-fourth ASEAN Summit (Nay Pi Taw, Myanmar, 10–11 May 2014).

[179] The author has argued for the creation of a proper ASEAN Legal Sevice in *Towards a Rules-Based Community: An ASEAN Legal Service* (Cambridge: Cambridge University Press, 2014), co-written with Jean-Claude Piris, formerly Director-General of the European Council Legal Service.

in the Secretariat. The understanding was that ASEAN Secretariat would be neutral and had the institutional memory of how the Charter and other implementing documents came into being.[180] When the Rules of Procedure on Interpretation of the ASEAN Charter[181] were promulgated however, it was explicitly stated that ASEC's interpretation was not binding, not authoritative and did not represent the view of ASEAN.[182] This is symptomatic of the lack of trust on the part of the member states in ASEC. In a valedictory paper submitted to the ASEAN Coordinating Council, the outgoing Secretary-General stated that one of the key questions confronting ASEAN was the extent to which the member states were prepared to empower ASEC. Creation of the ASEAN Community will not occur unless member states (and in particular their foreign ministries) are willing to put more faith in the institutions they have created.

Institutional memory

The only people working full-time on ASEAN affairs are the Secretary-General and his deputies, the Committee of Permanent Representatives, the officers on the ASEAN desk at the ministries of foreign affairs of the member states and the officials of ASEC. Given that the first three groups are only assigned for a limited period,[183] the long-term memory of ASEAN as an organisation resides with ASEC. Together, ASEC and the Secretary-General form a neutral centre in ASEAN affairs and provide the institutional memory of the organisation.

Finances and budget

As to the operational budget and finances of ASEC, *see* Article 30.

Making contracts, acquiring and disposing of property and conducting litigation

---

[180] This understanding is confirmed by Dr Termsak Chalermpalanupap in 'Life in ASEAN after the Entry into Force of the ASEAN Charter', 58. Dr Termsak assisted the HLTF in its work throughout the drafting process.

[181] Adopted by the ASEAN Coordinating Council on 2 Apr. 2012.

[182] *See* Rule 2(1) of the 2012 Rules of Procedure for the Interpretation of the ASEAN Charter. It is arguable that rule 2(1) goes far beyond procedural matters and impinges on substance. In so far as it is inconsistent with the rights and obligations of the member states contained in the Charter, it may be ineffective because of Article 52(2).

[183] Or in the case of non-political DSGs, can only serve for six years at most because of Article 11(6)(b).

The 2009 Agreement on the Privileges and Immunities of ASEAN[184] provides that ASEAN as an entity may enter into contracts, acquire and dispose of property and conduct litigation, whether as plaintiff or defendant. In conducting these activities, ASEAN may be represented by the Secretary-General, one of the DSGs or any member of the staff of ASEC authorised by the Secretary-General.[185] Rules of Authorisation for Legal Transactions under Domestic Laws pursuant to Article 2 of the 2009 Agreement on Privileges and Immunities of ASEAN were adopted by the Foreign Ministers at the Seventeenth ASEAN Summit (Hanoi, October 2010). The 2012 Host Agreement reaffirms the legal capacity of ASEAN under Indonesian law.[186]

8. The Secretary-General and the staff shall:

(a) uphold the highest standards of integrity, efficiency, and competence in the performance of their duties;

(b) not seek or receive instructions from any government or external party outside of ASEAN; and

See also Article 11(9) below regarding taking instructions from Member States.

(c) refrain from any action which might reflect on their position as ASEAN Secretariat officials responsible only to ASEAN.

Compare Article 100(1) of the Charter of the United Nations.

9. Each ASEAN Member State undertakes to respect the exclusively ASEAN character of the responsibilities of the Secretary-General and the staff, and not to seek to influence them in the discharge of their responsibilities.

---

[184] Adopted at the Fifteenth ASEAN Summit in Cha-Am Hua Hin, Thailand, on 25 Oct. 2009.

[185] Ibid., Article 2(1).

[186] 2012 Agreement between the Government of the Republic of Indonesia and the Association of Southeast Asian Nations on Hosting and Granting Privileges and Immunities to the ASEAN Secretariat, Article 2.

Compare Article 100(2) of the Charter of the United Nations.

This provision is necessary to ensure the political impartiality of the officials of the ASEAN Secretariat. Nothing would be more destructive of the *esprit de corps* of ASEC than to have pressure brought on officials by the member countries of which they are nationals. In practice, however, the Secretary-General and two of the four Deputy Secretaries-General are nominated by the member states. In the case of the Secretary-General, appointment is for one five-year non-renewable term: Article 11(1). The two political Deputy Secretaries-General serve for only three years, with no renewal: Article 11(6)(a). Life has to go on after service with ASEAN. It is impossible to build a long-term career in the ASEAN Secretariat as a political appointee. This can only compromise the neutrality of such appointees, even if the member states scrupulously adhere to the principle of non-influence.

Article 12. Committee of Permanent Representatives to ASEAN

The Eminent Persons Group (EPG) referred to the accreditation of Permanent Representatives (PRs) in only one paragraph of its report.[187] It was envisaged in general terms that the PRs would 'represent ASEAN member states' respective governments, particularly at meetings of ASEAN committees.' What this actually would mean in practice was not specified. The Committee of Permanent Representatives (CPR) was supposed to replace the ASEAN Standing Committee (ASC), a body that was established by the 1967 ASEAN Declaration to support the work of the Foreign Ministers. Initially, this comprised the ambassadors to the host of the next ASEAN Ministerial Meeting (AMM). In 1992 this was changed to Directors-General in charge of ASEAN at the respective foreign ministries, together with the Secretary-General.[188] The ASC, amongst other tasks, oversaw the ASEAN Secretariat, albeit from a distance. It only met three to four times a year.

When it came to the drafting of this provision of the Charter, the High Level Task Force (HLTF) had the invaluable advantage of the presence of Secretary-General Ong Keng Yong, who was intimately familiar with the workings of ASEAN. The elaborated list of functions of the CPR was the result of extensive discussions amongst the HLTF

---

[187] Report of the Eminent Persons Group on the ASEAN Charter, paras 38 and 62 'ASEAN Permanent Representatives'.

[188] Severino, *In Search of an ASEAN Community*, 22.

members and the Secretary-General. Some delegations wanted the PRs to have extensive powers similar to those of the PRs to the United Nations in New York or those of the PRs of the European Union member states. Others had reservations about this, being concerned that the role of the Senior Officials Meeting (SOM)[189] and directors-general of ASEAN affairs in the foreign ministries would be weakened. Pengiran Dato Paduka Osman Patra, the HLTF member from Brunei, notes that 'frankly, several members [of the HLTF] were not particularly convinced about how the potential of this Committee would be realised unless the capitals of ASEAN are ready to empower and entrust full responsibilities to their PRs in Jakarta'.[190] The text is the compromise between the two views. Even so, the exact nature of the duties of the CPR were not spelt out.

The Terms of Reference (TOR) for the Committee of Permanent Representatives to ASEAN were approved by the Forty-first ASEAN Ministerial Meeting in July 2008. This document was drafted by the PRs themselves, apparently with very little input from trained lawyers. Among the tasks specifically entrusted to the CPR are supporting the work of the ASEAN Coordinating Council (ACC) in the following manner:[191]

a. assisting in the preparation of the meetings of the ASEAN Summit;
b. coordinating the implementation of agreements and decisions of the ASEAN Summit;
c. acting as the approving authority for ASEAN projects funded from ASEAN central funds;
d. approving the operational budget of ASEC.[192]

The CPR is also supposed to assist in considering and coordinating the reports of the Community Councils, the Secretary-General's annual report and the report of the ASEAN Foundation. Paragraph 6 of the TOR gives the CPR power to oversee the operations of the ASEAN Secretariat and

---

189 This comprises officials from the foreign ministries. SOM was established to discuss political issues, especially sensitive ones, before submission to the ASEAN Ministerial Meeting. The SOM leader was generally the permanent secretary (or his equivalent in countries that did not adopt the British nomenclature) of the ministry.

190 *See* his chapter 'Heart Labour' in Koh, Manalo and Woon, eds., *Making of the ASEAN Charter*, 13–14. Pengiran Osman was for many years the Permanent Secretary of the Ministry of Foreign Affairs and Trade, Brunei.

191 *See* para 4 of the Terms of Reference of the Committee of Permanent Representatives to ASEAN.

192 Strictly speaking, it is the ACC that approves the budget on the recommendation of the CPR: *see* Article 30(3).

related ASEAN institutions. They also 'coordinate' with the Secretary-General in the performance of his role to monitor the implementation of ASEAN decisions and agreements.

1. Each ASEAN Member State shall appoint a Permanent Representative to ASEAN with the rank of Ambassador based in Jakarta.

The Eminent Persons Group on the ASEAN Charter (EPG) recommended the appointment of Permanent Representatives (PRs) based in Jakarta to represent the member states.[193] This would help streamline ASEAN meetings and avoid having senior officials shuttle constantly back and forth from the capitals. The idea for a CPR was first mooted in a report of the 1982–83 Task Force for the Strengthening of the ASEAN Secretariat chaired by Mr Anand Panyarachun of Thailand, and the 1991–92 report by a panel headed by Tan Sri Ghazali Shafie of Malaysia.[194] These PRs would take on the role hitherto played by the ASEAN Standing Committee.[195]

The first PRs were appointed in 2009, after the Terms of Reference for the Committee of Permanent Representatives to ASEAN were approved at the Forty-first ASEAN Ministerial Meeting.[196] The inaugural meeting was held at the ASEAN Secretariat on 21 May 2009.[197] The Rules of Procedure of the Committee of Permanent Representatives to ASEAN were also adopted at the Fourth Meeting of the ASEAN Coordinating Council on 21 July 2009. Some member states appointed a separate PR to ASEAN, while for others the Ambassador to Indonesia doubled up as PR. This had been envisaged by the EPG as an acceptable practice.

The Permanent Representatives enjoy diplomatic immunity.[198]

2. The Permanent Representatives collectively constitute a Committee of Permanent Representatives, which shall:

---

193 Report of the Eminent Persons Group on the ASEAN Charter, para 38.

194 Severino, *In Search of an ASEAN Community*, 23.

195 In an oversight, the ASEAN Standing Committee is still listed as a sectoral ministerial body under the Political-Security Community in Annex 1 of the Charter.

196 Held in Singapore from 17–24 July 2008, just before the Charter came into force in Dec. 2008.

197 Chalermpalanupap, 'Life in ASEAN after the Entry into Force of the ASEAN Charter', 55.

198 *See* Article 19(2) and the 2009 Agreement on the Privileges and Immunities of ASEAN, Article 7.

(a) support the work of the ASEAN Community Councils and ASEAN Sectoral Ministerial Bodies;

As to the ASEAN Community Councils, *see* Article 9. ASEAN Sectoral Ministerial Bodies are covered by Article 10. The CPR may amend the list of such bodies without having to go through the procedure of amending the Charter: Article 10(2).

(b) coordinate with ASEAN National Secretariats and other ASEAN Sectoral Ministerial Bodies;

As to the ASEAN National Secretariats, *see* Article 13; ASEAN Sectoral Ministerial Bodies, *see* Article 10.

(c) liaise with the Secretary-General of ASEAN and the ASEAN Secretariat on all subjects relevant to its work;

As to the work of the Secretary-General and ASEAN Secretariat, *see* commentary to Article 11. This function seems to have evolved into a supervisory one. For instance, under the Rules of Authorisation for Legal Transactions under Domestic Laws[199] the Secretary-General must submit a list of persons authorised to enter into transactions to the Committee of Permanent Representatives, which has a power of veto. Considering that the Permanent Representatives rank as ambassadors while the Secretary-General has ministerial status, this is incongruous to say the least.

(d) facilitate ASEAN cooperation with external partners; and

Article 41(6) vests the task of ensuring consistency and coherence in ASEAN's external relations with the ASEAN Foreign Ministers Meeting. The 1967 ASEAN Declaration provided for an annual meeting of Foreign Ministers, known as the ASEAN Ministerial Meeting (AMM).[200] To support the work of the Foreign Ministers, a standing committee (the ASEAN Standing Committee or ASC) was also created, under the chairmanship of the country hosting the AMM. Initially, this comprised the ambassadors to

[199] Made pursuant to Article 2 of the 2009 Agreement on Privileges and Immunities of ASEAN and adopted by the Foreign Ministers at the Seventeenth ASEAN Summit (Hanoi, Oct. 2010).

[200] Since the coming into force of the Charter in Dec. 2008 the ASEAN Ministerial Meeting has been redesignated as the ASEAN Foreign Ministers Meeting.

the host of the next AMM. In 1992 this was changed to directors-general in charge of ASEAN at the respective foreign ministries, together with the Secretary-General.[201] This function of supporting the Foreign Ministers Meeting has now been taken over by the Committee of Permanent Representatives. While the CPR is not mentioned in Chapter XII on External Relations, it was given a central role in the 2011 Rules of Procedure for the Conclusion of International Agreements by ASEAN.

(e) perform such other functions as may be determined by the ASEAN Coordinating Council.

As to the ASEAN Coordinating Council, *see* Article 8.

Role of the Committee of Permanent Representatives

Although Article 12(2)(c) speaks of liaison with the Secretariat and Secretary-General, it appears that the CPR has now taken on the role of supervision. Indeed, in conversation with the author, one PR expressed the view that the CPR is the board of directors to whom the Secretariat (and implicitly, the Secretary-General) reports. This view was not shared by all the PRs. The exact relationship between the CPR on one hand and the Secretary-General and ASEC on the other is not entirely clear even now. Is the Secretary-General subject to the direct supervision and control of the CPR? How far should the CPR go in overseeing the operations of ASEC? The problem is compounded by the fact that the Secretary-General is of ministerial rank[202] while the PRs are only ambassadors.[203] Indeed, the first Secretary-General after the coming into force of the Charter, Dr Surin Pitsuwan, was Foreign Minister of Thailand at one stage and clearly outranked all the PRs. The Secretary-General has identified the tension between the CPR and ASEC as a factor that undermines community-building efforts.

Nonetheless, the CPR now exercises close supervision over the ASEAN Secretariat.[204] It considers the budgetary requests of the Secretariat and

---

201 Severino, *In Search of an ASEAN Community,* 22.
202 *See* Article 7(1)(g).
203 *See* Article 12(1).
204 In contrast to the ASEAN Standing Committee, which only met three to four times a year, there were fifty meetings of the CPR and its working groups in 2011 alone. Not all of these CPR meetings dealt with matters pertaining to ASEC, but it is immediately apparent that the CPR is in a position to micro-manage ASEC if it is minded to do so. This in fact was a complaint of some PRs in conversation with the author.

even looks into personnel matters. Under the Rules of Authorisation for Legal Transactions under Domestic Laws[205] the Secretary-General must submit a list of persons authorised to enter into transactions to the Committee of Permanent Representatives, which has a power of veto. The CPR was also intimately involved in approving the ASEAN Secretariat Staff Regulations. This might be considered to be micro-management of matters more efficiently left to the Secretary-General's discretion. Indeed, the Secretary-General himself voiced the desire that he should be given more latitude to decide on human resource management and matters relating to the operations of ASEC. Some PRs expressed the view to this author that the CPR is spending too much time micro-managing the Secretariat at the expense of more strategic big-picture issues. It is perhaps inevitable that at the initial stage there should be some uncertainty over the precise scope of the CPR's mandate. This will have to be worked out pragmatically as the organisation evolves.

Of the other tasks specified in clause (2) of this article, the CPR has been involved mainly in coordination of the activities of the Political-Security pillar. This is not surprising, since the PRs are from the respective foreign ministries. The HLTF and EPG envisaged that the CPR would be a coordinating body cutting across all three pillars. The EPG stated that the PRs would represent the member states at meetings of ASEAN committees, the idea being that it should not be necessary to send officials from the capitals to each and every meeting.[206] This has not been easy to implement in practice. Some PRs expressed the view to this author that the CPR has not been able to play a significant role in coordinating across the Community Councils. Lack of manpower resources is one of the problems. Lack of a clear mandate is another. A third problem identified by some PRs to the author is the fact that the CPR is new and the domestic hierarchy had not been clearly worked out when the CPR came into existence. The economic pillar has its own autonomous existence and does not report to or through the CPR. Liaison between the CPR and the ASEAN Economic Community Council and related sectoral bodies is provided by the officials of the ASEAN Secretariat, who brief the CPR on what is happening in that area. The ASEAN Socio-Cultural Community Council is the most amorphous, comprising other ministries which have no long history of working together. Again, the various sectoral bodies

[205] Made pursuant to Article 2 of the 2009 Agreement on Privileges and Immunities of ASEAN and adopted by the Foreign Ministers at the Seventeenth ASEAN Summit (Hanoi, Oct. 2010).

[206] Report of the Eminent Persons Group on the ASEAN Charter, para 38.

and committees do not report to the CPR, which is kept informed only through the Secretariat. It is imperative to work out these problems if there is to be proper coordination of ASEAN activities.

In conversation with the author, several PRs expressed the opinion that for the CPR to function as envisaged, it will be necessary to appoint a Deputy PR and supporting officers to cover each of the other Community Councils in every Permanent Representation. The Deputy PRs and their officers will then be able to discuss and coordinate matters pertaining to their Community Council, reporting to the PR who will provide the coordination across the three pillars. Only if all ten Permanent Representations have such officers in Jakarta will this coordinating function work. If not all ten are present, officers from the parent ministries will have to be sent out for meetings. This is a matter of resources which the member states must resolve. Until the Permanent Representations are beefed up, the CPR will not be able to fulfil the role envisaged for it by the EPG and HLTF.

As far as cooperation with external partners is concerned, it appears that some of these see the CPR as a means of disseminating ideas and information to the ASEAN capitals. Instead of having ten ambassadors approach the relevant ministries in each capital, the Ambassador to ASEAN[207] can discuss matters with the CPR, who will then report back to the respective ministries. This is a more efficient mode of communication. Again, the practice in this area is evolving.

Finally, the CPR of its own initiative has taken on tasks that are not explicitly spelt out in the Charter. During the Indonesian chairmanship, the CPR went out of Jakarta to other locations in Indonesia in order to reach out to the wider public. This is in line with the aim of creating a 'people-centred' ASEAN. Engagement with academia, the media and civil society groups helps to spread knowledge of the work of ASEAN, which can only be an advantage in community building.

Article 13. ASEAN National Secretariats

Each ASEAN Member State shall establish an ASEAN National Secretariat which shall:

(a) serve as the national focal point;

(b) be the repository of information on all ASEAN matters at the national level;

---

[207] Accredited under Article 46.

(c) coordinate the implementation of ASEAN decisions at the national level;
(d) coordinate and support the national preparations of ASEAN meetings;
(e) promote ASEAN identity and awareness at the national level; and
(f) contribute to ASEAN community building.

The National Secretariats are among the oldest ASEAN organs, having been established by the 1967 ASEAN Declaration.[208] They generally reside in the Foreign Ministry of the respective member states, under the aegis of the Directors-General in charge of ASEAN affairs. The National Secretariats form the interface for ASEAN in the member states, together with the Committee of Permanent Representatives in Jakarta.[209] At the domestic level, the National Secretariats are generally the drivers for their country's chairmanship agendas, and serve as the main coordinating body and resource for their domestic counterparts' involvement in the various ASEAN sectoral bodies.

Article 14. ASEAN Human Rights Body

The Charter mentions human rights repeatedly in the Preamble, Article 1(7) and Article 2(2)(i). This was deliberately done to underline the importance of the promotion of human rights. While member states were happy to sign up to general statements of high principle, giving life to the human rights body proved to be the most contentious issue during the process of drafting the Charter.[210]

As early as 1993, the Twenty-sixth ASEAN Ministerial Meeting (AMM) agreed that ASEAN 'should consider the establishment of an appropriate regional mechanism on human rights'.[211] This was in response to the 1993 World Conference on Human Rights.[212] The Foreign Ministers affirmed ASEAN's commitment to human rights and fundamental freedoms as set out in the Vienna Declaration of 25 June 1993. They further stressed the indivisibility of civil, political, economic, social and cultural rights. The Foreign Ministers agreed that ASEAN should coordinate a common

---

208 1967 ASEAN Declaration, para 3(d).
209 *See* Article 12(2)(b).
210 *See* for example Myanmar HLTF member U Aung Bwa's comments in his chapter 'The Jewel in my Crown', 32–3.
211 Joint Communiqué of the Twenty-sixth ASEAN Ministerial Meeting, Singapore 23–24 July 1993, para 18.
212 Held in Vienna from 14–25 June 1993.

approach on human rights and to consider the establishment of 'an appropriate regional mechanism on human rights'. This was before the CLMV countries became part of ASEAN.

Nothing was done officially to follow up on the pious hope expressed by the Foreign Ministers regarding the establishment of the human rights mechanism. Partly this was on account of the increased political diversity of the new members and the advent of the 1997 financial crisis.[213] More likely, it was because of the ambivalent attitude of member states to such a mechanism. It was left to civil society to pick up the ball and run with it. Following the 1993 AMM, an informal non-governmental Working Group for an ASEAN Human Rights Mechanism (WG-AHRM) was set up.[214] This working group consisted of Track-2 representatives from academia and civil society. The Working Group were invited to present recommendations to the AMM on several occasions but had minimal impact on ASEAN policies.[215] The Chairman of the Working Group, Mr Marzuki Darusman of Indonesia, met the High Level Task Force on Drafting the ASEAN Charter at its seventh meeting in Bali.[216]

The idea of a human rights mechanism continued to float around for more than a decade after the 1993 AMM but did not form part of any concrete policy. Even the Report of the Eminent Persons Group (EPG) on the ASEAN Charter[217] was equivocal; it stated that the EPG had discussed the possibility of setting up an ASEAN human rights mechanism and 'noted that this worthy idea should be pursued further'.[218] This was a late addition to the report, accepted to accommodate the insistence of one EPG member. The very guarded language was the result of a compromise reflecting the lack of agreement on this issue among the EPG members.

---

213 Termsak Chalermpalanupap, 'Promoting and Protecting Human Rights in ASEAN', available at http://www.asean.org/archive/9 3-1 4248-HumanRightsArticle.pdf. Dr Termsak was Special Assistant to Secretary-General Ong Keng Yong at the time the Charter was being drafted.

214 This was noted in the Joint Communiqué of the Thirty-first ASEAN Ministerial Meeting, Manila 24–25 July 1998, para 28. It is now an Accredited Civil Society Organisation in Annex 2 of the Charter.

215 *See* Hao Duy Phan, *A Selective Approach to Establishing an ASEAN Human Rights Mechanism in Southeast Asia: The Case for a Southeast Asian Court of Human Rights* (Leiden: Koninklijke Brill, 2012), 85–9.

216 Held from 26–28 June 2007. Pak Marzuki's contribution was duly noted, but the subsequent drafting of the Terms of Reference proved too contentious for the HLTF to complete. The TOR was only finalised in July 2009, after the Charter had come into force.

217 Endorsed by the Heads of State/Government in the Cebu Declaration on the Blueprint of the ASEAN Charter, issued at the Twelfth ASEAN Summit in Cebu, the Philippines, on 13 Jan. 2007.

218 Report of the Eminent Persons Group on the ASEAN Charter, para 47.

The ASEAN human rights mechanism was not listed in the recommended organisational structure for ASEAN in the EPG Report.

1. In conformity with the purposes and principles of the ASEAN Charter relating to the promotion and protection of human rights and fundamental freedoms, ASEAN shall establish an ASEAN human rights body.

At the first meeting of the High Level Task Force (HLTF) for Drafting of the ASEAN Charter in Jakarta (4-6 February 2007), the EPG member from Malaysia Tan Sri Musa Hitam briefed the HLTF on the deliberations of the EPG. He mentioned the ASEAN Human Rights Commission as an area where the EPG Report could have gone further. However, as early as the second HLTF meeting in Siem Reap (28 February to 1 March 2007) doubts were already being expressed by some delegations about the acceptability of such a commission. The issue was referred to the Foreign Ministers at their Retreat (1-2 March 2007). Instructions were given that the HLTF should draft a provision on a human rights organ, not necessarily a commission.

There the matter rested until the seventh HLTF meeting in Bali (26-28 June 2007). Some delegations argued forcefully in favour of a robust human rights mechanism; others demurred.[219] Even the title proved contentious, some members pushing for a commission, others stoutly resisting. The term 'mechanism' was therefore adopted as a compromise.

The debate continued at the eighth HLTF meeting in Manila (26 July 2007), with no agreement being reached.[220] Cambodia, Laos, Myanmar and Vietnam opposed the creation of a Human Rights Commission, while Indonesia and Thailand pushed for one. Brunei, Malaysia the Philippines and Singapore were caught between the two camps.[221] The guidance of the Foreign Ministers was again sought. The ministers themselves were divided. The ministers from the Philippines, Indonesia, Malaysia and Singapore rejected the formula that the HLTF had put to them as being

---

[219] Malaysian HLTF member Tan Sri Ahmad Fuzi bin Abdul Razak alludes to this in his chapter 'Facing Unfair Criticisms', in Koh, Manalo and Woon, eds., *Making of the ASEAN Charter*, chapter 2, 21.

[220] Pengiran Dato Paduka Osman Patra, the HLTF member from Brunei, stated 'of all our debates, this was the most explosive and tense of all': *see* his 'Heart Labour', in Koh, Manalo and Woon, eds., *Making of the ASEAN Charter*, chapter 1, 7,

[221] *See* Koh, 'The Negotiating Process', in Koh, Manalo and Woon, eds., *Making of the ASEAN Charter*, chapter 5, 58-9. Koh took over as Chairman of the HLTF after this meeting.

weaker than the instructions given at the Foreign Ministers' Retreat in Siem Reap in March. A counter-proposal from the Philippines, supported by Indonesia, Malaysia and Thailand, was rejected by Cambodia, Laos, Myanmar and Vietnam. There were heated exchanges on the subject.[222] Secretary-General Ong Keng Yong suggested a compromise form of words for Article 14, which was finally agreed to by the ministers. This paragraph is the compromise text agreed to by the Foreign Ministers at the Fortieth ASEAN Ministerial Meeting in Manila (29–30 July 2007). It was instructed that the Terms of Reference of the Human Rights Body, as it came to be called, would be submitted by the HLTF but need not be included in the Charter. Following the eighth HLTF meeting the ASEAN Secretariat prepared a non-paper on the Terms of Reference of the Human Rights Body.

Like Frankenstein's monster, the human rights organ remained a body without a name. It was only after the Charter came into force that it was finally christened. At the Forty-second ASEAN Foreign Ministers' Meeting[223] it was decided that the body should be designated the ASEAN Intergovernmental Commission on Human Rights (AICHR), following negotiations to conclude its Terms of Reference by a High Level Panel on the ASEAN Human Rights Body (HLP).[224] The AICHR was finally established in October 2009 at the Fifteenth ASEAN Summit.[225] It held its first meeting at the ASEAN Secretariat from 28 March to 1 April 2010.

2. This ASEAN human rights body shall operate in accordance with the terms of reference to be determined by the ASEAN Foreign Ministers Meeting.

The tenth HLTF meeting in Chiang Mai from 10–14 September was the most difficult. Negotiations almost broke down at one point as delegations could not agree on the role and Terms of Reference (TOR) of the Human Rights Body. Cambodia, Laos, Myanmar and Vietnam insisted that the TOR be settled together with the Charter. If this could not be done, then there could be no agreement on the Charter as a whole. The Philippines,

---

[222] *See* Koh, 'The Negotiating Process', in Koh, Manalo and Woon, eds., *Making of the ASEAN Charter,* chapter 5, 59.

[223] Held in Phuket, Thailand, on 20 July 2009.

[224] Joint Communiqué of the Forty-second ASEAN Foreign Ministers' Meeting, para 8.

[225] Cha-Am Hua Hin Declaration on the Intergovernmental Commission on Human Rights, issued by the ASEAN leaders at the Fifteenth ASEAN Summit, 23 Oct. 2009.

Indonesia, Malaysia and Thailand disagreed to even have this placed on the meeting agenda. As for the role of the Human Rights Body, some delegations wanted it to have a monitoring function while others were vehemently opposed, insisting that it be consultative only. The Singapore Chair, supported by the Brunei delegation, shuttled between the various delegations seeking to broker a compromise.[226] In the end agreement was reached on this paragraph after much hard and sometimes heated bargaining, subject to the approval of the Foreign Ministers. It was agreed as a compromise that the TOR of the Human Rights Body need not be finalised before completion of the Charter, so that the Charter could be completed even though the scope of the Human Rights Body had not been settled.

The next meeting of the HLTF took place in New York on 26 September 2007. At the informal ASEAN Ministerial Meeting that followed, the Foreign Ministers were divided over the role of the Human Rights Body but gave instructions to the HLTF to press on. The Foreign Ministers also instructed that the TOR need not be submitted before the completion of the Charter. It was finally agreed at the twelfth HLTF meeting in Bandar Seri Begawan from 3–5 October that the TOR of the Human Rights Body would be taken up after the Charter was signed.

A High Level Panel on an ASEAN Human Rights Body (HLP) for drafting the TOR was established by the Foreign Ministers at their Retreat in Singapore on 20 February 2008. The HLP commenced work in July 2008 and settled the draft of the TOR on 14 February 2009 after eight meetings.[227] Meanwhile, the ASEAN Political-Security Community Blueprint[228] specifically committed ASEAN to establish the human rights body.[229] The finalised TOR was endorsed by the Forty-second ASEAN Foreign Ministers' Meeting held in Phuket, Thailand, on 20 July 2009.

---

[226] *See* Koh, 'The Negotiating Process', 63, and Pibulsonggram, 'The Thai Perspective', 89–90, in Koh, Manalo and Woon, eds., *Making of the ASEAN Charter*.

[227] Press Release by the Chair of the HLP issued on 14 Feb. 2009 at Luang Prabang, Laos.

[228] Adopted by the Heads of State/Government at the Fourteenth ASEAN Summit in Cha-Am, Thailand, on 1 Mar. 2009 as an annex to the Cha-am Hua Hin Declaration on the Roadmap for the ASEAN Community (2009–15).

[229] *See* para A.1.5(i) of the APSC Blueprint.

Terms of Reference of the ASEAN Intergovernmental Commission on Human Rights[230]

The purposes of the AICHR are:[231]

- To promote and protect human rights and fundamental freedoms of the peoples of ASEAN.
- To uphold the right of the peoples of ASEAN to live in peace, dignity and prosperity.
- To contribute to the realisation of the purposes of ASEAN as set out in the Charter.
- To promote human rights within the regional context.
- To enhance regional cooperation with a view to complementing national and international efforts on the promotion and protection of human rights.
- To uphold international human rights standards as prescribed by the Universal Declaration of Human Rights, the Vienna Declaration and Programme of Action, and international human rights instruments to which ASEAN member states are parties. Note the careful formulation of this paragraph. Not every ASEAN member state accepts or is party to all international human rights instruments.

The TOR states that the AICHR will pursue a constructive and non-confrontational approach in promotion and protection of human rights.[232] It is intergovernmental, consultative and an integral part of the ASEAN organisational structure.[233] The members of the Commission are the member states themselves, each appointing a representative accountable to the member state.[234] Since decisions have to be taken by consensus[235] every member state has a veto. The AICHR reports to the ASEAN Foreign Ministers' Meeting.[236]

---

[230] This is to be found at aichr.org/documents.
[231] Terms of Reference of the ASEAN Intergovernmental Commission on Human Rights, para 1.
[232] Terms of Reference of the ASEAN Intergovernmental Commission on Human Rights, para 2.4.
[233] Terms of Reference of the ASEAN Intergovernmental Commission on Human Rights, para 3.
[234] Terms of Reference of the ASEAN Intergovernmental Commission on Human Rights, para 5.
[235] Terms of Reference of the ASEAN Intergovernmental Commission on Human Rights, para 6.1.
[236] Terms of Reference of the ASEAN Intergovernmental Commission on Human Rights, para 6.6.

These provisions were no doubt inserted to assuage the concerns of the member states that did not want a human rights mechanism built into the Charter in the first place. It is quite clear from the TOR that the AICHR is a political rather than a legal animal. The foreign ministries of the member states will be firmly in control of the agenda. The fact that the foreign ministries control the AICHR suggests that only human rights issues that raise bilateral problems will be seriously considered. Given the guiding principle of non-interference in the internal affairs of member states,[237] one would be surprised if the AICHR were to be allowed officially to deal with human rights abuses wholly within an ASEAN member state. Nonetheless, not everything that happens within ASEAN is broadcast to the world. The AICHR may perhaps become a conduit for ASEAN states to informally and unofficially broach the sensitive issue of domestic human rights abuses, far from the glare of the media and civil society.

The ASEAN Human Rights Declaration

One of the major tasks of the ASEAN Intergovernmental Commission on Human Rights (AICHR) was to develop an ASEAN Human Rights Declaration (AHRD).[238] The AHRD was adopted by the ASEAN leaders at the Twenty-first ASEAN Summit in Phnom Penh, Cambodia, on 18 November 2012.

The AHRD affirms all the rights in the Universal Declaration of Human Rights: *see* the Preamble, Articles 10 and 26 of the AHRD. In addition, it explicitly sets out the following fundamental rights and freedoms:

- The right to life: AHRD Article 11
- The right to personal liberty and security: AHRD Article 12
- Freedom from servitude and slavery: AHRD Article 13
- Freedom from torture and cruel, inhuman or degrading treatment or punishment: AHRD Article 14
- Freedom of movement and residence within the borders of each state, and the right to leave and return to one's own country: AHRD Article 15
- The right to seek and receive asylum: AHRD Article 16. Note that this is qualified by the laws of the receiving state.
- The right to property: AHRD Article 17

---

[237] Found in Preamble and Article 2(2)(f) of the Charter and repeated in para 2.2(b) of the Terms of Reference of the ASEAN Intergovernmental Commission on Human Rights.

[238] Terms of Reference of the ASEAN Intergovernmental Commission on Human Rights, para 4.2.

- The right to nationality: AHRD Article 18. This right is also qualified by national law.
- The right to marry, found a family and divorce: AHRD Article 19. This right is confined to 'men and women of full age' and is subject to national law.
- The right to the presumption of innocence: AHRD Article 20(1)
- Protection against retroactive criminal laws: AHRD Article 20(2)
- Protection against double jeopardy: AHRD Article 20(3)
- Freedom from arbitrary interference with a person's privacy, family, home or correspondence (including personal data) and from attacks on his honour and reputation: AHRD Article 21
- Freedom of thought, conscience and religion: AHRD Article 22
- Freedom of opinion and expression: AHRD Article 23
- The right of peaceful assembly: AHRD Article 24
- The right to participate in the government of one's country, either directly or through democratically-elected representatives: AHRD Article 25(1)
- The right to vote in periodic and genuine elections: AHRD Article 25(2)
- The right to work: AHRD Article 27(1)
- The right to form and join trade unions: AHRD Article 27(2)
- Freedom from economic and social exploitation for children and young persons: AHRD Article 27(3)
- The right to an adequate standard of living: AHRD Article 28
- The right of access to health care and medical services: AHRD Article 29(1)
- The right to social security: AHRD Article 30(1)
- The right to education: AHRD Article 31(1)
- The right to take part in cultural life and enjoy the arts and benefits of scientific progress: AHRD Article 32
- The right to enjoy peace: AHRD Article 38

It is explicitly stated in AHRD Article 6 that 'the enjoyment of human rights and fundamental freedoms must be balanced with the performance of corresponding duties as every person has responsibilities to all other individuals, the community and the society where one lives'. Article 7 also provides that 'All human rights are universal, indivisible, interdependent and interrelated. All human rights and fundamental freedoms in this Declaration must be treated in a fair and equal manner, on the same footing and with the same emphasis. At the same time, the realisation of human rights must be considered in the regional and national context bearing in mind different political, economic, legal, social, cultural, historical and religious backgrounds.'[239] Furthermore, AHRD Article 8 provides that 'the human rights and fundamental freedoms of every person shall be exercised with due regard to the human rights and fundamental freedoms of others'.

Critics will of course carp about the fact that there is no supervisory mechanism. It is left entirely to each individual member state to translate the grand declarations of principle into concrete measures. However, considering the heated controversy that human rights provoked during the Charter-drafting process, it is an achievement to have gotten so far.[240] The AHRD, like the Charter itself, may not be perfect but it is a good basis on which to continue the evolution of ASEAN as a people-oriented, law-abiding, rules-based community. At the very least, the AHRD provides a standard to which the ASEAN member states have voluntarily signed up. There can be no excuses that these are norms made by others and imposed upon an unwilling ASEAN. The standards contained in the AHRD are those by which the behaviour of ASEAN member states will be judged, both by their own peoples and the world.

Article 15. ASEAN Foundation

1. The ASEAN Foundation shall support the Secretary-General of ASEAN and collaborate with the relevant ASEAN bodies to support ASEAN community building by promoting greater awareness of the ASEAN identity, people-to-people interaction, and close collaboration among the business sector, civil society, academia and other stakeholders in ASEAN.

It was decided at the First Informal ASEAN Summit (Jakarta, November 1996) to establish the ASEAN Foundation 'to promote ASEAN awareness, people-to-people contact through scholarships, fellowships and other exchanges'. The ASEAN Foundation Memorandum of Understanding was

[239] The first sentence of AHRD Article 7 is word for word the same as para 5 of the Vienna Declaration 1993. What follows however is significantly different. Whereas the Vienna Declaration states that human rights must be protected regardless of historical, cultural and religious factors, the AHRD emphasises the regional and national contexts. Again, this is doubtless to address the reservations of member states who are uncomfortable with the idea of foreigners imposing foreign norms on them.

[240] For a Vietnamese perspective, *see* Nguyen Trung Thanh, 'The Making of the ASEAN Charter in my Fresh Memories', in Koh, Manalo and Woon, eds., *Making of the ASEAN Charter*, chapters 7–8, 102–3.

signed on 15 December 1997 by the Heads of State/Government at the Second ASEAN Informal Summit held in Kuala Lumpur on the occasion of the thirtieth anniversary of the founding of ASEAN. Its objectives were:[241]

- 'to promote greater awareness of ASEAN, and greater interaction among the peoples of ASEAN as well as their wider participation in ASEAN's activities *inter alia* through human resources development that will enable them to realise their full potential and capacity to contribute to progress of ASEAN Member States as productive and responsible members of the society';
- 'to endeavour to contribute to the evolution of a development cooperation strategy that promotes mutual assistance, equitable economic development, and the alleviation of poverty'.

The inaugural meeting of the Board of Trustees of the ASEAN Foundation was held in Jakarta on 14 July 1998.[242] The headquarters of the Foundation are in Jakarta. The Foundation has its own website separate from that of ASEAN: *see* www.aseanfoundation.org. Like ASEAN itself, the working language of the Foundation is English.[243] The Foundation is governed by a Board of Trustees comprising the Executive Director, the Secretary-General of ASEAN and representatives appointed by the member states.[244] The Board appoints the Executive Director (who must be an ASEAN national) for a non-renewable terms of three years.[245]

The Foundation was envisioned as an autonomous body complementary to the ASEAN Secretariat, with its own funds and resources. Vision 2020 envisaged the ASEAN Foundation as 'one of the instruments to address issues of unequal economic development, poverty and socio-economic disparities'.[246] The Foundation's objectives have been elaborated over the years to include promotion of ASEAN awareness, people-to-people contact among ASEAN Member States including youth exchanges, and increasing disadvantaged communities'

[241] *See* the 1997 Memorandum of Understanding on the Establishment of the ASEAN Foundation, Article 2 and Article IV of the 2000 revision of the MoU.

[242] Joint Communiqué of the Thirty-first ASEAN Ministerial Meeting,Manila, 24–25 July 1998, para 51.

[243] 1997 Memorandum of Understanding on the Establishment of the ASEAN Foundation, Article 9 and Article XVI of the 2000 revision of the MoU.

[244] 2000 Revised Memorandum of Understanding on the Establishment of the ASEAN Foundation, Article IX(1).

[245] Ibid., Article X(1).

[246] Vision 2020 was adopted by the ASEAN Heads of State/Government on 15 Dec. 1997, the same day as the establishment of the ASEAN Foundation.

access to ICT.[247] It is to play a complementary role with the ASEAN Secretariat to help achieve ASEAN's objectives.[248]

In 2006, the EPG report acknowledged that the ASEAN Foundation required 'reinvigoration' – there being a sense that the Foundation was lacking in resources, and that its activities and leadership faced difficulties in remaining relevant and focusing on the organisation's mandate. The Foundation has since been involved in commissioning a study on Attitudes to and Awareness of ASEAN in 2010,[249] and a number of ICT and youth-related projects.

The ASEAN Institute

The Eminent Persons Group (EPG) on the ASEAN Charter recommended the establishment of an ASEAN Institute to 'support the Secretary-General in research, policy analysis, strategic planning and outreach programmes'.[250] This was discussed at the Tenth High Level Task Force (HLTF) meeting in Chiang Mai from 10–13 September 2007. The Philippines expressed a tentative offer to host the proposed ASEAN Institute. Some members of the HLTF expressed the view that instead of setting up a new institution, the ASEAN Secretariat could be given more resources to develop its own research and analysis capability and that existing think-tanks also could assist the Secretary-General in this respect. The HLTF came to the conclusion that while the Institute was a good idea which should be explored, the main problems were funding and the question of how to sustain its operations at the desired level. It was recommended that the Charter need not mention the ASEAN Institute. When the time was right, the Institute could be established by the ASEAN Summit. The Foreign Ministers concurred with the recommendation of the HLTF not to include the ASEAN Institute in the Charter at their informal meeting in New York on 27 September 2007.

---

[247] Hanoi Plan of Action (1998–2004), para 4.3, 9.1; Vientiane Action Programme (2004–10) ASEAN Security Community Ref. 1.1.5.4; ASEAN Socio-Cultural Community Blueprint, para 29(ii), 43(viii).

[248] 2000 Revised Memorandum of Understanding on the Establishment of the ASEAN Foundation, Article XIV(1). This provision was not found in the original MoU.

[249] Awareness of and Attitudes Toward ASEAN. Research conducted on behalf of the ASEAN Foundation by Dr Eric C. Thompson, National University of Singapore, and Dr Chulanee Thianthai, Chulalongkorn University, available at www.aseanfoundation.org/documents/FA-New_%20Asean_Convert_lowres.pdf.

[250] Report of the Eminent Persons Group on the ASEAN Charter, para 42.

2. The ASEAN Foundation shall be accountable to the Secretary-General of ASEAN, who shall submit its report to the ASEAN Summit through the ASEAN Coordinating Council.

As to the Secretary-General, *see* Article 11; ASEAN Summit, Article 7; ASEAN Coordinating Council, Article 8.

This provision is new in providing that the Foundation is accountable to the Secretary-General. Previously, the Board reported to the ASEAN Heads of Government through the ASEAN Ministerial Meeting and the ASEAN Standing Committee.[251]

[251] 2000 Revised Memorandum of Understanding on the Establishment of the ASEAN Foundation, Article IX(6).

CHAPTER V.

ENTITIES ASSOCIATED WITH ASEAN

The inclusion of this chapter and the reference to engagement with civil society was a nod to calls for ASEAN to become a more people-centred organisation. The Eminent Persons Group highlighted the need for ASEAN institutions to engage with the ASEAN Parliamentary Assembly, civil society groups and academia, and in fact proposed that the key bodies of ASEAN at Heads of Government and Ministerial level, as well as the Secretariat, should undertake regular consultations with such bodies.[1] Article 16 was originally part of the preceding chapter on 'Organs'. It was moved to a separate chapter as one HLTF delegation preferred that these entities be distinguished from the official organs of ASEAN.

Article 16. Entities Associated with ASEAN

1. ASEAN may engage with entities which support the ASEAN Charter, in particular its purposes and principles. These associated entities are listed in Annex 2.

The list in Annex 2 comprises non-governmental organisations that have sought accreditation with ASEAN. The list is meant to be exhaustive, since amendments can be done by the Secretary-General only upon the recommendation of the Committee of Permanent Representatives under clause 3 of this Article. However, the fact of accreditation in itself does not indicate the importance of an organisation's contributions to ASEAN community building. Rather accreditation is an indication they are non-

[1] Report of the Eminent Persons Group, para 48. The EPG itself consulted with parliamentarians, human rights groups and general civil society organisations.

objectionable to all ten member states. The list in Annex 2 is a combination of odd bedfellows, from large well-established organisations such as the ASEAN Inter-Parliamentary Assembly,[2] ASEAN-ISIS think-tank network and ASEAN Chambers of Commerce and Industry, to smaller organisations like the ASEAN Kite Council and ASEAN Thalassaemia Society. Some active civil society organisations with an interest in ASEAN and which seek to present recommendations to the ASEAN Summit annually (e.g., the ASEAN People's Assembly and FORUM-ASIA) are not accredited.

In spite of numerous statements of intention to engage and consult with ASEAN civil society actors as early as 1986, consultations have been ad hoc and sporadic, usually with selected organisations and based on the preferences of the member state hosting the ASEAN Summit or ministerial meetings.

2. Rules of procedure and criteria for engagement shall be prescribed by the Committee of Permanent Representatives upon the recommendation of the Secretary-General of ASEAN.

Guidelines on the Accreditation of Civil Society Organisations (CSOs) were first adopted by the ASEAN Standing Committee in 1986 and subsequently amended in 2006. The current Guidelines were adopted by the Committee of Permanent Representatives and noted by the ASEAN Coordinating Council in November 2012.

See Article 11 on the Secretary-General and Article 12 on the Committee of Permanent Representatives.

---

[2] The HLTF and Foreign Ministers had some discussions over how to classify the ASEAN Inter-Parliamentary Assembly (AIPA), which comprises representatives from member state governments but is not a formal body of ASEAN. AIPA professes the objective of the establishment of an ASEAN Parliament as a long term goal. Its predecessor organization was established in 1975 and its membership closely followed the expansion of ASEAN, while member states without functioning legislatures were admitted as special observers. At the time of the adoption of the Charter only eight ASEAN member states were full members of AIPA. AIPA was not therefore considered eligible to be classified as an organ of ASEAN. The Foreign Ministers' decision was to place AIPA in the Annex to Chapter V but to distinguish it in its own category apart from civil society organizations. Brunei and Myanmar subsequently established legislatures and took on full membership in 2009 and 2011 respectively. The question of AIPA or an ASEAN Parliament as an organ of ASEAN has yet to be revisited.

3. Annex 2 may be updated by the Secretary-General of ASEAN upon the recommendation of the Committee of Permanent Representatives without recourse to the provision on Amendments under this Charter.

This is another example of the limited discretion of the Secretary-General. The Secretary-General has no power to amend the Annex unless the Committee of Permanent Representatives (CPR) makes a recommendation. In practice, it is likely that a suggestion for amendment would originate from the ASEAN Secretariat, which would then get the CPR to make a recommendation for the Secretary-General to act upon. For example, the Guidelines on the Accreditation of Civil Society Organisations (CSOs) provide that applications for accreditation by a CSO should be made to the Secretary-General, who then will refer the matter to the appropriate sectoral ministerial body, which will then make a recommendation to the CPR for approval. If no appropriate sectoral ministerial body can be identified, the Secretary-General will 'make recommendations to the CPR for its consideration and approval'.[3] Strictly speaking this is not in conformity with Article 16(3), since the recommendation must come from the CPR. Only the most pedantic lawyer would quibble however.

---

3 *See* rule 6 of the Guidelines.

CHAPTER VI.
IMMUNITIES AND PRIVILEGES

Article 17. Immunities and Privileges of ASEAN

1. ASEAN shall enjoy in the territories of the Member States such immunities and privileges as are necessary for the fulfilment of its purposes.

Compare Article 105(1) of the Charter of the United Nations.

The draft agreement on privileges and immunities of ASEAN was approved ad referendum by the Forty-second Foreign Ministers' Meeting held in Phuket, Thailand, on 20 July 2009.[1] Subsequently, the 2009 Agreement on the Privileges and Immunities of ASEAN (API) was adopted at the Fifteenth ASEAN Summit.[2] The wording of this Agreement is based on the 1946 Convention on the Privileges and Immunities of the United Nations. According to the List of ASEAN Legal Instruments maintained by the ASEAN Secretariat only Singapore, the Philippines and Vietnam had ratified the API at the time of writing.[3]

The API provides for the following immunities:[4]

- Immunity from legal process of ASEAN's assets and property[5]
- Inviolability of the premises of ASEAN[6]

---

1 Joint Communiqué of the Forty-second ASEAN Foreign Ministers' Meeting, para 9. In ASEAN the term 'ad referendum' refers to approval by correspondence.

2 Held in Cha-Am Hua Hin, Thailand, 23–25 Oct. 2009.

3 *See* 'ASEAN Legal Instruments', agreement.asean.org.

4 These generally mirror those given to the UN in the 1946 Convention on the Privileges and Immunities of the United Nations; *see* Articles II and III.

5 2009 Agreement on the Privileges and Immunities of ASEAN, Article 3(1).

6 Ibid., Article 3(2).

- Inviolability of ASEAN communications and documents[7]
- Freedom to transfer funds, currency and gold without restriction[8]
- Exemption from direct taxes, customs duties and import and export restrictions[9]

2. The immunities and privileges shall be laid down in separate agreements between ASEAN and the host Member State.

An Agreement on Hosting and Granting Privileges and Immunities between ASEAN and Indonesia was signed in Phnom Penh, Cambodia, on 2 April 2012. It is always open to any member state to grant greater privileges and immunities to ASEAN than specified in the 2009 Agreement on the Privileges and Immunities of ASEAN.

Article 18. Immunities and Privileges of the Secretary-General of ASEAN and Staff of the ASEAN Secretariat

1. The Secretary-General of ASEAN and staff of the ASEAN Secretariat participating in official ASEAN activities or representing ASEAN in the Member States shall enjoy such immunities and privileges as are necessary for the independent exercise of their functions.

Compare Article 105(2) of the Charter of the United Nations.

The 2009 Agreement on the Privileges and Immunities of ASEAN (API) lists the following privileges and immunities of the Secretary-General and staff of the ASEAN Secretariat:[10]

- Immunity from legal process in respect of acts done in an official capacity[11]
- Exemption from taxation on salaries and emoluments paid by ASEAN[12]

---

[7] Ibid., Article 3(3).

[8] Ibid., Article 3(4). However, ASEAN must comply with domestic rules on movement of foreign exchange and reporting of funds: Article 3(5).

[9] Ibid., Article 3(7). Generally, this applies to articles imported or exported for official use.

[10] Compare the 1946 Convention on the Privileges and Immunities of the United Nations, Article V.

[11] 2009 Agreement on the Privileges and Immunities of ASEAN, Article 4(3)(a).

[12] Ibid., Article 4(3)(b).

- Immunity from national service obligations[13]
- Immunity from immigration restrictions and alien registration[14]
- Provision of the same exchange facilities as are accorded to officials of comparable ranks in diplomatic missions accredited to the government concerned[15]
- Provision of the same repatriation facilities in time of international crisis as diplomatic envoys[16]
- The right to import one car, furniture and personal effects free of duty when first taking up post[17]

In addition, the Secretary-General and Deputy Secretaries-General shall have all privileges and immunities accorded to diplomatic envoys according to international law.[18] The privileges and immunities do not apply to nationals and permanent residents of the granting member state, with the exception of the immunity from legal process in respect of official acts.[19]

2. The immunities and privileges under this Article shall be laid down in a separate ASEAN agreement.

These are provided for in Article 4 of the 2009 Agreement on the Privileges and Immunities of ASEAN.[20]

Article 19. Immunities and Privileges of the Permanent Representatives and Officials on ASEAN Duties

1. The Permanent Representatives of the Member States to ASEAN and officials of the Member States participating in official ASEAN activities or representing ASEAN in the Member States shall enjoy such immunities and privileges as are necessary for the exercise of their functions.

---

13 Ibid., Article 4(3)(c).

14 Ibid., Article 4(3)(d). This applies as well to spouses, dependent children and minor children.

15 Ibid., Article 4(3)(e).

16 Ibid., Article 4(3)(f). This also applies to spouses, relatives and children.

17 Ibid., Article 4(3)(g).

18 Ibid., Article 4(4). This applies also to their spouses and minor children.

19 Ibid., Article 4(5).

20 Adopted at the Fifteenth ASEAN Summit in Cha-Am Hua Hin, Thailand, on 25 Oct. 2009.

Compare Article 105(2) of the Charter of the United Nations.

Officials of the member states

'Officials of the member states' means persons who participate in official ASEAN activities on behalf of a member state and who either hold a diplomatic or official passport or are notified to the receiving member state as officials.[21] No defintion of 'official ASEAN activities' is given. It presumably covers attendance as part of an official delegation to the major meetings of the ASEAN organs (e.g., the Summit, the Community Councils and the sectoral ministerial bodies). There are hundreds of other meetings though. Which ones are covered will presumably be worked out pragmatically over time.

While participating in official ASEAN activities or representing ASEAN, such officials have the following privileges and immunities:[22]

- Immunity from personal arrest and detention and seizure of personal baggage
- Immunity from legal process in respect of acts done in an official capacity
- Inviolability of all papers and documents
- The right to use codes in communications with ASEAN and to receive correspondence by courier or in sealed bags
- Provision of the same facilities in respect of currency or exchange restrictions as accorded to representatives of foreign governments on temporary official missions
- The same privileges and immunities in respect of their personal baggage as are accorded to diplomatic envoys

These do not apply if the officials are nationals, permanent residents or officials (even formerly) of the member state granting the privileges and immunities.[23]

---

21 2009 Agreement on the Privileges and Immunities of ASEAN, Article 1(5).

22 Ibid., Article 9(1). Compare the 1946 Convention on the Privileges and Immunities of the United Nations, Article VI.

23 2009 Agreement on the Privileges and Immunities of ASEAN, Article 9(4).

Permanent Representatives and diplomatic staff of the Permanent Missions

While in Indonesia, the Host Member State, these persons enjoy diplomatic immunity.[24] When participating in ASEAN activities or representing ASEAN outside Indonesia, such persons have the same privileges and immunities as other officials of member states, as set out above.[25]

Experts on ASEAN missions

There is no explicit mention of experts on missions for ASEAN in the Charter. However, this category exists in the 1946 Convention on the Privileges and Immunities of the United Nations, which was used as a model for the 2009 Agreement on the Privileges and Immunities of ASEAN (API). There was no definition of what an 'expert' is in this context, because the High Level Legal Experts Group (HLEG) could not find a formula which was acceptable to all delegations. The 1946 Convention on the Privileges and Immunities of the United Nations also does not define 'expert'. There are a number of consultants based at the ASEAN Secretariat, some of whom occasionally travel to various member states for short-term projects. In so far as they are engaged in ASEAN business they may be given privileges and immunities under this Article.

Following the model of the 1946 Convention on the Privileges and Immunities of the United Nations, the HLEG decided that such experts may be accorded such privileges and immunities as are considered appropriate by the granting member state, including (but not limited to) the following:[26]

- Immunity from personal arrest and detention and seizure of personal baggage
- Immunity from legal process in respect of acts done in an official capacity
- Inviolability of all papers and documents
- The right to use codes in communications with ASEAN and to receive correspondence by courier or in sealed bags
- Provision of the same facilities in respect of currency or exchange restrictions as accorded to representatives of foreign governments on temporary official mission

---

24 Ibid., Article 7(1).

25 Ibid., Article 7(2).

26 Ibid., Article 5(1). Compare the 1946 Convention on the Privileges and Immunities of the United Nations, Article VI.

- The same privileges and immunities in respect of their personal baggage as are accorded to diplomatic envoys

The Secretary-General will notify the National Secretariat of the country concerned of the experts and the nature of their mission and will issue identity documents if necessary.[27]

2. The immunities and privileges of the Permanent Representatives and officials on ASEAN duties shall be governed by the 1961 Vienna Convention on Diplomatic Relations or in accordance with the national law of the ASEAN Member State concerned.

Permanent Representatives

The Permanent Representatives have diplomatic immunity while in Indonesia, which is the Host Member State for the ASEAN Secretariat.[28] This applies also to members of their families forming part of their households. When outside Indonesia Permanent Representatives have the following immunities while participating in official ASEAN activities or representing ASEAN:[29]

- Immunity from personal arrest and detention and seizure of personal baggage
- Immunity from legal process in respect of acts done in an official capacity
- Inviolability of all papers and documents
- The right to use codes in communications with ASEAN and to receive correspondence by courier or in sealed bags
- Provision of the same facilities in respect of currency or exchange restrictions as accorded to representatives of foreign governments on temporary official missions
- The same privileges and immunities in respect of their personal baggage as are accorded to diplomatic envoys

These do not apply if they are nationals, permanent residents or officials (even formerly) of the member state granting the privileges and immunities.[30]

---

27 Ibid., Article 5(3).
28 Ibid., Article 7(1).
29 Ibid., Article 9(1) read with 7(2).
30 Ibid., Article 9(4) read with 7(2)

Officials on ASEAN duties

'Officials on ASEAN duties' means persons having diplomatic rank appointed by a member state to be members of the permanent mission to ASEAN.[31] Such persons (and members of their households) enjoy diplomatic immunity while in Indonesia (which hosts the ASEAN Secretariat).[32] When participating in ASEAN activities or representing ASEAN outside Indonesia, such persons have the same privileges and immunities as other officials of member states, as set out above.[33]

The Permanent Mission and non-diplomatic staff

These are not mentioned in the Charter. The Permanent Mission has diplomatic immunity as provided for in the 1961 Vienna Convention on Diplomatic Relations.[34] The provisions of that Convention also apply to the administrative, technical and service staff of the Permanent Mission.[35]

1961 Vienna Convention on Diplomatic Relations or equivalent national law

The reference to 'the national law of the ASEAN Member State concerned' was inserted to accommodate Brunei, which was the only ASEAN member not party to the 1961 Vienna Convention on Diplomatic Relations (VCDR)[36] at the time of the adoption of the Charter. Brunei clarified that it however had enacted domestic legislation to provide the equivalent privileges for diplomatic and consular envoys. Brunei subsequently acceded to the 1961 VCDR on 24 May 2013.[37]

---

31 Ibid., Article 1(6).

32 Ibid., Article 7(1) and (2).

33 Ibid., Article 7(2).

34 Ibid., Article 6.

35 Ibid., Article 8(1) & (2).

36 1961 Vienna Convention on Diplomatic Relations, adopted in Vienna, Austria, on 18 Apr. 1961, 500 UNTS 95.

37 United Nations Treaty Collection: treaties.un.org/Pages/ViewDetails.aspx?src=TREATY&mtdsg_no=III-3&chapter=3&lang=en

CHAPTER VII.

DECISION-MAKING

Article 20. Consultation and Consensus

1. As a basic principle, decision-making in ASEAN shall be based on consultation and consensus.

Consensus decision-making is recognised as one of the core elements of the 'ASEAN Way',[1] and is the default for all ASEAN meetings and initiatives except for limited instances concerning the implementation of certain economic agreements.[2] These principles were accepted right from the beginning of ASEAN, originating from the Indonesian concepts of *musyawarah* and *mufakat.*[3]

The Eminent Persons Group on the ASEAN Charter (EPG) recommended that decisions normally be taken by consensus, especially in the sensitive areas of security and foreign policy.[4] In practice, consensus means that no member state feels strongly enough about a matter to block it; it does not mean that everyone agrees. Effectively, decision by consensus gives every member state a veto. It is hard to see how the organisation could function otherwise, as no state would agree to give up its vital interests on the basis of a vote. However, in other areas, the EPG said that majority voting might be introduced to avoid a deadlocked situation when consensus could not be achieved. At the Foreign Ministers Retreat in Siem Reap (1-2 March 2007) one minister stated that his leader could not accept the principle of voting. No doubt others entertained similar reservations. The proposal

---

1 The genesis of this set of unwritten principles is documented by former Secretary-General Rodolfo Severino. *See* Severino, *In Search of an ASEAN Community*.

2 *See* Article 21(2).

3 See Djani, 'A Long Journey', in *Making of the ASEAN Charter*, chapter 11,145.

4 Report of the Eminent Persons Group on the ASEAN Charter, para 63.

was therefore dropped. Consensus thus remains the rule, subject to any exceptions provided for in specific ASEAN instruments. The HLTF made some attempt at its fifth meeting in Hanoi to define 'sensitive' areas as proposed by the EPG but encountered an objection from one HLTF member that it would be 'too sensitive to define the sensitive areas'.

It is specifically provided that proposed amendments to the Charter must command consensus in the ASEAN Coordinating Council before being submitted to the ASEAN Summit for approval: *see* Article 48.

2. Where consensus cannot be achieved, the ASEAN Summit may decide how a specific decision can be made.

The EPG's recommendation for majority voting where consensus cannot be reached was rejected by the Foreign Ministers at their Retreat in Siem Reap (1–2 March 2007). This provision, drafted by the Foreign Ministers, was therefore necessary to provide a means to break deadlocks. It is a pragmatic compromise where the decisions of bodies below the Summit are concerned; the leaders can give appropriate instructions to enable a decision to be reached, even if this involves voting. However, when it comes to Summit decisions this provision is circular. Decisions of the Summit are made by consensus. If there is no consensus, the Summit will decide how to decide. But since there was no consensus in the first place, how is the decision to be taken? The resolution of such a situation would be entirely political rather than legal.

3. Nothing in paragraphs 1 and 2 of this Article shall affect the modes of decision-making as contained in the relevant ASEAN legal instruments.

This leaves open the possibility of majority voting in specific areas. In particular, the EPG recommended that the formulae of 'ASEAN minus X' or '2 plus X' could be applied in certain projects, as decided by the ASEAN Community Councils.[5] The ASEAN economic ministers (through the Senior Economic Officials Meeting) specifically requested that the ASEAN minus X formula be included in the Charter; *see* Article 21(2). This means that it is possible to progress on some projects without waiting for all members,[6] the laggards catching up later. 'Two plus X' refers to

---

5 Report of the Eminent Persons Group on the ASEAN Charter, paras 30 and 63.

6 *See* the 1992 Framework Agreement on Enhancing ASEAN Economic Cooperation, Article 1(2).

agreements entered into by some but not all ASEAN member states,[7] in the hope that others might later follow. An example would be the Treaty on Mutual Legal Assistance in Criminal Matters,[8] which initially was signed by Brunei, Cambodia, Indonesia, Laos, Malaysia, the Philippines, Singapore and Vietnam.

4. In the case of a serious breach of the Charter or non-compliance, the matter shall be referred to the ASEAN Summit for decision.

The Eminent Persons Group on the ASEAN Charter (EPG) contemplated that a member might be expelled in exceptional circumstances. Actually, it was phrased negatively, viz, that there should be no expulsion unless otherwise decided by the ASEAN Summit in exceptional circumstances.[9] The original draft submitted by Mr Ali Alatas of Indonesia stated that there should be no expulsion under any circumstances. Other EPG members disagreed, hence the rather guarded formula that found its way into the report. The EPG also recommended that ASEAN should have powers to ensure compliance with the Charter, including suspension from the rights and privileges of membership.[10] At their Retreat in Siem Reap (1–2 March 2007) most of the Foreign Ministers were against expulsion even if there were to be an egregious breach of the Charter. The problem would be getting a consensus for expulsion. A view had also been expressed by one minister that if there was to be mention of expulsion, withdrawal would also have to be provided for. In any case, it was felt that a provision for expulsion would be contrary to the family spirit of ASEAN. As a result, the Foreign Ministers gave instructions to the High Level Task Force (HLTF) that suspension, expulsion and withdrawal were not to be mentioned in the Charter.

Some HLTF delegations wanted a more robust statement regarding the consequences of a breach, but no consensus could be reached. The compromise was to simply provide that the ASEAN Summit would decide, without specifying how the decision would be taken or what measures are available. During the HLTF visit to Germany and Brussels in March 2007, our hosts pointed out that there was no formal mode of either suspension

---

7 This is the understanding of at least one former Secretary-General. *See* Severino, *In Search of an ASEAN Community*, 353.

8 Adopted in Kuala Lumpur, Malaysia, on 29 Nov. 2004. This did not start off as an ASEAN treaty. With the ratification by Thailand on 31 Jan. 2013, this treaty now is in force among all ten member states.

9 Report of the Eminent Persons Group on the ASEAN Charter, para 32.

10 Ibid., paras 31 and 61. Compare Articles 4 and 5 of the Charter of the United Nations.

or withdrawal in the European Union. The HLTF members were told by European officials that the suspension of Austria in 2000 was done with a proper legal basis. Following this example, *realpolitik* in ASEAN would probably allow similar action to be taken, though the political consequences for the organisation would probably be dire.

Rules for Reference of Non-Compliance to the ASEAN Summit were adopted by the Foreign Ministers on 2 April 2012 at the Twentieth ASEAN Summit in Phnom Penh, as an annex to the 2010 Protocol to the ASEAN Charter on Dispute Settlement Mechanism.

See also Article 7(2)(e) and Article 27(2).

Article 21. Implementation and Procedure

1. Each ASEAN Community Council shall prescribe its own rules of procedure.

As to the ASEAN Community Councils, *see* Article 9. The Rules of Procedure of the ASEAN Political-Security Community (APSC) Council were endorsed at the 2nd APSC Council Meeting in 2009.

The HLTF considered proposals for additional sub-articles in this section providing for voting on procedural matters and for meetings to be able to pass decisions without members who were 'voluntarily absent'. However, it was not possible to reach consensus on these provisions.

2. In the implementation of economic commitments, a formula for flexible participation, including the ASEAN Minus X formula, may be applied where there is a consensus to do so.

The Eminent Persons Group on the ASEAN Charter envisaged that the ASEAN minus X (ASEAN-X) formula might be used by all the Community Councils.[11] The ASEAN economic ministers (through the Senior Economic Officials Meeting) had specifically requested this to be included in the Charter. The Foreign Ministers accordingly instructed the High Level Task Force to do so, but only for economic matters. In this sphere, the ASEAN-X formula allows for a 'variable-geometry' ASEAN (e.g., the approval of a two-speed ASEAN Free Trade Area (AFTA) after the accession of the new member states).[12] The 2007 ASEAN Economic Community Blueprint

---

[11] Report of the Eminent Persons Group on the ASEAN Charter, para 30.

[12] The 1992 Framework Agreement on Enhancing ASEAN Economic Cooperation was amended by a Protocol in 1995 when Vietnam joined. This introduced Article 1(2A)

provides for the application of the formula in the liberalisation of services and the acceleration of agreed economic initiatives.[13] The HLTF's understanding was that ASEAN-X would be applied only in cases where there is a consensus to do so.

---

which allowed for the new members to accede to the Agreement on flexible terms.

[13] Adopted by the Heads of State/Government at the Thirteenth ASEAN Summit in Singapore on 20 Nov. 2007, then incorporated on 1 Mar. 2009 as an annex to the Cha-Am Hua Hin Declaration on the Roadmap for the ASEAN Community (2009–15). *See* paras 21(ix), 22(a) and 72(v).

CHAPTER VIII.
SETTLEMENT OF DISPUTES[1]

Overview

The original 1967 Bangkok Declaration that founded ASEAN made no provision for settlement of disputes among the member states. In 1971 ASEAN issued the Zone of Peace, Freedom and Neutrality Declaration (ZOPFAN) Declaration,[2] which was 'inspired by the worthy aims and objectives of the United Nations, in particular by the principles of respect for the sovereignty and territorial integrity of all states, abstention from threat or use of force, peaceful settlement of international disputes, equal rights and self-determination and non-interference in affairs of States,' according to its Preamble. This was the first explicit commitment to the peaceful settlement of disputes in ASEAN. At the First ASEAN Summit in 1976 the Declaration of ASEAN Concord (or the Bali Concord I, as it is now known) and the Treaty of Amity and Cooperation (TAC) were signed.[3] The Bali Concord I solemnly declared that 'Member states, in the spirit of ASEAN solidarity, shall rely exclusively on peaceful processes in the settlement of intra-regional differences.' The member states renounced the use of force and committed themselves to settlement of

[1] Material from the commentary to this Chapter has been used by the author in other published works, notably *Towards a Rules-Based Community*. Though that book was co-written with Mr Jean-Claude Piris, the material in question is the author's.

[2] Signed in Kuala Lumpur on 27 Nov. 1971 by the Foreign Ministers of Indonesia (Mr Adam Malik), Malaysia (Tun Abdul Razak, who was by then Prime Minister and Foreign Minister), the Philippines (Mr Carlos Romulo), Singapore (Mr S. Rajaratnam) and Thailand (Mr Thanat Khoman, then Special Envoy of the National Executive Council). For the background to this *see* Severino, *In Search of an ASEAN Community*, 166–7.

[3] Both were signed on 24 Feb. 1976 in Denpasar, Bali by the President of Indonesia (Mr Soeharto), the Prime Minister of Malaysia (Dr Hussein Onn), the President of the Philippines (Mr Ferdinand Marcos), the Prime Minister of Singapore (Mr Lee Kuan Yew) and the Prime Minister of Thailand (Mr Kukrit Pramoj). Brunei ratified the Treaty of Amity and Cooperation in Southeast Asia (TAC) on 6 June 1987, Vietnam on 30 May 1995, Cambodia on 25 July 1995, Myanmar on 10 July 1996 and Laos on 17 July 1996.

differences or disputes by peaceful means in Article 2 of the TAC. There was no legal mechanism set up to achieve this aim. The TAC was more a political document than a legal one. Troubles within the ASEAN family were meant to be settled by diplomacy or quietly allowed to fade into the background.[4]

A major shortcoming of ASEAN is the failure to fully implement the various declarations, blueprints, roadmaps and other grand declarations of intent. To remedy the deficiency in carrying out commitments, the Eminent Persons Group on the ASEAN Charter (EPG) recommended the establishment of dispute settlement mechanisms in all fields of ASEAN cooperation, including monitoring and enforcement mechanisms.[5] The ASEAN Secretariat was to be entrusted with monitoring compliance with ASEAN decisions, agreements and action plans. The Secretary-General was to report instances of non-compliance to the ASEAN Summit.[6]

These recommendations were largely implemented when it came to the drafting of the Charter. Some High Level Task Force (HLTF) delegations initially expressed a view that a court should be set up.[7] This idea was quickly scotched. ASEAN was not ready for a pan-ASEAN judicial institution. Although not explicitly articulated, it was clear that an ASEAN court could not be established as long as the rule of law was weak in some ASEAN states. Any court would have been compromised from the start if a judge had to take instructions from his country. Indeed, far from wanting a court, some member states appeared to be wary of any sort of compulsory adjudication, despite the clear recommendation of the EPG. One can only speculate as to the instructions that these delegations received, but it did appear that their preference was to keep the settlement of disputes on the political plane, to be dealt with by the ASEAN Summit.

The HLTF was conscious that there were existing dispute settlement mechanisms in the TAC and ASEAN Protocol on Enhanced Dispute Settlement Mechanism (the Vientiane Protocol or EDSM).[8] The decision

---

4 For instance, the dispute between Malaysia and the Philippines over Sabah which had led to a rupture of diplomatic relations between the two countries in 1963 remains unresolved even today. The Philippines has not yet formally dropped its claim to Sabah. *See* Severino, *In Search of an ASEAN Community*, 164–6.

5 Report of the Eminent Persons Group on the ASEAN Charter, paras 44–5.

6 Report of the Eminent Persons Group on the ASEAN Charter, para 45. *See now* Article 27(1).

7 This was an idea had also been discussed by the Eminent Persons Group, but there was no consensus and therefore it was left out of the Report.

8 Adopted by the Economic Ministers at the Tenth ASEAN Summit in Vientiane, Laos, on 29 Nov. 2004.

was taken to use these as the basis for Chapter VIII of the Charter, filling in the gaps as necessary.

The scheme of Chapter VIII is thus: the first line in settling a dispute is dialogue, consultation and negotiation: Article 22. This was a concession to those who had reservations about too much law being involved in the process of dispute settlement. Article 23(1) then goes on to provide that the parties to the dispute may agree to resort to good offices, conciliation or mediation. These are the voluntary, non-binding modes of settlement favoured by some member states. It is also provided in Article 23(2) that the parties to the dispute may request the Chairman of ASEAN or the Secretary-General to provide good offices, conciliation or mediation.

Article 24(1) then goes on to say that where a specific ASEAN instrument provides for dispute settlement, the mechanisms and procedures set out should be utilised.

The mechanism in the Treaty of Amity and Cooperation in Southeast Asia (TAC)[9] is to be used to resolve disputes that do not involve the interpretation or application of any ASEAN instrument: Article 24(2).

Article 24(3) provides that disputes concerning ASEAN economic agreements are to be settled in accordance with the Vientiane Protocol on the Enhanced Dispute Settlement Mechanism (Vientiane Protocol or EDSM)[10] where there is no specific provision. This is one of the most crucial provisions in the Charter. The creation of an ASEAN community will be driven by economic integration. This was explicitly recognised by the EPG in its report.[11] Economic integration cannot happen without some means of binding dispute settlement. Hence the push for the creation of an effective dispute settlement mechanism in the economic field. The Vientiane Protocol was meant to ensure that legally-binding decisions could be made and expeditiously enforced,[12] a vital prerequisite for the creation of an economic community.

Article 25 fills in the gaps by providing that appropriate dispute settlement mechanisms, including arbitration, should be established for disputes concerning the Charter or other ASEAN instruments. This was done by the 2010 Protocol to the ASEAN Charter on Dispute Settlement

---

9 Signed at the First ASEAN Summit in Denpasar, Bali, on 24 Feb. 1976.

10 Adopted by the Economic Ministers at the Tenth ASEAN Summit in Vientiane, Laos, on 29 Nov. 2004. Shortly before this an ASEAN Compliance Body (ACB) had been set up to enable member countries to use mediation and peer pressure in dispute settlement: *see* the Joint Media Statement of the Thirty-sixth ASEAN Economic Ministers Meeting (Jakarta, 3 Sept. 2004), para 10.

11 Report of the Eminent Persons Group on the ASEAN Charter, paras 14–15.

12 *See* the Joint Media Statement of the Thirty-sixth ASEAN Economic Ministers Meeting (Jakarta, Sept. 2004), paras 9–11.

Mechanisms (the DSM Protocol).[13] Finally, Article 28 preserves the right of member states to have recourse to the modes of dispute settlement prescribed in the UN Charter and other international legal instruments.

Any party affected by non-compliance with the result of a dispute settlement process may refer the matter to the Summit for a decision: Article 27(2). Unresolved disputes also go to the Summit for decision: Article 26. In time to come, the ASEAN Summit may evolve into a kind of final tribunal of appeal from dispute settlement bodies. This is a consummation devoutly to be wished. It is imperative to ensure that the decisions of the Summit are firmly rooted in law if ASEAN is to be taken seriously as a rules-based organisation adhering to the rule of law.[14]

Disputes among ASEAN organs

This Chapter is concerned solely with inter-state disputes. There is no provision covering disputes among ASEAN organs (e.g., between the Committee of Permanent Representatives (CPR) and the ASEAN Secretariat (ASEC), between the CPR and sectoral ministerial bodies and between the ASEAN Coordinating Council (ACC) and the three Community Councils). The outgoing Secretary-General in a valedictory report to the ACC identified the lack of clarity regarding the relations among the various organs as a major factor inhibiting the development of the ASEAN Community. There have been disagreements (one hesitates to call them turf battles) about the roles of various organs and councils, in particular between ASEC and the CPR. In the absence of any mechanism to delineate these roles, ultimately the ASEAN Summit as supreme policy-making organ must decide.[15]

---

[13] Signed by the Foreign Ministers at the Sixteenth ASEAN Summit held in Hanoi, 8–9 Apr. 2010. This is not yet in force according to the Table of Ratifications maintained by the ASEAN Secretariat: *see* ASEAN Legal Instruments at agreement.asean.org.

[14] The latest reiteration of this is to be found in Bali Concord III (signed by the ASEAN leaders in Nov. 2011), where it is stated that the ASEAN common platform on global issues is to be based on 'a strengthened ASEAN Community centred on ASEAN as a rules-based organisation, with the ASEAN Charter as the foundation'.

[15] It might delegate the role to some subsidiary body (e.g., the ACC) but this would not solve the problem of overlapping jurisdiction of the three Community Councils, or disagreements about hierarchy and reporting lines.

Article 22. General Principles

1. Member States shall endeavour to resolve peacefully all disputes in a timely manner through dialogue, consultation and negotiation.

The 1976 Declaration of ASEAN Concord[16] declared that 'Member states, in the spirit of ASEAN solidarity, shall rely exclusively on peaceful processes in the settlement of intra-regional differences'. The member states renounced the use of force and committed themselves to settlement of differences or disputes by peaceful means in Article 2 of the Treaty of Amity and Cooperation in Southeast Asia (TAC).[17] Article 13 of the TAC requires the High Contracting Parties to settle disputes among themselves through 'friendly negotiations'. The principle in this clause hardly needs stating, since the first recourse in the resolution of a dispute between member states would be dialogue, consultation and negotiation. It is only when bilateral relations have reached a nadir that the assistance of outside parties may be necessary. In that case, the Chair of ASEAN or the Secretary-General (or indeed any other concerned ASEAN member) may offer to bring the parties together. Good offices, conciliation and mediation are provided for in the next Article.

The 2010 Protocol to the ASEAN Charter on Dispute Settlement Mechanisms[18] provides that a party may request consultations regarding any dispute concerning the interpretation of the Charter or other non-economic ASEAN instruments without specific dispute settlement mechanisms.[19] The respondent must reply within 30 days, enter into consultations within 60 days and complete the process within 90 days or such longer period as the parties agree.[20] If any of these deadlines is missed, the complaining party may request arbitration.[21]

---

[16] Adopted at the First ASEAN Summit in Bali, Indonesia, on 24 Feb. 1976.

[17] Signed by the leaders of the five original ASEAN Member States on the same date as the Bali Concord.

[18] Signed by the Foreign Ministers at the Sixteenth ASEAN Summit held in Hanoi, 8–9 Apr. 2010. This is not yet in force according to the list maintained by the ASEAN Secretariat. 'ASEAN Legal Instruments,' ASEAN Secretariat, online: agreement.asean.org.

[19] 2010 Protocol to the ASEAN Charter on Dispute Settlement Mechanisms, signed on 8 Apr. 2010 in Hanoi, Vietnam, Article 5(1).

[20] Ibid., Article 5(3).

[21] Ibid., Article 8(1). As to arbitration, *see* commentary to Article 25 of the Charter (*supra*).

2. ASEAN shall maintain and establish dispute settlement mechanisms in all fields of ASEAN cooperation.

The dispute settlement mechanism for the ASEAN Economic Community is the most advanced. Economic disputes are settled in accordance with the Vientiane Protocol on the Enhanced Dispute Settlement Mechanism (Vientiane Protocol or EDSM)[22] where there is no specific provision made: Article 24(3). For non-economic disputes, there is now a Protocol to the ASEAN Charter on Dispute Settlement Mechanisms. This was negotiated by the High-Level Legal Experts' Group (HLEG).[23] It was signed by the Foreign Ministers at the Sixteenth ASEAN Summit in Hanoi on 8 April 2010 and opened for ratification in April 2012 following the addition of Annex 5 on Unresolved Disputes and Annex 6 on Non-Compliance. Vietnam became the first member state to ratify the Protocol in August 2012.[24]

Article 23. Good Offices, Conciliation and Mediation

1. Member States which are parties to a dispute may at any time agree to resort to good offices, conciliation or mediation in order to resolve the dispute within an agreed time limit.

The aim of good offices, conciliation or mediation is to achieve an amicable settlement of the dispute, viz, one under which neither party loses face. Given the consensual nature of ASEAN relations, this is likely to be the preferred mode of dispute settlement. The 2010 Protocol to the ASEAN Charter on Dispute Settlement Mechanisms (the DSM Protocol)[25] provides detailed rules of procedure for this in Annexes 1–3.[26] Note the rather

---

[22] Adopted by the Economic Ministers at the Eleventh ASEAN Summit in Vientiane, Laos, on 29 Nov. 2004.

[23] This was set up to look into the legal issues arising from the implementation of the ASEAN Charter. *See* the Joint Communiqué of the Forty-first ASEAN Foreign Ministers' Meeting (Singapore, 17–14 July 2008), para 11.

[24] *See* Government of Vietnam, Report to the President on the Ratification of the Protocol to the ASEAN Charter on Dispute Settlement Mechanisms, Official Note 213/TTr-CP, 29 Aug. 2012, available at http://baodientu.chinhphu.vn/Uploaded_VGP/dothanhhoai/20120904/QD%20213.pdf.

[25] Signed by the Foreign Ministers at the Sixteenth ASEAN Summit held in Hanoi, 8-9 Apr. 2010. This is not yet in force according to the list maintained by the ASEAN Secretariat: *see* 'ASEAN Legal Instruments,' agreement.asean.org.

[26] Strictly speaking, these rules apply when the ASEAN Coordinating Council has ordered good offices, etc., pursuant to Article 9 of the 2010 Protocol to the ASEAN Charter on Dispute Settlement Mechanisms. However, there is nothing to stop the parties using this framework voluntarily.

strict and artificial distinction between mediation and conciliation. The role of the mediator is to 'help facilitate communication and negotiation between the parties'.[27] A conciliator, in contrast, may make proposals for settlement of the dispute.[28]

In practice, mediation often blends into conciliation in a seamless manner. For example in 2011 Indonesian Foreign Minister Marty Natalegawa mediated the dispute between Cambodia and Thailand over the temple of Preah Vihear.[29] Not only did he shuttle between the parties, he also brokered a ceasefire and suggested the insertion of Indonesian observers. It would be unwise to keep the two modes as distinct as the DSM Protocol envisages.

2. Parties to the dispute may request the Chairman of ASEAN or the Secretary-General of ASEAN, acting in an ex-officio capacity, to provide good offices, conciliation or mediation.

In the economic sphere, Article 4 of the Vientiane Protocol on the Enhanced Dispute Settlement Mechanism (Vientiane Protocol or EDSM)[30] specifically provides that the Secretary-General of ASEAN may offer good offices, conciliation or mediation with a view to assisting in the settlement of a dispute, giving him a potentially significant role in the resolution of such disputes. This should be contrasted to this clause, which contemplates the involvement of the Secretary-General[31] or the Chairman of ASEAN[32] only upon the request of the disputing parties. This is deliberate. When drafting the Charter some of the delegations of the High Level Task Force (HLTF) were concerned to ensure that the Secretary-General did not become too activist and independent of the member states. In general, foreign ministry officials have been more suspicious of outside involvement in dispute settlement than officials from other ministries, preferring to keep control of the process at a political level.

Though this clause refers to a request by the disputing parties, it would accord with the spirit of the Charter (which provides that disputes

---

27 Annex 2 to the 2010 Protocol to the ASEAN Charter on Dispute Settlement Mechanisms, rule 2.

28 Annex 3 to the 2010 Protocol to the ASEAN Charter on Dispute Settlement Mechanisms, rule 4(3).

29 This is discussed in more detail in the commentary to Article 28.

30 Adopted by the Economic Ministers at the Eleventh ASEAN Summit in Vientiane, Laos, on 29 Nov. 2004.

31 As to the role of the Secretary-General, *see* Article 11.

32 As to the Chair of ASEAN, *see* Articles 31 and 32.

should be resolved peacefully in a timely manner)[33] as well as the recommendations of the Eminent Persons Group if any party could make such a request, even in the absence of agreement by the other party. Otherwise, an intransigent party could block settlement of the dispute indefinitely. This would hardly conduce to creating a community based on the rule of law, which is one of the primary aims of the Charter.[34]

Similarly, there is in practice nothing to stop the Secretary-General offering his good offices, etc. When trouble broke out between Cambodia and Thailand in 2003 over alleged remarks by a Thai actress regarding ownership of Angkor Wat, the incumbent Secretary-General Ong Keng Yong offered ASEAN's assistance in resolving matters; unfortunately, he was rebuffed by Cambodia.[35]

The Chairman of ASEAN may also offer good offices, etc. Indeed, Article 32(c) states that it is part of the role of the Chairman to 'ensure an effective and timely response to urgent issues or crisis situations affecting ASEAN.' In 2008, a dispute flared up between Cambodia and Thailand over the Temple of Preah Vihear. Singaporean Foreign Minister George Yeo, who occupied the Chair at that time, hosted an informal gathering of ASEAN Foreign Ministers at the Botanic Gardens in Singapore. At first the Thai Foreign Minister declined to attend. However, Foreign Minister Yeo managed to persuade him to go to Singapore. The ASEAN Foreign Ministers offered the 'facilities of ASEAN' to mediate the dispute, recognising the importance of maintaining peace and stability of the region.[36] A proposal was made for the formation of an ASEAN Contact Group to help support the efforts of the disputing parties to find a peaceful solution. There was no consensus among the group however, neither Cambodia nor Thailand being willing at that point to have ASEAN involved. Subsequently in 2010, Cambodian Foreign Minister Hor Namhong wrote to Vietnamese Foreign Minister Pham Gia Khiem in his capacity as ASEAN Chair requesting mediation of the dispute under the Charter.[37] This time Thailand again declined to let the ASEAN Chair mediate.[38] When fighting broke out between Cambodia and Thailand

---

33 *See* Article 22(1) above.

34 *See* the Preamble and Articles 1(7), 2(2)(h), 2(2)(n) above.

35 Severino, *In Search of an ASEAN Community*, 14–15. Confirmed to the author by Mr Ong himself.

36 *See* Statement by Singaporean Minister for Foreign Affairs George Yeo, 22 July 2008. Available on the website of the Singapore Ministry of Foreign Affairs: www.mfa.gov.sg.

37 *International Crisis Group Asia Report* no. 215, 'Waging Peace: ASEAN and the Thai-Cambodian Border Conflict' (6 Dec. 2011), fn. 105.

38 Ibid., 15.

over the temple in 2011[39] Indonesian Foreign Minister Marty Natalegawa, who held the Chair at the time, took the initiative to mediate the dispute and finally brokered a ceasefire.

Power of the ASEAN Coordinating Council make an order

The 2010 Protocol to the ASEAN Charter on Dispute Settlement Mechanisms (DSM Protocol) states that a party to a dispute may request consultations, failing which it may make a request for arbitration.[40] If the respondent fails to agree to arbitration, the matter may be referred to the ASEAN Coordinating Council (ACC).[41] The ACC may make an order directing the parties to resolve the dispute through good offices, mediation, conciliation or arbitration.[42] In that event, the rules contained in Annexes 1–3 of the DSM Protocol will apply.

Good offices, etc under the Treaty of Amity and Cooperation in Southeast Asia

The 1976 Treaty of Amity and Cooperation in Southeast Asia (TAC)[43] makes provision for a High Council to take cognisance of disputes or situations likely to disturb regional peace and harmony. This consists of one representative at ministerial level from each of the ten ASEAN member states together with representatives of non-ASEAN states which are directly involved in the dispute.[44] If negotiations do not succeed in settling the dispute, the High Council's role is to recommend 'appropriate means of settlement such as good offices, mediation, inquiry or conciliation'.[45] The High Council itself may offer its good offices. If the parties agree, the High Council may constitute itself as a committee of mediation, inquiry or conciliation.

---

[39] Discussed in the commentary to Article 28.

[40] 2010 Protocol to the ASEAN Charter on Dispute Settlement Mechanisms, Articles 5 and 8(1).

[41] This consists of the Foreign Ministers, *see* Article 8.

[42] 2010 Protocol to the ASEAN Charter on Dispute Settlement Mechanisms, Article 9(1).

[43] Signed on 24 Feb. 1976 in Denpasar, Bali by the leaders of the five original member states. Brunei ratified the Treaty of Amity and Cooperation in Southeast Asia (TAC) on 6 June 1987, Vietnam on 30 May 1995, Cambodia on 25 July 1995, Myanmar on 10 July 1996 and Laos on 17 July 1996.

[44] Treaty of Amity and Cooperation in Southeast Asia, Article 14 (as amended by the First Protocol, signed in Manila on 15 Dec. 1987) and Rule 3 of the Rules of Procedure (adopted on 23 July 2001 in Hanoi).

[45] Treaty of Amity and Cooperation in Southeast Asia, Article 15.

Article 24. Dispute Settlement Mechanisms in Specific Instrument

1. Disputes relating to specific ASEAN instruments shall be settled through the mechanisms and procedures provided for in such instruments.

Some ASEAN instruments allow for arbitration or reference to the International Court of Justice, with the consent of the other party.[46] The main weakness of this clause is that the dispute settlement 'mechanism' in some ASEAN instruments will likely prove ineffective in resolving disputes. For example, the 2002 ASEAN Agreement on Transboundary Haze Pollution provides that disputes will be settled amicably by consultation or negotiation,[47] which hardly inspires confidence that problems will be resolved in a legally binding manner. The solution would be to bring such ineffective 'mechanisms' within the purview of the 2010 Protocol to the ASEAN Charter on Dispute Settlement Mechanisms. This would accord with the spirit of the Eminent Persons Group's recommendations and the Charter as a whole.

2. Disputes which do not concern the interpretation or application of any ASEAN instrument shall be resolved peacefully in accordance with the Treaty of Amity and Cooperation in Southeast Asia and its rules of procedure.

The 1976 Declaration of ASEAN Concord (Bali Concord)[48] declared that 'Member states, in the spirit of ASEAN solidarity, shall rely exclusively on peaceful processes in the settlement of intra-regional differences.' The member states renounced the use of force and committed themselves to settlement of differences or disputes by peaceful means in Article 2 of the Treaty of Amity and Cooperation in Southeast Asia (TAC).[49] Chapter IV of the TAC covers the Pacific Settlement of Disputes.

The dispute settlement mechanism under the TAC consists of a High Council comprising one representative at ministerial level from each of

---

[46] *See* for example the 1995 Treaty on the Southeast Asia Nuclear Weapon-Free Zone, Article 21.

[47] *See* Article 27 of the Treaty, which was signed in Kuala Lumpur on 10 June 2002. It has been ratified by all ASEAN member states save Indonesia, from which the haze principally originates.

[48] Adopted at the First ASEAN Summit in Bali, Indonesia, in Feb. 1976.

[49] Signed by the leaders of the five original ASEAN Member States on the same date as the Bali Concord.

the ten ASEAN member states together with representatives of non-ASEAN states which are directly involved in the dispute.[50] This High Council is supposed to take cognizance of any 'disputes or situations likely to disturb regional peace and harmony.'[51] If negotiations do not succeed in settling the dispute, the High Council's role is to recommend 'appropriate means of settlement such as good offices, mediation, inquiry or conciliation'.[52] The High Council itself may offer its good offices. If the parties agree, the High Council may constitute itself as a committee of mediation, inquiry or conciliation.

There are three glaring weaknesses in the scheme set up in Chapter IV of the TAC. Firstly and most significantly, Articles 14 and 15 do not apply unless the parties to the dispute agree.[53] Any of the disputants can block the use of the dispute settlement mechanism. The non-mandatory nature of the procedure means that it will be used only if there is a significant change in the political mindset of the High Contracting Parties in favour of objective dispute settlement. As things stand, the solution to any dispute threatening to disturb peace and harmony in the region will be political rather than legal. This tends to be the preference of foreign ministries, which generally do not like to have their freedom of action constrained by legal niceties.

The second weakness as far as ASEAN member states are concerned is that the TAC procedure allows countries other than ASEAN member states to get involved in the dispute settlement process. At the Third ASEAN Summit held in Manila in 1987 the TAC was amended to allow for the accession of states outside Southeast Asia. Under rule 14 of the Rules of Procedure, non-ASEAN member states may be represented as observers at meetings of the High Council. This means that these non-ASEAN states will be able to watch and (with the permission of the High Council) speak at meetings. The washing of dirty linen in public is bad enough; washing it in full view of people outside the family is worse. There is a view among some ASEAN members, ventilated during the negotiations on the ASEAN Charter, that 'outsiders' should not be part of any dispute settlement mechanism. This is probably the underlying motive for the amendment of the TAC in 1987 and 2010 to provide that a non-ASEAN High Contracting Party will not form part of the High

[50] Treaty of Amity and Cooperation in Southeast Asia, Article 14 (as amended by the First Protocol, signed in Manila on 15 Dec. 1987) and Rule 3 of the Rules of Procedure (adopted on 23 July 2001 in Hanoi).

[51] Treaty of Amity and Cooperation in Southeast Asia, Article 14.

[52] Ibid., Article 15.

[53] 1976 Treaty of Amity and Cooperation in Southeast Asia, Article 16.

Council unless that party is directly involved in a dispute to which the TAC applies.[54] 'Regional solutions for regional problems' is the mantra. Although this view does not command the unanimous agreement of all the ASEAN member states, it nonetheless remains strongly held in some quarters. In the light of the history of Southeast Asia, the wariness about interference by outside powers is entirely understandable. This wariness appears to extend even to international adjudication of political (as opposed to economic) disputes.[55]

The third weakness is that there is no explicit provision for arbitration or adjudication by a court or tribunal. Good offices, mediation, inquiry and conciliation essentially are non-legal modes of dispute settlement. They supplement direct political negotiations. This reluctance to submit to binding dispute settlement has characterised the 'ASEAN way' from the very start. Any dispute settlement under the TAC will have to be consensual rather than confrontational. More importantly, there will not be a public loss of face. This approach accords with the primary role of ASEAN as a mechanism to foster trust among the member states. One suspects that this is driven by *realpolitik* rather than principle. International courts and arbitrators cannot be controlled by governments. In countries where the rule of law is weak, it is perhaps too much to expect that a government would willingly cede the power to decide an international political dispute to neutral outside parties. Nonetheless, neutral dispute settlement is vital if ASEAN is to progress towards a rules-based community. The question is whether there is sufficient political will to do so within the time-frame agreed.

The drafters of the TAC clearly recognized the limitations of the dispute settlement mechanism that they had created. In Article 17 it is specifically provided that nothing in the TAC shall preclude recourse to the modes of settlement in Article 33(1) of the UN Charter,[56] though the High Contracting parties are 'encouraged' to solve disputes by 'friendly negotiations' before resorting to such other modes of dispute settlement.

---

[54] *See* the First and Third Protocols Amending the Treaty of Amity and Cooperation in Southeast Asia, signed respectively in Manila on 15 Dec. 1987 and Hanoi on 23 July 2010.

[55] In the case of economic disputes, all ASEAN states are also members of the World Trade Organisation (WTO), which involves signing up to the WTO dispute settlement mechanism. The benefits of membership of the WTO are sufficient to overcome the aversion to compulsory adjudication of disputes. In the view of at least some ASEAN member states there is no such imperative for the settlement of political disputes, which often involve zero-sum outcomes.

[56] This provision is mirrored in Article 28 of the ASEAN Charter, below.

The TAC might have been invoked in the dispute between Malaysia and Indonesia over the islands of Sipadan and Ligitan. These two small islands lie in the Celebes Sea off the northeast coast of the island of Borneo. In colonial times Borneo was divided between the British (who controlled Brunei, Sarawak and British North Borneo, now known as Sabah) and the Dutch (the southern portion of Borneo being part of the Netherlands East Indies). The two islands in question were in the British sphere and in due course were taken over by Malaysia. Malaysian sovereignty over Ligitan and Sipadan was contested by Indonesia. Indonesia wanted to bring the Ligitan/Sipadan dispute to the High Council but Malaysia refused, fearing that other ASEAN members would be partial to Indonesia.[57] Malaysia had territorial disagreements with practically all her neighbours.[58] In the end the dispute was referred to the ICJ instead.[59] Interestingly, the Special Agreement for submission of the case to the ICJ stated in the preamble that the parties desired 'that this dispute should be settled in the spirit of friendly relations existing between the Parties as enunciated in the 1976 Treaty of Amity and Cooperation in Southeast Asia'.[60]

A more recent occasion for possible invocation of the TAC was the dispute between Thailand and Cambodia over the area surrounding the Temple of Preah Vihear.[61] The original dispute about sovereignty over the Temple was settled by the decision of the International Court of Justice in 1962.[62] The ICJ held by nine votes to three that the temple stood in territory under the sovereignty of Cambodia. The dispute flared up again when Cambodia applied to have the ruins of Preah Vihear accepted as a

---

57 *See* Severino, *In Search of an ASEAN Community*, 12–13.

58 In 1979 Malaysia issued a map entitled 'Territorial Waters and Continental Shelf Boundaries of Malaysia' which purported to extend the maritime area claimed by Malaysia. This attracted protests from Brunei, China, Indonesia, the Philippines, Singapore, Thailand and Vietnam. This map was not relevant to the Sipadan/Ligitan matter; however, given the fact that Malaysia had provoked opposition by all her neighbours to her territorial claims, it is not surprising that it was felt that a High Council consisting of those neighbours would not be sympathetic.

59 President Soeharto decided to submit the matter to the ICJ despite the objections of his officials. Indonesia lost the case. See *Case Concerning Sovereignty over Pulau Ligitan and Pulau Sipadan*, judgment 17 Dec. 2002).

60 The Special Agreement was signed on 31 May 1997 by Mr Ali Alatas, Foreign Minister of Indonesia, and Datuk Abdullah Ahmad Badawi, Foreign Minister of Malaysia. Mr Alatas was a member of the Eminent Persons Group that conceptualised the Charter. Datuk Abdullah Badawi was Prime Minister of Malaysia when the Charter was presented to the Thirteenth ASEAN Summit in Singapore.

61 This is discussed in the commentary to Article 28.

62 *Case Concerning the Temple of Preah Vihear (Merits)*, judgment dated 15 June 1962. Available at http://www.icj-cij.org/docket/files/45/4871.pdf.

UNESCO World Heritage site in 2008.[63] Although Thailand under Prime Minister Thaksin Shinawatra and his successor was initially supportive, the issue became entangled in Thai domestic politics. Prime Minister Thaksin had been deposed by a coup in 2006 and his political foes used the Preah Vihear issue as a weapon to destabilise the government. The UNESCO listing took place in July 2008.

In that same month an informal meeting of the ASEAN Foreign Ministers took place in Singapore, which held the Chair of ASEAN. Singapore's Foreign Minister George Yeo announced that the ministers had placed ASEAN's facilities at the disposal of the parties for the settlement of the dispute.[64] The possibility of using the TAC was raised briefly but was not accepted by the parties. A proposal was made for a Contact Group to support the parties in their effort to reach a peaceful resolution. However, the parties would not accept the assistance of their ASEAN colleagues at that time. Without the cooperation of the disputing parties, ASEAN could do nothing further.

The TAC mechanism is not likely to be used to settle disputes between ASEAN member states. The process is too public, involving the convening of a High Council at which non-ASEAN High Contracting Parties may be represented as observers. Rather, the TAC is likely be used as an inspirational document, committing the High Contracting Parties to peaceful settlement of their disputes, as happened in the Ligitan/Sipadan case between Indonesia and Malaysia. If a legally binding result is desired, the TAC does allow other international dispute settlement mechanisms to be invoked. This might even mean recourse to the ICJ, as in the Sipadan/Ligitan case. It is also possible that the TAC route will lead indirectly to the arbitration procedure now provided in the 2010 Protocol to the ASEAN Charter on Dispute Settlement Mechanisms,[65] if the High Council is so minded to recommend arbitration as a means of settlement.[66]

As for disputes with non-member states of ASEAN, the TAC is also more likely to be invoked as an inspirational document rather than a settlement mechanism. At the time of writing, China is embroiled in a series of territorial disputes with some ASEAN member states (notably

---

[63] The background to this is recounted in *International Crisis Group Asia Report* no. 215, 'Waging Peace: ASEAN and the Thai-Cambodian Border Conflict' (6 Dec. 2011), 4–6, 9–12.

[64] *See* Statement by Singaporean Minister for Foreign Affairs George Yeo, 22 July 2008, available on the website of the Ministry of Foreign Affairs, Singapore: www.mfa.gov.sg.

[65] *See* 2010 Protocol to the ASEAN Charter on Dispute Settlement Mechanisms, Article 8 and Annex 4.

[66] Article 15 of the 1976 Treaty of Amity and Cooperation in Southeast Asia gives the High Council power to recommend 'appropriate means of settlement'.

Vietnam and the Philippines) over claims in the South China Sea. The 2002 Declaration of Conduct of Parties in the South China Sea,[67] the 2012 Six-Point Principles on the South China Sea issued by the ASEAN Foreign Ministers[68] and the Joint Statement of the Fifteenth ASEAN-China Summit[69] all refer to the TAC, but no steps have yet been taken to invoke the High Council procedure.

3. Where not otherwise specifically provided, disputes which concern the interpretation or application of ASEAN economic agreements shall be settled in accordance with the ASEAN Protocol on Enhanced Dispute Settlement Mechanism.

Economic integration is now the cornerstone of ASEAN community. Of the three pillars, this is the most advanced. The creation of an ASEAN Economic Community cannot take place without the existence of some means of settling disagreements amongst the member states over interpretation and implementation of the various economic agreements. The creation of such a dispute settlement mechanism was an early priority of ASEAN.

Article 9 of the 1992 Framework Agreements on Enhancing ASEAN Economic Cooperation provided for the establishment of a dispute settlement mechanism, but it took four more years before the member states signed the Manila Protocol on Dispute Settlement Mechanism (sic). The Manila Protocol was superseded in 2004 by the Protocol on Enhanced Dispute Settlement Mechanism (the Vientiane Protocol or EDSM), signed in Vientiane by the economic ministers at the Tenth ASEAN Summit.[70]

The Vientiane Protocol is administered by the Senior Economic Officials Meeting (SEOM). It applies to disputes arising under the 1992 Framework Agreements on Enhancing ASEAN Economic Cooperation or other economic agreements set out in Appendix I to the Protocol, as well as future ASEAN economic agreements (referred to as 'covered agreements'). The coverage of the Vientiane Protocol has now been extended to all ASEAN economic agreements by this clause of the Charter.[71] Article 4 of the Vientiane Protocol provides for good offices,

---

[67] Signed by the ten member states and China at the Eighth ASEAN Summit in Phnom Penh, Cambodia, on 4 Nov. 2002.

[68] Issued at the Forty-fifth ASEAN Foreign Ministers' Meeting in Phnom Penh, Cambodia, 20 July 2012.

[69] Issued in Phnom Penh, Cambodia, on 19 Nov. 2012.

[70] Held in Vientiane, Laos, from 29–30 Nov. 2004.

[71] It is possible to exclude the operation of the Vientiane Protocol; *see* for example the

conciliation or mediation. It specifically states that the Secretary-General of ASEAN may offer good offices, conciliation or mediation with a view to assisting in the settlement of a dispute, giving him a potentially significant role in resolution of such disputes. The High Level Task Force on ASEAN Economic Integration recommended the creation of an ASEAN Compliance Body (ACB) modelled on the Textile Monitoring Body of the WTO.[72] This provides an informal non-binding means of resolving disputes. A request may be made for ACB members from states not involved in the dispute to review the case and make findings within a stipulated timeframe. If a finding of non-compliance is made, the guilty state should correct the situation; otherwise the matter has to go to formal dispute settlement. The ACB was established by the ASEAN Economic Ministers in 2004.

The core of the dispute settlement mechanism is the mandatory procedure prescribed by the Vientiane Protocol. If there is any dispute under the covered agreements, the aggrieved party may request consultations.[73] The other party must reply within 10 days and enter into consultations within 30 days. If it fails to do so, the complainant may raise the matter to SEOM.[74] Similarly, the matter may go to SEOM if consultations do not result in a satisfactory resolution of the problem within 60 days.

Once the dispute is raised to SEOM, a panel will be established unless SEOM decides by consensus not to do so.[75] This means in practice that all the members of SEOM must either agree not to do so or acquiesce in that decision. SEOM has 45 days to decide. The decision will be taken either at a SEOM meeting or by circulation. It is specifically provided that non-reply by any member is taken as agreement to the establishment of a panel. This is to avoid the well-known tactic of keeping silent and hoping that the problem will go away. Thus, the default position is that a panel will be established.

The panel's function is to make a report to SEOM, having objectively considered the facts and provisions of the relevant agreements.[76] The panel is obliged to submit its report and recommendations within 60

2012 ASEAN Agreement on the Movement of Natural Persons, Article 11(2).

[72] This report was annexed to Bali Concord II, adopted at the Ninth ASEAN Summit (Oct. 2003). The body was referred to as the ASEAN Compliance Monitoring Body.

[73] 2004 Protocol on Enhanced Dispute Settlement Mechanism, Article 3.

[74] Ibid., Article 5(1).

[75] Contrast this to the 2010 Protocol to the ASEAN Charter on Dispute Settlement Mechanisms, where there is no mandatory procedure for the establishment of an arbitral panel.

[76] 2004 Protocol on Enhanced Dispute Settlement Mechanism, Articles 6–7.

days.[77] SEOM must adopt the report within 30 days unless there is a consensus not to do so or a party notifies its decision to appeal.[78] If the decision to adopt is not made at a formal meeting, it will be done by circulation and a non-reply is again treated as agreement to adopt.[79]

Appeals go to an appellate body established by the ASEAN Economic Ministers Meeting.[80] An appeal must be concluded within 60 days.[81] Appeals are limited to issues of law and interpretation. The Appellate Body's report shall be adopted by SEOM within 30 days unless there is a consensus not to do so.[82] The disputing parties are obliged to accept the report unconditionally and comply within 60 days of the report of the panel or Appellate Body, as the case may be.[83] SEOM is to oversee compliance.[84] Non-compliance attracts sanctions under the Protocol. The offending party may be ordered to pay compensation. Article 16(2) of the Protocol sets out a timeframe within which negotiations for compensation must be entered into. If no satisfactory compensation has been agreed within the stipulated period, the aggrieved party may request authorization from SEOM to suspend concessions or other obligations under the covered agreements.[85] SEOM is obliged to grant such authorization unless there is a consensus to reject the request.[86] Compensation and suspension of concessions are temporary measures. The offending state is obliged to comply with its obligations under the covered agreements.[87] If the offending party continues to be recalcitrant, the matter may be referred to the ASEAN Summit for a decision under Article 27(2) of the Charter.

The Vientiane Protocol has clear similarities to the dispute settlement procedure of the World Trade Organisation,[88] especially with its strict timelines and provisions to ensure that the panel and appellate reports are adopted unless there is a consensus against it. Such a mechanism is vital if the ASEAN Free Trade Area is to function properly. It has never been

---

[77] Ibid., Article 8(2). Exceptionally, it may take a further ten days if necessary.
[78] Ibid., Article 9(1).
[79] Ibid., Article 9(2).
[80] Ibid., Article 12.
[81] Ibid., Article 12(5); exceptionally, the Appellate Body may take longer, but the maximum is 90 days.
[82] Ibid., Article 12(13).
[83] Ibid., Article 15(1).
[84] Ibid., Article 15(6).
[85] Ibid., Article 16(2).
[86] Ibid., Article 16(6).
[87] Ibid., Article 16(1) and (9).
[88] *See* the WTO's Understanding on Rules and Procedures Governing the Settlement of Disputes.

invoked, so no assessment of its effectiveness can be made.[89] According to a senior ASEAN official the main problems are lack of resources, the unenthusiastic attitude of the member states (who prefer consultation and mediation) and the fact that the timelines are not workable.

However, the WTO Dispute Settlement Mechanism has been invoked by Singapore against Malaysia,[90] Singapore against the Philippines and the Philippines against Thailand.[91] The Singapore case against Malaysia was withdrawn after the underlying cause of complaint was addressed. The second Singapore case against the Philippines was settled amicably after consultations between then-Minister of Trade and Industry George Yeo and his Filipino counterpart Mar Roxas. The two had excellent relations, which allowed the matter to be resolved without convening a panel. The Philippines paid some compensation. This is the way that many incipient disputes are handled before they get too serious: by quiet diplomacy out of the spotlight. ASEAN provides the framework within which political leaders get to meet regularly and develop ties of friendship.

The Philippine case against Thailand is the only one to have proceeded to adjudication. The Philippines requested consultations with Thailand on 7 February 2008. A panel was established and duly presented its final report, finding in favour of the Philippines. Thailand appealed and lost. The Appellate Body's report was adopted on 15 July 2011. On 11 August 2011 Thailand informed the Dispute Settlement Body that it intended to implement the recommendations and rulings 'in a manner that respects its WTO obligations'. Thailand was given a reasonable time to do this after negotiations with the Philippines.[92] The sharp contrast with the Preah Vihear case should be noted.[93] This matter arose at almost exactly the same time as the Preah Vihear problem. The WTO proceedings did not provoke the kind of reaction that Preah Vihear elicited in Thailand. One infers that this was because the issue did not become politicised by contending factions in Thailand.

The Philippines/Thailand dispute could have been resolved in accordance with the Vientiane Protocol.[94] It was not. In conversation with

---

[89] A senior ASEAN official told the author that ASEAN's consultants from the EU had said that the timelines were not realistic. Scepticism as to the effectiveness of the system has also been expressed to the author by some diplomats based in Jakarta.

[90] Dispute DS1, 1995.

[91] Dispute DS371, 2008. The panel report recommending that Thailand bring the offending measures into conformity with its obligations was adopted on 15 July 2011.

[92] Dispute DS371, 2008. The panel report recommending that Thailand bring the offending measures into conformity with its obligations was adopted on 15 July 2011.

[93] This is discussed in more detail in the commentary to Article 28.

[94] *See* Dispute DS371. The Philippines had requested consultations with Thailand on 7 Feb. 2008. The Vientiane Protocol came into force on 29 Nov. 2004.

the author, a senior ASEAN official expressed the view that member states are still not confident of the effectiveness of the ASEAN dispute settlement mechanism. If this is true, it is a bad portent for the creation of a rules-based ASEAN Economic Community by the declared deadline. One can only speculate as to the exact nature of the reservations on the part of the Philippines, which was the complainant state. From the point of view of the Ministry of Foreign Affairs of any ASEAN state, invoking a binding dispute settlement mechanism is a serious step. When given the choice between a tested mechanism and an untested one, caution dictates that the tested mechanism should be chosen. This leads to a policy dilemma: if no member state chooses to use the Vientiane Protocol, it will never be tested; but if the Protocol is invoked and something goes wrong, there will be recriminations. No one wants to be first into uncharted waters. Therefore, a policy decision has to be made at the highest level to prefer the ASEAN route to the WTO one. If ASEAN Member States are serious about creating an economic community, they need to take the Vientiane Protocol seriously when disagreements arise.

Article 25. Establishment of Dispute Settlement Mechanisms

Where not otherwise specifically provided, appropriate dispute settlement mechanisms, including arbitration, shall be established for disputes which concern the interpretation or application of this Charter and other ASEAN instruments.

During the Charter-drafting process a serious difference of opinion emerged over the wording of Article 25. There was some hard bargaining before agreement was reached on this Article. An initial proposal to require the establishment of appropriate dispute settlement mechanisms 'including adjudication' ran into resistance. It was apparent during the negotiations that some member states preferred less formal means of dispute settlement. The feeling was that there should be non-legal avenues for dispute settlement rather than a formal process. This view did not commend itself to the majority of the HLTF members. It was felt that any dispute settlement mechanism that did not allow for a legally binding settlement of disputes could not be taken seriously. The compromise reached is encapsulated in the phrase 'including arbitration'.

After the signing of the Charter, a High-Level Legal Experts' Group (HLEG) was set up by the Forty-first ASEAN Ministerial Meeting in

Singapore to look into the legal aspects of implementation,[95] specifically mentioning the dispute settlement mechanisms. The deadline was supposed to have been December 2008. The task proved more difficult than anticipated.[96] The HLEG was given more time to finalise the dispute settlement mechanisms by the Forty-second Foreign Ministers' Meeting held in Phuket, Thailand, on 20 July 2009.[97] It was only at the Sixteenth ASEAN Summit[98] that the Protocol on Dispute Settlement Mechanisms by the Foreign Ministers was finally signed.[99]

The Protocol to the ASEAN Charter on Dispute Settlement Mechanisms (the DSM Protocol) covers other disputes that concern the interpretation or application of the ASEAN Charter or other ASEAN instruments.[100]

Good offices, conciliation and mediation

The parties to a dispute may agree to resort to good offices, conciliation or mediation.[101] The DSM Protocol provides detailed rules of procedure for this in Annexes 1-3.[102] However, it would be unwise to have a dispute settlement mechanism based entirely on consensual mechanisms. Clearly something more robust is required if disputes between member states are to be settled in a final and legally binding fashion.

Arbitration

Arbitration is now provided for in Articles 10-17 and annex 4 of the DSM Protocol. The first step is a request for consultations. The DSM Protocol provides that a Complainant may request consultations, which must be completed within 90 days unless the parties otherwise agree.[103] If the

---

95 Joint Communiqué of the Forty-first ASEAN Foreign Ministers' Meeting, para 11.

96 The HLEG also had to complete the agreement on privileges and immunities; *see* commentary to Chapter VI above.

97 Joint Communiqué of the Forty-second ASEAN Foreign Ministers' Meeting, para 9.

98 Held in Hanoi, 8-9 Apr. 2010. The Protocol is not yet in effect. *See* the list maintained by the ASEAN Secretariat. 'ASEAN Legal Instruments,' ASEAN Secretariat, online: agreement.asean.org.

99 Even then, it was not opened for ratification until Apr. 2012 when the final two annexes were completed.

100 Protocol to the ASEAN Charter on Dispute Settlement Mechanisms 2010, Article 2(1).

101 *See* the commentary to Article 23(1) above.

102 Strictly speaking, these rules apply when the ASEAN Coordinating Council has ordered good offices, etc., pursuant to Article 9 of the DSM Protocol. However, there is nothing to stop the parties using this framework voluntarily.

103 Protocol to the ASEAN Charter on Dispute Settlement Mechanisms 2010, Article 5.

Respondent does not agree to enter into consultations or the consultations do not result in a settlement of the dispute, the Complainant may request the appointment of an arbitral tribunal.[104] If the respondent does not agree to the appointment of an arbitral tribunal, the matter will be referred to the ASEAN Coordinating Council (ACC),[105] which comprises the Foreign Ministers of the ASEAN members.[106] The ACC can direct the parties to settle the dispute by good offices, conciliation, mediation or arbitration.[107] The ACC has a maximum of 75 days to do this.[108] If the ACC cannot come to a decision, the matter may be referred to the Summit as an unresolved dispute.[109] Contrast this to the 'negative consensus' system under the Vientiane Protocol. Under that Protocol a panel will be established unless there is a consensus not to do so; in other words, the respondent cannot block the establishment of a panel. Under the DSM Protocol there must be a consensus to refer the matter to arbitration. It will be realised that an intransigent party can insist on a political solution (or even no solution) by preventing the ACC from coming to a consensus. There will of course be a political price to be paid for this.

Generally, an arbitral tribunal will consist of three arbitrators.[110] Arbitrators are to be chosen from a list maintained by the Secretary-General, each member state being entitled to nominate ten persons.[111] Crucially, arbitrators must be independent of the parties and not take instructions from them.[112] Each party appoints one arbitrator. They must concur on the third arbitrator, failing which the appointment will be made by the Chair of the ACC on the recommendation of the Secretary-General (who has to consult the Committee of Permanent Representatives).[113] Significantly, Article 11(3) implicitly recognises that

---

[104] Ibid., Article 8(1).

[105] Ibid., Article 8(4).

[106] *See* Article 8(1) of the ASEAN Charter, above.

[107] Protocol to the ASEAN Charter on Dispute Settlement Mechanisms 2010, Article 9(1).

[108] Ibid., Article 9(2) and 9(3).

[109] Ibid., Article 9(4). Rules for Reference of Unresolved Disputes to the ASEAN Summit were incorporated as Annex 5 to the DSM Protocol on 27 Oct. 2010.

[110] Rule 1(1) of Annex 4 to the DSM Protocol. Where more than one member state is involved in the dispute, there may be more arbitrators subject to agreement among the parties: Rule 6(1) to Annex 4 of the DSM Protocol.

[111] Rule 5 of Annex 4 to the DSM Protocol. Some members may have capacity problems in populating the list. It is not expressly provided that member states can only nominate their nationals, so it is always open to them to appoint eminent jurists who are not their nationals, though one expects that this will be rare.

[112] Protocol to the ASEAN Charter on Dispute Settlement Mechanisms 2010, Article 11(2)(c).

[113] Rule 1(4)(b) of Annex 4 to the Protocol to the ASEAN Charter on Dispute Settlement

arbitrators can come from outside ASEAN, since it is stated that the Chair of the arbitral panel shall 'preferably' be a national of an ASEAN state. However, this will happen only in exceptional circumstances.[114] This is another example of the desire to keep matters within the family when it comes to dispute settlement.

As a mechanism to produce a legally binding settlement, the DSM Protocol is set up to fail. This is a consequence of second thoughts by the foreign ministries after the adoption of the ASEAN Charter. As previously explained, some ASEAN member states were reluctant to have a system of compulsory dispute settlement. Having been induced to concede the point during the negotiations on the Charter, they got their way when the DSM Protocol was drafted.

A dispute will only go to arbitration if there is a positive decision on the part of the ACC to allow it. Since ASEAN works on consensus, this will only happen if all the members agree (or can be induced by peer-pressure to acquiesce). Thus, it is likely that disputes will continue to be settled by political means, the DSM Protocol notwithstanding. Ratification of the Protocol has been slow. The willingness of the member states to do so is a litmus test of the true depth of their commitment to creating a rules-based organisation.

Article 26. Unresolved Disputes

When a dispute remains unresolved, after the application of the preceding provisions of this Chapter, this dispute shall be referred to the ASEAN Summit, for its decision.

An 'unresolved dispute' means a dispute over the interpretation or application of the Charter or of other ASEAN instruments which has not been settled by mutual agreement or the application of Article 9 of the 2010 Protocol to the ASEAN Charter on Dispute Settlement Mechanisms (DSM Protocol).[115]

A purposive reading of this article would encompass all disputes between member states, since the previous provisions of this Chapter are

---

Mechanisms 2010. Note the implicit desire to circumscribe the freedom of action of the Secretary-General.

[114] Rule 1(4)(d) of Annex 4 to the Protocol to the ASEAN Charter on Dispute Settlement Mechanisms 2010.

[115] Protocol to the ASEAN Charter on Dispute Settlement Mechanisms 2010, Article 1(e). Strictly speaking, this definition applies only to the Protocol, but it is likely it will be adopted to interpret this Article as well.

meant to comprehensively cover all such problems. This would accord with the spirit of the Charter, one of ASEAN's guiding principles being reliance on peaceful settlement of disputes: *see* Article 2(2)(d). Disputes between member states cannot be swept under the carpet in the hope that future generations will have greater wisdom in dealing with them. This only creates time-bombs that blow up without warning.

For example, the Philippines opposed the formation of Malaysia in 1963 because of its claim to Sabah,[116] a claim which has not been dropped even today. In 1968, information surfaced about a Filipino plot to infiltrate saboteurs in Sabah.[117] Continued tensions between Malaysia and the Philippines over Sabah had led to the postponement of the Fourth ASEAN Ministerial Meeting, which was supposed to have been held in 1970 in Manila.[118] After that, the two countries decided to downplay their differences. But ignoring the problem did not solve it. In February 2013 hundreds of armed Filipinos landed near the town of Lahad Datu in Sabah, claiming to be the Royal Army of Sulu.[119] The defunct Sultanate of Sulu once held sway over Sabah. This incursion ended in bloodshed. Malaysian security forces are still continuing to watch out for subversive elements in eastern Sabah.

Clearly, a policy of benign (or not so benign) neglect merely pushes responsibility for solving the problem to succeeding generations. The first object of ASEAN is 'to maintain and enhance peace, security and stability and further strengthen peace-oriented values in the region': Article 1(1). A vital first step would be to have the Summit deal with territorial disputes within ASEAN, if necessary recommending that they be resolved by reference to an international judicial or arbitral body. Given that several ASEAN states are embroiled in territorial disputes with outside powers at the time of writing,[120] settling intra-ASEAN disputes would seem to be a logical development in order to maintain cohension and trust within the organisation in the face of external challenges.

---

[116] *See* Severino, *In Search of an ASEAN Community*, 164–6.

[117] Ibid., 164. *See also* http://countrystudies.us/philippines/93.htm. This website contains online versions of books previously published by the Federal Research Division of the Library of Congress.

[118] The Fourth AMM finally took place in Mar. 1971.

[119] *See* http://www.bbc.co.uk/news/world-asia-21656732.

[120] In particular, China's claims in the South China Sea put it at odds with Vietnam, the Philippines, Brunei and Malaysia. The Philippines instituted arbitral proceedings against China under Annex VII of the UN Convention on Law of the Sea on 22 Jan. 2013: *see* press release of the International Tribunal for the Law of the Sea dated 25 Apr. 2013. In May 2014 China moved a drilling rig into disputed waters around the Paracel Islands, provoking serious riots in Vietnam: *see* 'Vietnam anti-China protest: factories burnt', 14 May 2014 http://www.bbc.com/news/world-asia-27403851.

Referral to the ASEAN Summit

Rules for Reference of Unresolved Disputes and the Instrument of Incorporation into the 2010 Protocol to the ASEAN Charter on Dispute Settlement Mechanisms as Annex 5 were signed by the Foreign Ministers at the Seventeenth ASEAN Summit.[121]

The notification to the ASEAN Summit is to be done through the ASEAN Coordinating Committee (ACC).[122] The ACC will try to get the parties to settle the matter without having to involve the Summit.[123] If the problem cannot be resolved, the matter must be referred to the Summit within 90 days or any timeframe deemed appropriate by the ACC.[124] The ACC will annex a report with its recommendations when the matter is referred to the Summit.

Once the matter goes to the ASEAN Summit, the resolution of the dispute will not be entirely on the basis of the law. Inevitably, the recommendations of the ACC will be political and not legal in nature. However, there is nothing to prevent the Summit from establishing a legal panel of some sort to assist the leaders in deciding what to do if there is an unresolved dispute. This would accord with ASEAN's ambition to be a rules-based organisation subscribing to the rule of law. Clearly it would not be in the interests of the parties - or of ASEAN itself - that disputes between member states should remain unresolved after being referred to the apex organ of ASEAN.

Article 27. Compliance

1. The Secretary-General of ASEAN, assisted by the ASEAN Secretariat or any other designated ASEAN body, shall monitor the compliance with the findings, recommendations or decisions resulting from an ASEAN dispute settlement mechanism, and submit a report to the ASEAN Summit.

As to the Secretary-General and ASEAN Secretariat, *see* Article 11.

---

[121] Rules for Reference of Unresolved Disputes to the ASEAN Summit, adopted on 27 Oct. 2010 in Hanoi, Vietnam. Instrument of Incorporation of the Rules for Reference of Unresolved Disputes to the ASEAN Summit to the Protocol to the ASEAN Charter on Dispute Settlement Mechanisms signed on 27 Oct. 2010 in Hanoi, Vietnam.

[122] Rule 2 of the Rules for Reference of Unresolved Disputes to the ASEAN Summit.

[123] Rule 3 of the Rules for Reference of Unresolved Disputes to the ASEAN Summit.

[124] Rule 4(1) of the Rules for Reference of Unresolved Disputes to the ASEAN Summit.

A party to a dispute settled under the 2010 Protocol to the ASEAN Charter on Dispute Settlement Mechanisms is obliged to provide the Secretary-General with a status report in writing regarding its compliance with any arbitral award or settlement agreement.[125]

2. Any Member State affected by non-compliance with the findings, recommendations or decisions resulting from an ASEAN dispute settlement mechanism, may refer the matter to the ASEAN Summit for a decision.

Rules for Reference of Non-Compliance to the ASEAN Summit and the Instrument of Incorporation into the 2010 Protocol to the ASEAN Charter on Dispute Settlement Mechanisms (DSM Protocol) as Annex 6 were adopted at the Twentieth ASEAN Summit.[126]

The notification to the ASEAN Summit is to be done through the ASEAN Coordinating Committee (ACC),[127] at least where the matter concerns an arbitral award or settlement agreement under the DSM Protocol. Nothing is expressly provided in the DSM Protocol regarding non-compliance with awards under the Vientiane Protocol or settlements pursuant to the Treaty of Amity and Cooperation. One expects that a similar procedure will be followed in such cases despite the absence of explicit rules. The ACC is to facilitate consultations among the parties to settle the matter without having to involve the Summit.[128] If the problem cannot be resolved, the matter must be referred to the Summit within 90 days or such longer period as the parties to the dispute may agree.[129] The ACC will annex a report with its recommendations when the matter is referred to the Summit.[130]

Once the matter goes to the ASEAN Summit, the resolution of the dispute will not be entirely on the basis of the law. As supreme

---

125 Protocol to the ASEAN Charter on Dispute Settlement Mechanisms 2010, Article 16(2).

126 Rules for Reference of Non-Compliance to the ASEAN Summit, adopted on 2 Apr. 2012 in Phnom Penh, Cambodia. Instrument of Incorporation of the Rules for Reference of Non-Compliance to the ASEAN Summit, signed on 2 Apr. 2012 in Phnom Penh, Cambodia.

127 Rule 1(b) of the Rules for Reference of Non-Compliance to the ASEAN Summit. There are also Rules for Reference of Unresolved Disputes to the ASEAN Summit, which were incorporated as Annex 5 to the DSM Protocol on 27 Oct. 2010. Confusingly, rule 2(1) of Annex 5 characterises non-compliance with the instructions of the ACC as an unresolved dispute. As to the ACC, *see* Article 8 of the ASEAN Charter, above.

128 Rule 3 of the Rules for Reference of Non-Compliance to the ASEAN Summit.

129 Rule 5(a) of the Rules for Reference of Non-Compliance to the ASEAN Summit.

130 Rule 5(b) of the Rules for Reference of Non-Compliance to the ASEAN Summit.

policymaking organ, the Summit's powers are not constrained. Inevitably, the recommendations of the ACC will be political and not legal in nature. However, there is nothing to prevent the Summit from establishing a legal panel of some sort to assist the leaders in deciding what to do if there is a case of non-compliance with the decision of a dispute settlement body. If ASEAN is serious about becoming a rules-based organisation, it would be far better that some independent legal body advise the leaders instead of having them decide on the basis of the political recommendations of the ACC. It would be immensely damaging to ASEAN's credibility if the result of an arbitration or other dispute settlement process could be overturned or modified on political grounds. Trust in institutions is vital if ASEAN is to fulfil its declared ambitions. That trust can only be fostered if the member states respect the decisions of the dispute settlement mechanisms they have agreed to establish.

Article 28 United Nations Charter Provisions and Other Relevant International Procedures

Unless otherwise provided for in this Charter, Member States have the right of recourse to the modes of peaceful settlement contained in Article 33(1) of the Charter of the United Nations or any other international legal instruments to which the disputing Member States are parties.

This Article preserves the right of ASEAN member states to resort to other dispute settlement mechanisms, in particular those mentioned in Article 33(1) of the UN Charter, viz, 'negotiation, enquiry, mediation, conciliation, arbitration, judicial settlement, resort regional agencies or arrangements'. Thus far none of the ASEAN mechanisms listed in the Charter have ever been invoked. Member states seem to be much more comfortable with referring disputes to established mechanisms outside the ASEAN framework.

Singapore and Malaysia have been particularly assiduous in using third party adjudication mechanisms to settle disputes. Singapore invoked the WTO Dispute Settlement Mechanism against Malaysia in 1995.[131] The complaint was eventually withdrawn when the underlying cause was redressed. On 5 September 2003 Malaysia submitted a Request for Provisional Measures to the International Tribunal on Law

[131] Dispute DS1, 1995. This was the very first matter to be referred to WTO dispute settlement.

of the Sea (ITLOS) in relation to Singapore's land reclamation activities near their common maritime boundary.[132] The parties eventually came to a settlement of their differences. Finally there was the dispute between Malaysia and Singapore over the island of Pedra Branca. This went to the International Court of Justice and was resolved in 2007 largely in Singapore's favour.

Two other territorial disputes between ASEAN member states have reached the stage of judicial resolution by the International Court of Justice (ICJ): between Cambodia and Thailand over the Temple of Preah Vihear, which predated the formation of ASEAN; and between Indonesia and Malaysia over the islands of Sipadan and Ligitan.

The only other case between ASEAN member states is the Philippine case against Thailand which proceeded to adjudication under the WTO Dispute Settlement Mechanism in 2008.

The actual result of these cases is not of crucial importance. More significant is the light that these instances throw on the dynamics of dispute resolution in ASEAN and the attitude of the member states to formal legal proceedings as opposed to diplomacy.

The cases before the International Court of Justice

(1) Sipadan-Ligitan

Sipadan and Ligitan are two small islands lying in the Celebes Sea off the north-east coast of the island of Borneo. In colonial times Borneo was divided between the British (who controlled Brunei, Sarawak and British North Borneo, now known as Sabah) and the Dutch (the southern portion of Borneo being part of the Netherlands East Indies). The two islands in question were in the British sphere and in due course were taken over by Malaysia. Malaysian sovereignty over Ligitan and Sipadan was contested by Indonesia. The Philippines also had a claim to Sabah, which had led to problems between the two countries in the early days after the founding of ASEAN.[133]

---

[132] *See* Case Concerning Land Reclamation by Singapore in and around the Straits of Johor (Malaysia v Singapore). ITLOS Case no. 12.

[133] *See* Severino, In Search of an ASEAN Community, 164–6. The Philippines has never formally abandoned its claim. The issue again came to prominence in early 2013 when a group of armed Filipinos landed in Sabah near the town of Lahad Datu claiming to be the Royal Army of Sulu, which supposedly exercised sovereignty over Sabah: *See* http://www.bbc.co.uk/news/world-asia-21656732. This incursion ended in bloodshed.

Indonesia wanted to bring the Ligitan/Sipadan dispute to the High Council under the 1976 Treaty of Amity and Cooperation in Southeast Asia but Malaysia refused, fearing that other ASEAN members would be partial to Indonesia.[134] At the time Malaysia had territorial disagreements with practically all her neighbours.[135] In the end the dispute was referred to the International Court of Justice (ICJ) instead.[136] Interestingly, the Special Agreement for submission of the case to the ICJ stated in the preamble that the parties desired 'that this dispute should be settled in the spirit of friendly relations existing between the Parties as enunciated in the 1976 Treaty of Amity and Cooperation in Southeast Asia'.[137] An application by the Philippines to intervene on the basis of her claim to Sabah was refused by the ICJ.[138]

In the end Indonesia lost the case. The ICJ ruled almost unanimously that sovereignty over Sipadan and Ligitan belonged to Malaysia.[139] The result of this loss was a noticeable reluctance on the part of Indonesia to submit to international dispute resolution henceforth.[140] The ICJ judgment may have settled the issue before it, but it did not make resolution of other boundary disputes between Malaysia and Indonesia easier.[141]

---

[134] *See* Severino, *In Search of an ASEAN Community*, 12–13.

[135] In 1979 Malaysia issued a map entitled 'Territorial Waters and Continental Shelf Boundaries of Malaysia' which purported to extend the maritime area claimed by Malaysia. This attracted protests from Brunei, China, Indonesia, the Philippines, Singapore, Thailand and Vietnam. This map was not relevant to the Sipadan/Ligitan matter; however, given the fact that Malaysia had provoked opposition by all her neighbours to her territorial claims, it is not surprising that it was felt that a High Council consisting of those neighbours would not be sympathetic.

[136] Case Concerning Sovereignty over Pulau Ligitan and Pulau Sipadan (Judgment 17 Dec. 2002). President Soeharto decided to submit the matter to the ICJ despite the objections of his officials. *See* Severino, *In Search of an ASEAN Community*, 12–13.

[137] The Special Agreement was signed on 31 May 1997 by Mr Ali Alatas, Foreign Minister of Indonesia, and Datuk Abdullah Ahmad Badawi, Foreign Minister of Malaysia. The agreement may be found at http://www.icj-cij.org/docket/files/102/7177.pdf.

[138] *See* the judgment of the ICJ on the application, 23 Oct. 2001; available at http://www.icj-cij.org/docket/files/102/7698.pdf.

[139] *See* the judgment dated 17 Dec. 2002; available at http://www.icj-cij.org/docket/files/102/7714.

[140] This was plain during the negotiations on this Chapter. A senior Indonesian diplomat subsequently confirmed to the author that Indonesia would be reluctant to resort to the ICJ again in future.

[141] For example, the dispute over Ambalat, a region in the Celebes Sea. Malaysia's 1979 map entitled 'Territorial Waters and Continental Shelf Boundaries of Malaysia' (which purported to extend the maritime area claimed by Malaysia) and the Sipadan/Ligitan matter contributed to tension between the two countries. *See* 'Pembicaraan Soal Ambalat' (Discussions on the Question of Ambalat) reported by BBC Indonesia.com on 10 June 2009; available at http://www.bbc.co.uk/indonesian/news/story/2009/06/090610_ambalattalks.shtml.

(2) Pedra Branca

The island of Pedra Branca lies at the eastern entrance of the Straits of Singapore twenty-four nautical miles to the northeast of Singapore island. In 1847 the government of the Straits Settlements[142] took possession of the island and built a lighthouse on it. Horsburgh Lighthouse has been in operation since 1851, first under the control of the British and subsequently of Singapore. In 1979 Malaysia issued a map entitled 'Territorial Waters and Continental Shelf Boundaries of Malaysia' which indicated that Pedra Branca lay within Malaysian waters. Singapore protested. Negotiations took place but did not produce a result.[143] Singapore's position had always been that if negotiations could not resolve the issue, the matter should be referred to international adjudication. Malaysia was reluctant to do so. However, on 17 September 1994 Malaysia finally agreed to refer the Pedra Branca issue to the ICJ. At that time Malaysia was also embroiled in its dispute with Indonesia over Sipadan and Ligitan. It took a further four years to settle the Special Agreement to give jurisdiction to the ICJ. Despite the fact that the Special Agreement had been finalized, Malaysia declined to sign it for a further four years, until 6 February 2003. Indeed, it was not until 17 May 2003 that Malaysia finally ratified the Special Agreement.[144]

Unlike in the case of the Special Agreement to refer the Ligitan/Sipadan to the ICJ, there was no reference to the spirit of friendly relations embodied in the Treaty of Amity and Cooperation in Southeast Asia.[145] In fact, bilateral relations between Malaysia and Singapore were at a low ebb.[146] Nonetheless, it was an act of political maturity on both sides to agree to submit the dispute to the ICJ instead of continually bickering over the island. The ICJ ruled in favour of Singapore on 23 May 2008 as far as Pedra Branca was concerned.[147] It awarded sovereignty over Middle Rocks (two clusters of small rocks 0.6 nautical miles south of Pedra Branca) to Malaysia. The court left the status of South Ledge (a rock formation

---

[142] A British colony, of which Singapore was the capital.

[143] The history of the dispute is recounted in S Jayakumar and Tommy Koh, *Pedra Branca: The Road to the World Court* (Singapore: NUS Press, 2009).

[144] On 17 Dec. 2002 the ICJ had ruled in Malaysia's favour in its dispute with Indonesia. The timing of the Malaysian ratification is probably not a coincidence.

[145] The Special Agreement is available at http://www.icj-cij.org/docket/file/130/1785.pdf.

[146] This was especially so during the reign of Malaysian Prime Minister Mahathir Mohamed. Relations improved considerably when he was succeeded by Dato' Seri Abdullah Badawi, who by coincidence was Foreign Minister of Malaysia when the Special Agreement with Indonesia was signed.

[147] The judgment is available at http://www.icj-cij.org/docket/files/130/14492.pdf.

visible only at low tide) ambiguous, holding that sovereignty lay with the state in whose territorial waters it lay. The resolution of the dispute over Pedra Branca allowed the two countries to move on in their bilateral relations without this thorn in the side continually scratching. However, delimitation of the maritime boundaries between Pedra Branca and Middle Rocks has still not taken place.

(3) Preah Vihear

While the hearings on the Pedra Branca were going on in the Hague, the ASEAN Charter was signed at the Thirteenth ASEAN Summit in Singapore.[148] The Eminent Persons Group (EPG) set up to conceptualise the Charter had recognised that ASEAN's main problem was not lack of vision; the main problem was following up on the grand declarations, plans of action and roadmaps. This has been a constant shortcoming identified by the current and former Secretaries-General not only to the EPG but also to the High Level Task Force (HLTF) on Drafting of the ASEAN Charter. It was stated baldly that 'ASEAN must establish a culture of honouring and implementing its decisions and agreements, and carrying them out on time'.[149] To remedy the deficiency in carrying out commitments, the EPG recommended the establishment of dispute settlement mechanisms in all fields of ASEAN cooperation, including monitoring and enforcement mechanisms.[150]

A High Level Legal Experts Group (HLEG) was tasked with fleshing out the dispute settlement mechanism.[151] The HLEG's recommendations resulted in the Protocol to the ASEAN Charter on Dispute Settlement Mechanisms (the DSM Protocol), signed by the Foreign Ministers of the ASEAN states on 8 April 2010 in Hanoi.[152] Territorial disputes between ASEAN member states would fall within the Treaty of Amity and Cooperation in Southeast Asia (TAC) or DSM Protocol. The dispute between Thailand and Cambodia over the Temple of Preah Vihear might

---

148 The Charter was presented to the ASEAN Foreign Ministers by this author as leader of the Singapore delegation. Singapore was then the Chair of ASEAN.

149 Report of the Eminent Persons Group on the ASEAN Charter, para 44. This remains a matter of concern even now; in conversation with this author, this issue was repeatedly raised by ASEAN officials and former Secretaries-General.

150 Report of the Eminent Persons Group on the ASEAN Charter, Executive Summary, para 6.

151 *See* the Joint Communiqué of the Forty-first ASEAN Ministerial Meeting, para 11.

152 This is not yet in force. *See* the list maintained by the ASEAN Secretariat. 'ASEAN Legal Instruments,' ASEAN Secretariat, online: agreement.asean.org.

have been resolved under either of those instruments.[153] As it turned out, neither the TAC nor the DSM Protocol was invoked.

The Preah Vihear dispute is both the earliest and the latest case involving ASEAN member states. Cambodia was not one of the original five ASEAN Member States, having joined only in 1999.[154] Only by looking back at history can one understand the nature of the problem. The Siamese and the Khmers are traditional foes. The kingdom of Angkor arose in the ninth century.[155] This kingdom exercised control over a territory that today extends into southern Laos and north-eastern Thailand.

The Temple of Preah Vihear dates from the eleventh century, though it can be traced back to a ninth century hermitage founded by Prince Indrayudha, the son of King Jayavarman II.[156] From the thirteenth century Angkor was increasingly challenged by Thai kingdoms, principally Ayutthaya to the west. The borders shifted with the ebb and flow of power of the competing polities. The temple complex of Angkor Wat and the city of Angkor Thom were eventually abandoned (though not forgotten, despite French claims to have 'discovered' the ruins in the nineteenth century) and the capital moved eastwards near the present-day Phnom Penh. The historic rivalry between Cambodia and Thailand lends a particular sensitivity to claims of sovereignty on that border. Siem Reap, where Cambodia's premier national symbol Angkor Wat is located, is roughly translated as 'Victory over Siam'. Even the false accusation that a Thai actress had questioned the sovereignty of Cambodia over Angkor Wat was sufficient to provoke anti-Thai riots in Phnom Penh in 2003.

The disputed border was demarcated in 1907 by treaty between the Kingdom of Siam and the French colonial authorities who had control over Cambodia, a process which was not entirely accepted by the Thais. After the fall of France in 1940, Siam took the opportunity to regain the 'lost'

---

[153] Although the DSM Protocol was not in force, there was nothing to stop the two disputants from having recourse to its provisions to resolve their dispute. They had both already signed up to it.

[154] Cambodia's membership was delayed on account of the uncertain political situation following hostilities between supporters of the two co-Prime Ministers, Prince Norodom Ranariddh and Hun Sen. *See* the Joint Statement of the Special Meeting of the ASEAN Foreign Ministers on Cambodia (Kuala Lumpur, July 1997) and Severino, *In Search of an ASEAN Community*, 57–67. In reality, Hun Sen had launched a coup against his co-Prime Minister Prince Ranariddh.

[155] For a general introduction to the historical background *see* Ricklefs, *New History of Southeast Asia*, chapters 3, 5 and 10.

[156] *See* the Historical Description on the UNESCO World Heritage List website: whc.unesco.org.

territory in a short war against the French colonial authorities in 1941.[157] The end of the Pacific War saw the return of these territories to French control.[158] Despite this, Thailand occupied portions of the Cambodian province of Kompong Thom, including Preah Vihear, in 1949.[159] Prince Norodom Sihanouk took control of Cambodia's government in 1952 and won recognition for an independent Cambodia at the Geneva Conference in 1954, which had been convened to reach a settlement of the First Indochina War.[160] That same year Thai troops occupied the ruins of Preah Vihear.[161]

In 1959 Cambodia instituted proceedings against Thailand in the International Court of Justice. Both countries had filed declarations accepting the compulsory jurisdiction of the court.[162] Notwithstanding this, Thailand contended that its declaration was ineffective and sought to have the case summarily dismissed. The Court rejected the Thai arguments and held that it had jurisdiction.[163] The original dispute about sovereignty was settled by the decision of the International Court of Justice in 1962.[164] The ICJ held by nine votes to three that the temple stood in territory under the sovereignty of Cambodia. This judgment did not solve the problem, merely postponed the reckoning. The ICJ only trimmed the weeds without digging out the roots.

The dispute flared up again when Cambodia applied to have the ruins of Preah Vihear accepted as a UNESCO World Heritage site in 2008.[165]

---

[157] *See* Britannica Online www.britannica.com under 'Thailand: The Phibun Dictatorship and World War II'.

[158] Thailand was allied to Japan. It managed nonetheless to escape post-war retribution beyond retrocession of territories taken from Burma, Malaya, Cambodia and Laos during the War. *See* Ricklefs, *New History of Southeast Asia*, 299–300, 360–2. France never accepted the forcible annexation by Thailand of the territories in French Indochina in 1941. These territories were retroceded in an accord dated 17 Nov. 1946: *see* Annex VI to Cambodia's Application Instituting Proceedings in the *Case Concerning the Temple of Preah Vihear* (15 Sept. 1959), 79, para 2.

[159] Para 1 of the Application Instituting Proceedings in the *Case Concerning the Temple of Preah Vihear (*15 Sept. 1959).

[160] *See* Britannica Online www.britannica.com under 'Cambodia: Independence'.

[161] Para 1 of the Application Instituting Proceedings in the *Case Concerning the Temple of Preah Vihear* (15 Sept. 1959).

[162] Thailand on 20 May 1950 and Cambodia on 19 Sept. 1957. A check on the ICJ website (www.icj-cij.org) reveals that Thailand no longer accepts the compulsory jurisdiction of the ICJ.

[163] *Case Concerning the Temple of Preah Vihear*, judgment dated 21 May 1961. Available at http://www.icj-cij.org/docket/files/45/4857.pdf.

[164] *Case Concerning the Temple of Preah Vihear (Merits)*, judgment dated 15 June 1962. Available at http://www.icj-cij.org/docket/files/45/4871.pdf.

[165] The background to this is recounted in *International Crisis Group Asia Report* no.

Although Thailand under Prime Minister Thaksin Shinawatra and his successor was initially supportive, the issue became entangled in Thai domestic politics. Prime Minister Thaksin had been deposed by a coup in 2006 and his political foes used the Preah Vihear issue as a weapon to destabilise the government. The UNESCO listing took place in July 2008.

In that same month an informal meeting of the ASEAN Foreign Ministers took place in Singapore, which held the Chair of ASEAN. Singapore's Foreign Minister George Yeo announced that the ministers had placed ASEAN's facilities at the disposal of the parties for the settlement of the dispute.[166] The possibility of using the TAC was raised but not accepted by the parties. A proposal was made for a Contact Group to support the parties in their effort to reach a peaceful resolution. However, the parties would not accept the assistance of their ASEAN colleagues at that time. Indeed, the Thai Foreign Minister stated that a constitutional amendment (introduced after the coup that deposed Prime Minister Thaksin Shinawatra) precluded him from negotiating territorial matters, on pain of being charged with treason. This constitutional prohibition was raised by successive Thai Foreign Ministers when pressed by their ASEAN colleagues to negotiate a settlement.

Sporadic fighting broke out at the site from October 2008 to early 2009.[167] Nothing moved during the chairmanship of Thailand the following year, as might be expected. The domestic political situation in Thailand remained extremely volatile.[168] Vietnam took over the chair of ASEAN in 2010. Cambodian Foreign Minister Hor Namhong wrote to Vietnamese Foreign Minister Pham Gia Khiem requesting mediation of the dispute under Article 32(c) of the ASEAN Charter, but Thailand declined.[169] On 4 February 2011, in an escalation of the dispute, fighting broke out between Thailand and Cambodia in the vicinity of Preah Vihear.

ASEAN was lucky to have had Indonesia in the Chair at that precise moment in time. It was pure serendipity; Brunei was supposed to have

---

215, 'Waging Peace: ASEAN and the Thai-Cambodian Border Conflict' (6 Dec. 2011), 4-6, 9-12.

[166] *See* Statement by Singaporean Minister for Foreign Affairs George Yeo, 22 July 2008, available on the website of the Ministry of Foreign Affairs, Singapore: www.mfa.gov.sg.

[167] *International Crisis Group Asia Report* no. 215, 'Waging Peace: ASEAN and the Thai-Cambodian Border Conflict' (6 Dec. 2011), 6.

[168] Clashes between different political factions had forced the cancellation of the ASEAN+1, ASEAN+3 and East Asia Summits that were to have been held in Pattaya in April, an enormous humiliation for Thailand. *See* BBC news, 11 Apr. 2009, available on the website of the BBC: news.bbc.co.uk.

[169] 'Waging Peace: ASEAN and the Thai-Cambodian Border Conflict', Asia Report no. 215, (International Crisis Group Asia, 6 Dec. 2011), 15.

taken the Chair of ASEAN, but had at Indonesia's request swapped slots. Indonesian Foreign Minister Marty Natalegawa was a seasoned diplomat. He had been Indonesia's Permanent Representative to the United Nations and Director-General in charge of ASEAN matters in the Indonesian Foreign Ministry and therefore was intimately familiar with how the system worked. He was immediately on the phone to Cambodian Foreign Minister Hor Namhong and Thai Foreign Minister Kasit Piromya. On 7 and 8 February 2011 he was in Phnom Penh and Bangkok for talks. The Thais preferred to keep the dispute at a bilateral level. The Cambodians, no doubt calculating that they would be seen as the wronged party, insisted on bringing the matter to the UN Security Council.

On 14 February 2011 Indonesian Foreign Minister Marty Natalegawa, speaking as the Chair of ASEAN, told the Security Council that ASEAN wanted an observer mission. The Security Council, which had more pressing matters to deal with than a minor border skirmish in Southeast Asia, left it to ASEAN to sort out.[170] Armed with this mandate, Foreign Minister Natalegawa began shuttling between the disputing parties, as the Cambodian and Thai Foreign Ministers would not meet face-to-face. With the backing of the other ASEAN Foreign Ministers, he persuaded the Thais and the Cambodians that a continuing dispute would not be good for ASEAN solidarity. There were no threats of armed intervention, economic sanctions or even diplomatic isolation. The appeal was to enlighten self-interest.

An informal (i.e., previously unscheduled) meeting of ASEAN Foreign Ministers was held on 22 February 2011 in Jakarta. Foreign Minister Natalegawa briefed the other ministers on the result of his visits to Phnom Penh and Bangkok and his appearance before the Security Council. Thai Foreign Minister Kasit Piromya and Cambodian Foreign Minister Hor Namhong presented their countries' respective positions. A statement was issued by the Foreign Ministers[171] welcoming Indonesia's efforts in her capacity as Chair of ASEAN and requesting that those efforts continue. The disputing parties accepted (with varying degrees of enthusiasm) the proposal that Indonesian observers be deployed on both sides of the border to prevent a resumption of hostilities. Singaporean Foreign Minister George Yeo shed some light on the manoeuvres behind the

---

[170] ASEAN Secretariat, Press Release, 'Historic Firsts: ASEAN Efforts on Cambodian-Thai Conflict Endorsed by UNSC' (21 Feb. 2011), online: www.asean.org/news/asean-secretariat-news/item/historic-firsts-asean-efforts-on-cambodian-thai-conflict-endorsed-by-unsc.

[171] Statement by the Chairman of ASEAN on 22 Feb. 2011.

scenes when he answered a parliamentary question on 3 March 2011. He revealed that even though the Thais had been unwilling to accept Indonesian observers initially, faced with peer pressure from the other nine members, they eventually relented.[172] The Foreign Ministers requested Indonesia to continue ASEAN's efforts to find a peaceful resolution of the dispute.

This unfortunately did not lead to the settlement of the problem. Although the Thai government may have agreed to accept Indonesian observers, the Thai military remained recalcitrant. The Cambodians pursued a parallel dispute settlement process, applying to the ICJ for interpretation of its 1962 judgment[173] and for provisional measures[174] on 28 April 2011. In the application for provisional measures, the Thais again tried to have the case dismissed summarily on the ground that the court had no jurisdiction. The ICJ pronounced its decision regarding provisional measures on 18 July 2011.[175] Thailand's objection to the jurisdiction of the court was rejected. Both parties were ordered to withdraw their military personnel from a defined provisional demilitarized zone and refrain from taking any action to aggravate the situation. The parties were enjoined to 'continue the co-operation which they have entered into within ASEAN and, in particular, allow the observers appointed by that organization to have access to the provisional demilitarized zone'.

The Indonesian observers were not deployed in the end. This was a matter of *realpolitik* rather than law. The primary object of ASEAN's intervention was to end the hostilities. Once the shooting stopped, there was no further need. On 11 November 2013 the ICJ delivered judgment largely in favour of Cambodia while enjoining the parties to 'cooperate between themselves and with the international community in the protection of the site as a world heritage'.[176]

The active involvement of the Chair of ASEAN is noteworthy. The observers may not have been deployed, but the fighting stopped. The Security Council recognised the important role played by ASEAN in

---

[172] Ministry of Foreign Affairs (Singapore) Press Release, 'Remarks by Minister for Foreign Affairs George Yeo in Parliament during Committee of Supply Debate on 3 Mar. 2011,' online: www.mfa.gov.sg/content/mfa/media_centre/press_room/pr/2011/201103/press_20110303_01.html.

[173] Under Article 60 of the Statute of the Court and Article 98 of the Rules of Court.

[174] Under Article 41 of the Statute and Article 73 of the Rules.

[175] Request for the Interpretation of the Judgment of 15 June 1962 in the Case Concerning the Temple of Preah Vihear, Order dated 18 July 2011. Available at http://www.icj-cij.org/docket/files/151/16564.

[176] Request for the Interpretation of the Judgment of 15 June 1962 in the *Case Concerning the Temple of Preah Vihear,* judgment dated 11 Nov. 2013, para 106.

bringing about this result. One can only hope that this is a precedent that will be followed in future.

The cases involving the WTO Dispute Settlement Mechanism

The WTO Dispute Settlement Mechanism has been invoked on two occasions by ASEAN member states: by Singapore against Malaysia[177] and by the Philippines against Thailand.[178] There was another occasion where a bilateral trade dispute did not actually reach the stage of formal dispute settlement, between Singapore and the Philippines. The Singapore case against Malaysia was withdrawn after the underlying cause of complaint was addressed. The Singapore case against the Philippines was settled amicably after consultations between then Minister of Trade and Industry George Yeo and his Filipino counterpart Mar Roxas. The two had excellent relations, which allowed the matter to be resolved without convening a panel. The Philippines paid some compensation. The Philippine case against Thailand is the only one to have proceeded to adjudication.

The Philippines requested consultations with Thailand on 7 February 2008. A panel was established and duly presented its final report, finding in favour of the Philippines. Thailand appealed and lost. The Appellate Body's report was adopted on 15 July 2011. On 11 August 2011 Thailand informed the Dispute Settlement Body that it intended to implement the recommendations and rulings 'in a manner that respects its WTO obligations'. Thailand was given a reasonable time to do this after negotiations with the Philippines. The sharp contrast with the Preah Vihear case should be noted. This matter arose at almost exactly the same time as the Preah Vihear problem. The WTO proceedings did not provoke the kind of reaction that Preah Vihear elicited in Thailand. One infers that this was because the issue did not become politicised by contending factions in Thailand.

Some general observations on the resolution of disputes

Three key points emerge from the Ligitan/Sipadan, Pedra Branca and Preah Vihear cases.

Firstly, recourse to a binding mode of dispute settlement is rare. It is vital to appreciate that recourse to arbitration or an international tribunal

[177] Dispute DS1, 1995.
[178] Dispute DS371, 2008.

is a political decision, not a legal one. Unlike in the case of domestic dispute settlement, the complainant has to factor in the cost in terms of damage to bilateral relations with the respondent[179] and possibly with other ASEAN states that may have urged the parties to come to an amicable settlement. The strength of the complainant's legal case is only one factor to be considered. It may not even be the decisive factor. Once a complainant crosses the Rubicon by invoking a binding dispute settlement mechanism, the die is cast; anything short of victory means a loss of face and domestic political credibility. Where the government is weak domestically, political opponents can hijack nationalistic sentiments for short-term political advantage. Only a secure government can afford to run the political risk; ironically, a democratic government facing elections or dependant on coalition partners may be less willing to resort to binding international dispute settlement than an authoritarian regime.

It is no coincidence that the government of President Soeharto in Indonesia and the governments of Malaysia and Singapore were firmly entrenched when the Ligitan/Sipadan case between Indonesia and Malaysia[180] and the Pedra Branca case between Malaysia and Singapore[181] were submitted to the ICJ. Both of these cases might have been dealt with under the TAC, but that procedure is more political than judicial. The submission of the Ligitan/Sipadan dispute to the ICJ was a decision taken at the highest level, despite the reservations of officials.[182] Interestingly, in submitting the dispute to the ICJ the parties explicitly referred to the TAC.[183] Similarly, the Pedra Branca case was submitted to the Court

[179] In the Preah Vihear case bilateral relations between the disputing parties were at a low ebb when reference was made to the ICJ. At one point the Cambodian government appointed ousted Thai Prime Minister Thaksin Shinawatra as adviser to Prime Minister Hun Sen, a move that could only have been calculated to irritate the Thais. *See International Crisis Group Asia Report* no. 215, 'Waging Peace: ASEAN and the Thai-Cambodian Border Conflict' (6 Dec. 2011), 12–13. Relations improved with the election of the new government under Khun Thaksin's sister Prime Minister Yingluck Shinawatra.

[180] *Case Concerning Sovereignty over Pulau Ligitan and Pulau Sipadan*, judgment dated 17 Dec. 2002.

[181] *Case Concerning Sovereignty over Pedra Branca/Pulau Batu Puteh, Middle Rocks and South Ledge*, judgment dated 23 May 2008.

[182] Indonesia had tried to bring the Ligitan/Sipadan dispute to the High Council under the TAC but Malaysia refused, fearing that other ASEAN members would be partial to Indonesia: *see* Severino, *In Search of an ASEAN Community*, 12–13. President Soeharto decided to submit the dispute to the ICJ, overriding the objections of his officials.

[183] The Special Agreement (signed on 31 May 1997 by the Foreign Ministers of the two countries, viz, Mr Ali Alatas and Datuk Abdullah Badawi) stated in the preamble that the parties desired 'that this dispute should be settled in the spirit of friendly relations

after negotiations had proven unsuccessful. In both instances there was sufficient political will to have the matter resolved finally by adjudication. In contrast, Thailand's government was shaky at the time the Cambodians brought the matter to the ICJ.

Whatever the situation may be in Europe, to which ASEAN is often compared, nationalism in Southeast Asia is not dead. The colonial interlude kept the regional disputes in check. The Preah Vihear case reminds us that these problems still fester. The disagreement over Preah Vihear became a piece in a rowdy game of domestic political one-upmanship in Thailand.[184] Governments may be willing to be bound by international norms, but they may be constrained by domestic politics in what they can do. A strong military with a history of political interventionism does not help. Political groups may use territorial disputes to whip up jingoistic nationalistic feelings for domestic advantage. In such a situation, the last thing that a weak government may want to do is invite impartial dispute settlement. It should be noted that Thailand challenged the jurisdiction of the court both in 1961 and 2011. Thailand's reluctance can be explained in a large part by the volatility of its domestic politics.[185] However, the procedure under Article 60 of the Statute of the ICJ allows one party to request interpretation and that was sufficient for the Court to be seised of the matter despite the opposition of the Thais.

By coincidence, at the same time as the Preah Vihear matter the Philippines and Thailand were also embroiled in a trade dispute. That case was decided under the WTO dispute settlement mechanism.[186] The Philippines requested consultations with Thailand on 7 February 2008. A panel was established and duly presented its final report, finding in favour of the Philippines. Thailand appealed and lost. The Appellate Body's report was adopted on 15 July 2011. On 11 August 2011 Thailand informed the Dispute Settlement Body that it intended to implement the recommendations and rulings 'in a manner that respects its WTO obligations'. The mature Thai reaction to the WTO decision provides a sharp contrast to the raucous political theatre

---

existing between the Parties as enunciated in the 1976 Treaty of Amity and Cooperation in Southeast Asia'.

[184] The political background is explained in detail in the *International Crisis Group Asia Report* no. 215, 'Waging Peace: ASEAN and the Thai-Cambodian Border Conflict' (6 Dec. 2011).

[185] *See* the *International Crisis Group Asia Report* no. 215, 'Waging Peace: ASEAN and the Thai-Cambodian Border Conflict' (6 Dec. 2011), 11–12, 21–2.

[186] Dispute DS371. The WTO dispute settlement mechanism is compulsory.

surrounding Preah Vihear which was going on at exactly the same time. This was possible because the WTO matter did not become enmeshed in the web of Thai domestic politics.[187]

Second point: the three ICJ cases highlight the weakness of the adjudication process where territorial delimitation is the issue. It is a zero-sum game. There is always a loser. The loss may rankle a generation after the court decision, as the Preah Vihear case demonstrates. The loser loses face. That is not desirable in an ASEAN context, the *raison d'être* of ASEAN being to foster trust among the member states. The reluctance to submit territorial disputes to binding adjudication is not confined to ASEAN, as the current spat between Japan and South Korea (Dokdo/Takeshima), and China (Diaoyutai/Senkaku), demostrates. Moreover, it often happens that the loser then decides that it will never again be placed in such a position.[188] This is again not a phenomenon unique to ASEAN. When the ICJ ruled against Colombia in a recent case on territorial delimitation,[189] the latter reacted by withdrawing from the Pact of Bogotá,[190] under which it had accepted the compulsory jurisdiction of the court.

The ASEAN way is to seek compromise, using the Charter and peer pressure as levers. On Armistice Day 2013 the ICJ clarified its 1962 judgment on Preah Vihear. Thailand was obliged to withdraw its forces from the promontory of Preah Vihear and ensure access to the Temple from the Cambodian side.[191] One wonders whether the second pronouncement will have any greater effect than the first in dealing with the roots of the dispute. More promising would be the efforts within ASEAN to find a solution that does not result in a loss of face for one party; a possibility

---

[187] *See* the *International Crisis Group Asia Report* no. 215, 'Waging Peace: ASEAN and the Thai-Cambodian Border Conflict' (6 Dec. 2011), 11–12, 21–2.

[188] Thailand had at one time submitted to the compulsory jurisdiction of the ICJ. A check on the website of the ICJ (www.icj-cij.org) reveals that the Declaration of Thailand recognising compulsory jurisdiction of the ICJ filed on 20 May 1950 appears to have been withdrawn. During the negotiations on the drafting of the ASEAN Charter, Indonesia was keen on not creating a compulsory dispute settlement mechanism. One can only speculate as to the underlying motives in these two examples, but it is probably a fair inference that being on the losing side in the Preah Vihear and Ligitan/Sipadan cases respectively played a part in shaping these countries' attitudes towards compulsory jurisdiction in the settlement of inter-state disputes.

[189] *Territorial and Maritime Dispute (Nicaragua v Colombia)*, judgment dated 19 Nov. 2012. Available at http://www.icj-cij.org/docket/files/124/17164.pdf.

[190] American Treaty on Pacific Settlement, in force on 6 May 1949. Colombia was one of the original signatories on 30 Apr. 1948. It denounced the treaty on 27 Nov. 2012. It was reported that Colombia's president had said, 'Never again should we have to face what happened to us on November 19'. See *The Economist* , 8–14 Dec. 2012, 55.

[191] Request for the Interpretation of the Judgment of 15 June 1962 in the *Case Concerning the Temple of Preah Vihear,* judgment dated 11 Nov. 2013.

would be some sort of joint cooperation to exploit the potential of the area. When two neighbours argue about the ownership of a durian tree, it does not make any sense to let the durians fall and rot on the ground while they try to settle their differences.

What of the ASEAN Charter provisions? At the time that the Preah Vihear dispute was referred to the ICJ, the 2010 Protocol had already been signed, though it was not yet in force. The weakness of the Charter is that there is no mechanism to force a settlement of any dispute. Recourse to the TAC is provided for in Article 24(2) of the Charter, but the TAC mechanism is voluntary. Even if it were mandatory, the TAC route would not produce a legally binding result.

This leads to the third major point: the existence of the ASEAN Charter gave the ASEAN Chair the cover needed to attempt to effect a peaceful resolution of disputes. This happened both in 2008 when Singapore held the Chair and in 2011 when Indonesia was the incumbent. The first attempt by Singaporean Foreign Minister George Yeo proved abortive in the face of resistance by the disputants; one cannot force unwilling parties to compromise, short of sending in troops or imposing sanctions. This is not practical in an ASEAN context, or indeed in any international context.[192] The second attempt by Indonesian Foreign Minister Marty Natalegawa to broker a deal in his capacity as ASEAN Chair was more successful. Faced with peer pressure from the other nine members, the Thais agreed to accept the Indonesian suggestion for the deployment of observers.[193] Whatever the exact words of the Charter may be, it is clear that the actions of the Chair were considered to be fully in accordance with the spirit of the treaty. The Statement issued after the informal Foreign Ministers meeting[194] explicitly referred to the TAC and the Charter as the basis for the intervention of the Chair in the dispute.

The Preah Vihear case is illuminating also because it demonstrates graphically the limitations under which a politically appointed Secretary-General works. The Secretary-General at the time, Dr Surin Pitsuwan, had been Foreign Minister of Thailand in the past and was a member of the ruling Democrat Party. He clearly could not be a neutral interlocutor

[192] Those who complain about the ineffectiveness of the ASEAN Way should ask whether the international community has been any more successful in brokering peace among unwilling parties over the last half century. One need only mention the current situation in Syria and Gaza.

[193] Even though the observers never deployed in the end, the fact is that the fighting stopped and the disputing parties pulled back from the brink. The Security Council recognised the crucial role that ASEAN had played in bringing about this result.

[194] Statement issued by the Chairman after the Informal Meeting of the Foreign Ministers of ASEAN on 22 Feb. 2011.

in a case between his country and Cambodia.[195] However, this was a problem not with the office of the Secretary-General as such but rather with the person who held the post. Under the Charter disputing parties may request the Secretary-General to provide good offices, conciliation or mediation.[196] Potentially, the Secretary-General can play a pivotal role in the settlement of disputes within ASEAN. A Secretary-General who is perceived to be impartial and not beholden to his country of origin could have considerable influence in bringing disputing parties together. So much depends on the personalities involved, however.

The resolution of territorial disputes is primarily a political matter not a legal one. Foreign ministries will take the lead. Although ASEAN states have signed the ASEAN Charter, thereby committing themselves to the rule of law and peaceful settlement of disputes, for the moment *realpolitik* rather than principle will likely continue to govern. Nonetheless, there is some hope for the future. The Chair of ASEAN and the Secretary-General have a potentially significant role to play. It remains to be seen whether the political will can be mustered to follow through on the grand ambitions to create a rules-based ASEAN.

---

[195] When asked how he might assist in resolving the dispute, Dr Surin reportedly quipped, 'This is a dispute between two Buddhist countries over a Hindu temple. What can I, a Muslim, do?'

[196] ASEAN Charter, Article 23(2).

CHAPTER IX.

BUDGET AND FINANCE

Article 29. General Principles

1. ASEAN shall establish financial rules and procedures in accordance with international standards.

These are to be determined by the ASEAN Coordinating Committee upon the recommendation of the Committee of Permanent Representatives: Article 30(4). The ASEAN Secretariat Financial Rules and Procedure (AFRP) were adopted on 8 April 2010.[1] The AFRP are in accordance with International Public Sector Accounting Standards (IPSAS).[2]

Rigorous financial rules and procedures were a pressing matter for ASEAN at the time that the Charter was being drafted. The perennial issue of serious resource constraints prevented the ASEAN Secretariat from playing a more effective role and in particular from hiring and retaining qualified staff. Despite the drastic increases in the number of ASEAN meetings in various sectors and the resultant increased workload for the Secretariat, member states had been generally resistant to all but minimal budget increases. The implications of this policy were highlighted when the Secretariat's financial staff struggled to explain inconsistencies in their own procedures to the working groups tasked with following up on implementation of the Charter. To make matters worse, it had become clear that a number of member states were consistently in arrears in the contributions, despite repeated reminders.

---

[1] Joint Communiqué of the Forty-third ASEAN Foreign Ministers Meeting, 19-20 July 2010 in Hanoi, Vietnam, para 8. The ASEAN Secretariat Financial Rules and Procedure were adopted by the Sixth Meeting of the ASEAN Coordinating Council.

[2] ASEAN Secretariat Financial Rules and Procedure, adopted on 8 Apr. 2010 in Hanoi, Vietnam. *See* 'Introduction.'

2. ASEAN shall observe sound financial management policies and practices and budgetary discipline.

This would seem obvious, but it was included to make it clear that there could be no *carte blanche* for waste. Member states are ever mindful that international organisations are notorious for their cost.

3. Financial accounts shall be subject to internal and external audits.

The ASEAN Secretariat Financial Rules and Procedure (AFRP) provide that the Internal Audit and Evaluation Division (IAED) is responsible for internal audit. The functions and responsibilities of the IAED are set out in Chapter 8, rule 2 of the AFRP. According to the organisational chart of the ASEAN Secretariat[3] the IAED is directly under the Secretary-General's office. External audit is covered in rule 3 of Chapter 8 of the AFRP. The external auditor presents its report to an ASEAN Audit Committee (AAC) convened by the member states.

Article 30. Operational Budget and Finances of the ASEAN Secretariat

1. The ASEAN Secretariat shall be provided with the necessary financial resources to perform its functions effectively.

Securing sufficient resources for the Secretariat is a perennial problem for ASEAN. Member states are generally wary of creating an expensive bureaucracy on the European model.

The budget of the ASEAN Secretariat was US$14.33 million in 2011, US$15.76 million in 2013 and US$16.3 million in 2013, hardly an extravagant sum. Even then, the budget could not be fully utilized due to the high staff turnover, which left many positions vacant. Some members of the Committee of Permanent Representatives saw this as evidence that no increase need be considered until ASEC's management was improved.

Separately, the EPG recommended that the operational budget could be supplemented by a Special Fund specifically for projects to narrow

---

3 Available at www.asean.org/asean-secretariat/organisational-structure.

the development gap in ASEAN.[4] Despite the desire of some High Level Task Force (HLTF) delegations to enshrine this, the foreign ministers instructed that there was no need to mention in detail matters of funding in a constitutional document like the ASEAN Charter.[5]

2. The operational budget of the ASEAN Secretariat shall be met by ASEAN Member States through equal annual contributions which shall be remitted in a timely manner.

The Eminent Persons Group (EPG) on the ASEAN Charter had recommended that the principle of equal contribution by member states be retained.[6] When it came to drafting the Charter, however, there was some suggestion initially that the richer member states should contribute more. This was a view espoused by at least one member of the EPG who spoke to the HLTF, but strongly opposed by other EPG members. As a result the EPG's recommendation was to continue with the equal contributions formula in place since the founding of the ASEAN Secretariat. When the HLTF visited Germany and Brussels in early 2007 to be briefed on the European Parliament and the European Union (at the invitation of the German government), it was clarified that Luxembourg, for example, did not pay more than Germany in absolute terms, even though in per capita terms its contribution was greater. Considering the disparity in absolute size of the economies of the ASEAN countries, the larger middle-income members of ASEAN would end up paying more than the small ones. The principle of equal contributions was therefore left in place.

Apart from contributions from the member states, ASEAN receives funds from dialogue partners as well as external organisations. This was one of the reasons for the recommendation that ASEAN should be given a legal personality.[7] The EPG had also urged that 'efforts should also be made to attract more resources from the private business sector, international organisations and ASEAN's friends and partners'.[8] The outgoing Secretary-General in his valedictory report to the ASEAN

---

4 See paras 34 and 65 of the Report of the Eminent Persons Group on the ASEAN Charter.

5 Malaysian HLTF member Tan Sri Ahmad Fuzi bin Abdul Razak states that 'Many within the HLTF itself were unhappy with its inability to achieve a consensus on this': *see* 'Facing Unfair Criticisms', 22.

6 Report of the Eminent Persons Group on the ASEAN Charter, para 33.

7 *See* commentary to Article 3.

8 Report of the Eminent Persons Group on the ASEAN Charter, para 33.

Coordinating Council stated that contributions from dialogue partners exceeded those from member states.

3. The Secretary-General shall prepare the annual operational budget of the ASEAN Secretariat for approval by the ASEAN Coordinating Council upon the recommendation of the Committee of Permanent Representatives.

As to the Secretary-General, *see* Article 11; the ASEAN Coordinating Council, *see* Article 8; the Committee of Permanent Representatives, *see* Article 12.

4. The ASEAN Secretariat shall operate in accordance with the financial rules and procedures determined by the ASEAN Coordinating Council upon the recommendation of the Committee of Permanent Representatives.

The ASEAN Secretariat Financial Rules and Procedure (AFRP) were adopted by the ASEAN Coordinating Council on 8 April 2010.

CHAPTER X.

ADMINISTRATION AND PROCEDURE

Article 31. Chairman of ASEAN

1. The Chairmanship of ASEAN shall rotate annually, based on the alphabetical order of the English names of Member States.

This has been the practice since the inception of ASEAN, initially in respect of the ASEAN Ministerial Meeting.[1] There have been occasional departures from the strict sequence, as for example when Indonesia swopped places with Brunei in 2011 and Myanmar's postponement of its chairmanship from 2006 until 2014. As regards the role of the Chairman, *see* Article 32.

2. ASEAN shall have, in a calendar year, a single Chairmanship by which the Member State assuming the Chairmanship shall chair:

(a) the ASEAN Summit and related summits;
(b) the ASEAN Coordinating Council;
(c) the three ASEAN Community Councils;
(d) where appropriate, the relevant ASEAN Sectoral Ministerial Bodies and senior officials; and
(e) the Committee of Permanent Representatives.

This clause is broadly in line with the recommendation of the Eminent

[1] The 1967 ASEAN Declaration provided for an annual meeting of the Foreign Ministers to be hosted in rotation: *see* Article 3(a).

Persons Group on the ASEAN Charter.[2] The rationale was to improve coordination. Some delegations had suggested that all meetings up to ministerial level should be chaired, though not necessarily hosted, by the ASEAN chair. The majority of the High Level Task Force (HLTF) thought that this was not feasible given the logistical stress of coordinating over 700 ASEAN meetings annually. It was decided at the twelfth meeting of the HLTF that the single chairmanship should be restricted to the Summit, ACC, Community Councils, key sectoral ministerial bodies (ASEAN Foreign Ministers Meeting, ASEAN Economic Ministers Meeting, ASEAN Defence Ministers Meeting, and the ASEAN Finance Ministers Meeting) and Committee of Permanent Representatives (CPR) due to resource constraints.

As to the ASEAN Summit, *see* Article 7; the ASEAN Coordinating Council, *see* Article 8; the ASEAN Community Councils, *see* Article 9; ASEAN sectoral ministerial bodies, *see* Article 10; the Committee of Permanent Representatives, *see* Article 12.

Article 32. Role of the Chairman of ASEAN

The Member State holding the Chairmanship of ASEAN shall:

(a) actively promote and enhance the interests and well-being of ASEAN, including efforts to build an ASEAN Community through policy initiatives, coordination, consensus and cooperation;

Holding the Chair gives a member state international visibility and the opportunity to host world leaders. Each member state that holds the Chair attempts to have at least one major 'deliverable' during the period of its chairmanship. Often, this is no more than a declaration of some sort (often not followed up, which is a major shortcoming of ASEAN, but it would be unrealistic to expect major initiatives every year).

(b) ensure the centrality of ASEAN;

The 'centrality of ASEAN' and its associated concept of ASEAN as a 'primary driving force' or 'in the driver's seat' came into use in the 1990s as ASEAN expanded its role as a convenor in regional and international relations in forums such as the ASEAN Regional Forum (established in 1994) and

2 *See* Report of the Eminent Persons Group, paras 25 and 39.

the ASEAN Plus Three meetings (established in 1997). What this entails was explained by Mr George Yeo, the Foreign Minister of Singapore, in a statement at the closing ceremony of the Forty-first ASEAN Ministerial Meeting when Singapore handed over the Chairmanship to Thailand:[3]

> With the rise of China and India changing the polarity of the world, we must make sure that the political, economic and security architecture of the region takes into account the interest of ASEAN. Over the years, ASEAN, in a peaceful non-threatening way, has helped to bring countries in the region together. We have been able to do this through enlightened diplomacy and by offering our hand of friendship to all the major powers. We must never lose this position. We must take an active interest in regional and global affairs and play a role which is helpful to others. We ensure the centrality of ASEAN in the evolving regional architecture, not by force or assertion but by the openness and neutrality of our position and by our usefulness to others.

ASEAN is open to engagement with all countries and international organisations. The ASEAN Regional Forum brings together the major players in Asia to discuss security issues.[4] Meetings with dialogue partners are a regular feature of ASEAN Summits and Foreign Ministers' Meetings. The 1976 Treaty of Amity and Cooperation in Southeast Asia (TAC) is open to accession by any state, even ones far removed geographically from Southeast Asia.[5]

See also Articles 1(15) and 41(3) regarding the centrality of ASEAN.

---

[3] Issued in Singapore on 24 July 2008. Available on the ASEAN website under the Political-Security Community, Forty-first AMM: www.asean.org/communities/asean-political-security-community.

[4] For an early articulation of centrality of ASEAN in the ARF process, *see* 'ASEAN Regional Forum: A Concept Paper', adopted by the Second ASEAN Regional Forum in Bandar Seri Begawan on 1 Aug. 1995.

[5] At the time of writing the following have acceded to the TAC (*see* the ASEAN Legal Instruments list: http://agreement.asean.org): Papua New Guinea (10 Aug. 1989); the People's Republic of China (8 Oct. 2003); India (8 Oct. 2003); Japan (2 July 2004); Pakistan (2 July 2004); Republic of Korea (27 Nov. 2004); the Russian Federation (29 Nov. 2004); Australia (28 July 2005); Mongolia (28 July 2005); New Zealand (28 July 2005); France (13 Jan. 2007); Timor Leste (13 Jan. 2007); Bangladesh (1 Aug. 2007); Sri Lanka (1 Aug. 2007); the European Communities and European Union (28 May 2009); the Democratic People's Republic of Korea (24 July 2008); the United States of America (22 July 2009); Canada (23 July 2010); Turkey (23 July 2010); Brazil (17 Nov. 2012); the United Kingdom (3 July 2012); Norway (1 July 2013). Serbia has also expressed interest in acceding to the TAC: *see* the Chairman's Statement of the Twenty-first ASEAN Summit (Phnom Penh, Nov. 2012).

(c) ensure an effective and timely response to urgent issues or crisis situations affecting ASEAN, including providing its good offices and such other arrangements to immediately address these concerns;

Provision of good offices by the Chair is covered by Article 23(2). An excellent example of the key role that the Chair can play in dealing with crisis situations is provided by the Preah Vihear case.[6] In 2008 Singaporean Foreign Minister George Yeo convened a meeting in Singapore to help defuse the problem; unfortunately, this proved abortive. In 2011 Indonesian Foreign Minister Marty Natalegawa, who held the Chair at the time, took the initiative to mediate the dispute and managed to broker a ceasefire. He also appeared before the UN Security Council to present ASEAN's position on the issue. The involvement of the Chairman of ASEAN in dispute settlement gives a greater significance to the role of the ASEAN Chair. The effectiveness of the Chair depends largely on the personality of the foreign minister and head of government of the country that holds it; effectiveness is not a function of size alone.

There was an attempt to expand the role of the ASEAN Chair in 2000 by creating an ASEAN Troika at the level of the Foreign Ministers. This was an ad hoc body comprising the current Chair together with the past and future Chair.[7] The idea was to more effectively cooperate on issues affecting peace and stability of the region. Although the idea of the Troika was agreed to by the ASEAN Summit in 1999 and a concept paper adopted in 2000, the troika was never convoked.[8] It nonetheless remains a tantalizing possibility.

(d) represent ASEAN in strengthening and promoting closer relations with external partners; and

As to external partners, *see* Article 41.

---

6 Discussed in the commentary to Articles 23 and 28.

7 An earlier use of a 'troika' was during the Cambodian political crisis of 1997. The 1997 troika was not based on the ASEAN Chairmanship (then held by Malaysia) but comprised the Philippine Secretary of Foreign Affairs Domingo Siazon, Thai Foreign Minister Prachuab Chaiyasarn, and Indonesian Foreign Minister Ali Alatas; *see* Severino, *In Search of an ASEAN Community*, 58.

8 Chairman's Press Statement of the Third Informal ASEAN Summit issued in Manila, Philippines, 28 Nov. 1999. *The ASEAN Troika: A Concept Paper* was adopted at the Thirty-third ASEAN Ministerial Meeting in Bangkok, Thailand, 24–25 July 2000.

(e) carry out such other tasks and functions as may be mandated.

Article 33. Diplomatic Protocol and Practices

ASEAN and its Member States shall adhere to existing diplomatic protocol and practices in the conduct of all activities relating to ASEAN. Any changes shall be approved by the ASEAN Coordinating Council upon the recommendation of the Committee of Permanent Representatives.

Protocol for the use of the ASEAN flag, emblem and anthem has been set out in various guidelines approved by the ACC.[9] A handbook on ASEAN Protocol and Practices was issued by the ASEAN Secretariat in 1995.[10]

As to the ASEAN Coordinating Committee, *see* Article 8; the Committee of Permanent Representatives, *see* Article 12.

Article 34. Working Language of ASEAN

The working language of ASEAN shall be English.

This is a pragmatic choice. None of the other official languages of the ASEAN member states is widely spoken throughout Southeast Asia. The nearest thing to a common language would be Malay, which is the language of Indonesia, Malaysia and Brunei and an official language in Singapore. However, it is not understood in the rest of ASEAN. English was introduced into the former British colonies and protectorates of Malaysia, Singapore and Brunei, as well as the former US colony of the Philippines. English-language competence in these countries tends to be higher than in the other ASEAN member states. Though Myanmar was also a British colony, knowledge of the English language does not seem to be widespread.

From the start, ASEAN functioned in English. The 1967 ASEAN Declaration is written in that language, as are practically all other ASEAN treaties, instruments, declarations, roadmaps, workplans etc. The most significant exception is the Treaty of Amity and Cooperation in Southeast

---

[9] *See* the commentary to Articles 37, 38 and 40 respectively.

[10] ASEAN Secretariat, *Handbook on ASEAN Protocol and Practices* (Jakarta: ASEAN Secretariat, 1995).

Asia (TAC),[11] which was drawn up in the official languages of the original five member states with an agreed common translation into English.[12]

Article 53 provides that the authoritative text of this Charter is the English version, though there are translations into other ASEAN languages. Often the phraseology is curious, which is the result of officials whose first language is not English trying to draft documents in that language. If ASEAN is to progress as a rules-based organisation, at some point a core of competent English-speaking legal draughtsmen will have to be formed. Thus far, drafting of documents has been extremely ad hoc and dependent on the overworked Secretariat and contributions (often of patchy quality) from the legal services of the member states.

The ASEAN Socio-Cultural Community Blueprint[13] states that English is to be promoted as an international business language in the workplace.[14] Interaction with ASEAN's dialogue partners is in the English language.

---

[11] Signed on 24 Feb. 1976 by the Heads of State/Government in Bali at the First ASEAN Summit.

[12] *See* Article 20 of the Treaty of Amity and Cooperation in Southeast Asia.

[13] Adopted by the Heads of State/Government at the Fourteenth ASEAN Summit in Cha-am, Thailand, on 1 Mar. 2009 as an annex to the Cha-Am Hua Hin Declaration on the Roadmap for the ASEAN Community (2009–15).

[14] *See* section A.2 para 12(ii).

CHAPTER XI.

IDENTITY AND SYMBOLS

Article 35. ASEAN Identity

ASEAN shall promote its common ASEAN identity and a sense of belonging among its peoples in order to achieve its shared destiny, goals and values.

The idea of a regional identity for ASEAN was first mentioned in the Bali Concord I, which proposed the study of ASEAN in schools and the support of scholars, writers, artists and mass media representatives to foster a sense of regional identity.[1]

The Vientiane Action Programme[2] and ASEAN Socio-Cultural Community Blueprint[3] list several measures to build an ASEAN identity, none of which have really great potential impact. The challenge is to create an identity common to such a disparate group of countries. Note however Article 2(2)(l), which states the guiding principle of 'respect for the different cultures, languages and religions of the peoples of ASEAN, while emphasising their common values in the spirit of unity in diversity'.

The ASEAN Ministers Responsible for Culture and the Arts have been meeting irregularly since their inaugural meeting in Kuala Lumpur in 2003. ASEAN now has its own anthem, 'The ASEAN Way', composed

---

1 Declaration of ASEAN Concord, signed by the Heads of State/Government at the First ASEAN Summit in Bali on 24 Feb. 1976. Preamble, para 8 and para D(3).

2 Vientiane Action Programme (2004–10), adopted by the ASEAN Heads of State/Government at the Tenth ASEAN Summit on 29–30 Nov. 2004, ASEAN Socio-Cultural Community Plan of Action, Annex 3, section 3.4.

3 Adopted by the Heads of State/Government at the Fourteenth ASEAN Summit in Cha-Am, Thailand, on 1 Mar. 2009 as an annex to the Cha-Am Hua Hin Declaration on the Roadmap for the ASEAN Community (2009–15). *See* section E of the Blueprint, Building ASEAN identity.

by Kittikhun Sodprasert, Sampow Triudom and Payom Valaipatchra: *see* Article 40 below. ASEAN day is 8 August, the day the ASEAN Declaration was signed in 1967: *see* Article 39. An ASEAN flag was adopted by the Foreign Ministers at the Twenty-seventh ASEAN Ministerial Meeting in Bangkok in July 1994:[4] *see* Article 37. The flag, together with the ASEAN emblem, are probably the most recognisable ASEAN symbols.

A 2007 study on ASEAN awareness and identity commissioned by the ASEAN Foundation among university students in all ten countries found that over 75 per cent had positive attitudes towards ASEAN and would consider themselves citizens of ASEAN. Enthusiasm about ASEAN was strongest in the newer member states of the CLMV, while ambivalence was highest in Singapore.[5] Nonetheless, not even the most optimistic of ASEAN's supporters could realistically claim that there is anything like a pan-ASEAN identity, even in an embryonic form. There is no generally accepted word as yet to designate a citizen of ASEAN, as one might speak of a European or African or Latin American. It is not generally accepted practice to call people from ASEAN 'Southeast Asians' or perhaps 'Aseanese'.

Article 36. Asean Motto

The ASEAN motto shall be: 'One Vision, One Identity, One Community'

This was originally the theme of the Eleventh ASEAN Summit, held in Kuala Lumpur, Malaysia, from 12–14 December 2005. The Kuala Lumpur Declaration on the Establishment of the ASEAN Charter was signed at this summit. The Eminent Persons Group on the ASEAN Charter (EPG) was also established then. The EPG recommended the adoption of this phrase as ASEAN's motto.[6]

---

4 Joint Communiqué of the Twenty-seventh ASEAN Ministerial Meeting, 22–23 July 1994 in Bangkok, Thailand, para 27.

5 *Awareness of and Attitudes Toward ASEAN.* Research conducted on behalf of the ASEAN Foundation by Dr Eric C. Thompson, National University of Singapore and Dr Chulanee Thianthai, Chulalongkorn University, available at www.aseanfoundation.org/documents/FA-New_%20Asean_Convert_lowres.pdf.

6 Report of the Eminent Persons Group on the ASEAN Charter, para 68.

Article 37. ASEAN Flag

The ASEAN flag shall be as shown in Annex 3.

The ASEAN flag was first adopted by the Foreign Ministers at the Twenty-seventh ASEAN Ministerial Meeting (Bangkok, July 1994) as 'a symbol of ASEAN cooperation and solidarity in promoting the common aspirations of Member Countries for peace and prosperity in the region'.[7] At that time there were only six rice stalks, representing the ASEAN-6. The new flag with ten rice stalks was adopted in 1997. The red, yellow and blue colours were chosen to represent the main colours of the flags of the ASEAN member states of the time (prior to Myanmar's change of flag in 2010). Blue represents peace and stability; red represents courage and dynamism; white denotes purity; yellow symbolises prosperity. The ten stalks 'represent the dream of ASEAN's Founding Fathers for an ASEAN comprising all the ten countries of Southeast Asia bound together in friendship and solidarity'. The circle represents the unity of ASEAN.[8]

Guidelines on the Use of the ASEAN Flag were adopted by the ASEAN Coordinating Council at its eighth meeting in Jakarta on 6 May 2011.[9] The flag is displayed at diplomatic and consular missions of ASEAN member states alongside the national flag.

Article 38. ASEAN Emblem

The ASEAN emblem shall be as shown in Annex 4.

The ASEAN emblem predates the ASEAN flag. Originally, it had five rice stalks to represent the original five member states. These were coloured brown to stand for strength and stability. They were set in a yellow field with the word 'ASEAN' below them. The number of rice stalks was increased to ten on the occasion of ASEAN's thirtieth anniversary in 1997.[10]

The significance of the ASEAN Emblem is similar to that of the flag. The colours reflect the main colours of the crests of all ASEAN member states. The Emblem itself represents a stable, peaceful, united and dynamic ASEAN. Blue represents peace and stability; red represents courage and

---

[7] Joint Communiqué of the Twenty-seventh ASEAN Ministerial Meeting, 22-23 July 1994 in Bangkok, Thailand, para 27.

[8] Annex 3 of the ASEAN Charter.

[9] 'ASEAN Flag,' ASEAN Secretariat, online: www.asean.org/asean/about-asean/asean-flag.

[10] *See* 'The Founding of ASEAN', the first chapter in Flores and Abad, *ASEAN at 30*, available at http://www.asean.org/news/item/asean-at-30'.

dynamism; white denotes purity; yellow symbolises prosperity. The ten stalks 'represent the dream of ASEAN's Founding Fathers for an ASEAN comprising all the ten countries of Southeast Asia bound together in friendship and solidarity'. The circle represents the unity of ASEAN.[11]

Guidelines on the Use of the ASEAN Emblem were approved by the ASEAN Coordinating Council (ACC) at its sixth meeting in Hanoi, Vietnam, on 8 April 2010.[12] Member states are encouraged to use the emblem at ASEAN-related functions, placed to the right of the national symbols.

Article 39. ASEAN Day

The eighth of August shall be observed as ASEAN Day.

This is the day on which the ASEAN Declaration (also known as the Bangkok Declaration) was signed in 1967 by the Foreign Ministers of the five founding states, viz, Indonesia, Malaysia, the Philippines, Singapore and Thailand.

Article 40. ASEAN Anthem

ASEAN shall have an anthem.

The ASEAN anthem is 'The ASEAN Way', composed by Kittikhun Sodprasert and Sampow Triudom, with lyrics by Payom Valaipatchra. It was chosen after the adoption of the Charter, through an ASEAN song competition launched in August 2008 and open to the public in all ten ASEAN countries. The top prize was US$20,000.[13] The new anthem was first publicly sung at the ceremony to mark the coming into force of the ASEAN Charter held at the ASEAN Secretariat on 15 December 2008.[14] 'The ASEAN Way' replaced the unofficial 'ASEAN Hymn' composed by Ryan Cayabyab, with lyrics by Nicanor Tiongson.[15]

---

[11] Annex 4 of the ASEAN Charter.

[12] *See* 'ASEAN Emblem,' ASEAN Secretariat, online: www.asean.org/asean/about-asean/asean-emblem.

[13] '$20,000 ASEAN Song-Writing Contest on,' *Inquirer.net* (11 Sept. 2008), online: http://globalnation.inquirer.net/news/breakingnews/view/20080911-159959/20000-ASEAN-song-writing-contest-on

[14] *See* 'New ASEAN Anthem Sung', reported in *Viva News* 16 Dec. 2008. The English translation of the report is available at http://us.en.news.viva.co.id/news/read/15885-new_asean_anthem_sung.

[15] *See* the website of the Southeast Asian Ministers of Education Organization (SEAMEO), available at http://www.seameo-innotech.org/SEAtoolkit/index.php/teaching-materials-images/itemlist/category/9-audio.

Guidelines on the Use of the ASEAN Anthem were adopted by the ASEAN Coordinating Council at its sixth meeting in Hanoi on 8 April 2010.[16] The guidelines prescribe that the anthem is not to be used for commercial purposes or political propaganda. The anthem is to be played at ASEAN formal meetings and activities, including those with dialogue partners. The guidelines declare that the anthem is 'under the copyright of ASEAN'. The Secretariat is entrusted with the role of overseeing its proper use.

The member states are encouraged to translate the lyrics into their local languages. The English lyrics are as follows:[17]

> Raise our flag high, sky high
> Embrace the pride in our heart
> ASEAN we are bonded as one
> Looking out to the world
> For peace, our goal from the very start
> And prosperity to last.
> We dare to dream, we care to share
> Together for ASEAN
> We dare to dream
> We care to share, for it's the way of ASEAN.

It has been remarked that the lyrics reflect little understanding of the 'ASEAN Way' as that term is commonly understood in diplomatic and official circles since the 1970s. Diplomatically speaking, the 'ASEAN Way' is an unwritten set of principles emphasising respect for the sovereignty of member states, non-interference in one another's internal affairs and consensus-based decision making.[18] The Charter itself makes no reference to this term. The misunderstanding of the term in the ASEAN Anthem is due to the fact that the songwriters were not diplomats or officials.

---

16 'ASEAN Anthem,' ASEAN Secretariat, available at: www.asean.org/asean/about-asean/asean-anthem.

17 The music and lyrics are reproduced at the end of the ASEAN Annual Report. *See* the latest 2012-13 Annual Report, 88.

18 *See* Severino, *In Search of an ASEAN Community*, chapter 1.

CHAPTER XII.
EXTERNAL RELATIONS

Article 41. Conduct of External Relations

1. ASEAN shall develop friendly relations and mutually beneficial dialogue, cooperation and partnerships with countries and sub-regional, regional and international organisations and institutions.

The aim of ASEAN diplomacy is to have friendly relations with everyone and to keep Southeast Asia peaceful and free of big-power rivalries.

From its early beginnings in the '70s ASEAN's external relations have grown significantly. There are now eleven dialogue partners,[1] a ministerial level 'sectoral partnership' with Pakistan, and regular contacts with other international and regional organisations. The Post-Ministerial Conferences (PMC) held after the ASEAN Ministerial Meetings (AMM) provide an opportunity to engage these partners, as do the meetings in conjunction with the year-end ASEAN Summits. In 1997 an ASEAN plus Three (APT) process was inaugurated, bringing ASEAN together with China, Japan and South Korea. This involves an annual summit between ASEAN and the three countries, usually (but not invariably) held back-to-back with the ASEAN Summit.[2] An East Asia Summit (EAS) was established in 2005, involving the Heads of State/Government of the ASEAN member states as

---

[1] ASEAN's dialogue partners are Australia, Canada, China, the European Union, India, Japan, New Zealand, the Republic of Korea, Russia, the United Nations Development Programme and the United States. For a full list of ASEAN's external relations partners see http://www.asean.org/asean/external-relations. *See* commentary to Articles 42 and 44.

[2] An ASEAN plus Three (APT) Commemorative Summit was held in Phnom Penh on 19 Nov. 2012 to mark the 15th anniversary of APT cooperation.

well as Australia, China, India, Japan, South Korea and New Zealand.[3] In 2011 Russia and the United States joined the EAS process.

The ASEAN Regional Forum (ARF)[4] was established after the Twenty-sixth ASEAN Ministerial Meeting and Post-Ministerial Conference, held in Singapore on 23–25 July 1993 to discuss security in Southeast Asia and the wider region.[5] The first ARF, comprising Foreign Ministers of the ARF member countries, was held in Bangkok on 25 July 1994.[6]

The ASEAN Defence Ministers' Meeting (ADMM) has been broadened into the ADMM Plus[7] to discuss five areas of practical cooperation, viz, maritime security, counter-terrorism, humanitarian assistance and disaster relief, peacekeeping operations and military medicine. The inaugural meeting took place in Hanoi on 12 October 2010.

As regards the status of external parties and relations with international organisations, *see* commentary to Articles 44 and 45.

2. The external relations of ASEAN shall adhere to the purposes and principles set forth in this Charter.

One of the key guiding principles of ASEAN in its external relations is that it should remain outward-looking, inclusive and non-discriminatory: *see* Article 2(2)(m). Keeping Southeast Asia peaceful and free of big-power rivalries has been the cornerstone of ASEAN since its inception, and certainly since the promulgation of the Zone of Peace, Freedom and Neutrality Declaration (ZOPFAN) Declaration.[8]

---

3 *See* the Chairman's Statement of the Tenth ASEAN Summit held in Vientiane (Nov. 2004) para 21.

4 A paper setting out the aims of the ARF was adopted at the Second ASEAN Regional Forum in Bandar Seri Begawan on 1 Aug. 1995: see the ASEAN Regional Forum: A Concept Paper.

5 Joint Communiqué of the Twenty-sixth ASEAN Ministerial Meeting and Post-Ministerial Conference in Singapore, 23–25 July 1993, para 8.

6 The current participants besides the ASEAN member states are Australia, Bangladesh, Canada, China, North Korea, the European Union, India, Japan, Mongolia, New Zealand, Pakistan, Papua New Guinea, South Korea, Russia, Sri Lanka, Timor-Leste and the United States of America.

7 This includes eight other countries: Australia, China, India, Japan, New Zealand, South Korea, Russia and the United States.

8 Signed in Kuala Lumpur on 27 Nov. 1971 by the Foreign Ministers of Indonesia (Mr Adam Malik), Malaysia (Tun Abdul Razak, who was by then Prime Minister and Foreign Minister), the Philippines (Mr Carlos Romulo), Singapore (Mr S. Rajaratnam) and Thailand (Mr Thanat Khoman, then Special Envoy of the National Executive Council). For the background to this *see* Severino, *In Search of an ASEAN Community*, 166–7.

3. ASEAN shall be the primary driving force in regional arrangements that it initiates and maintain its centrality in regional cooperation and community building.

The 'centrality of ASEAN' and its associated concept of ASEAN as a 'primary driving force' or 'in the driver's seat' came into use in the 1990s as ASEAN expanded its role as a convenor in regional and international relations in forums such as the ASEAN Regional Forum (established in 1994)[9] and the ASEAN Plus Three (established in 1997). What this entails was explained by Mr George Yeo, the Foreign Minister of Singapore, in a statement at the closing ceremony of the Forty-first ASEAN Ministerial Meeting when Singapore handed over the Chairmanship to Thailand:[10]

> 'With the rise of China and India changing the polarity of the world, we must make sure that the political, economic and security architecture of the region takes into account the interest of ASEAN. Over the years, ASEAN, in a peaceful non-threatening way, has helped to bring countries in the region together. We have been able to do this through enlightened diplomacy and by offering our hand of friendship to all the major powers. We must never lose this position. We must take an active interest in regional and global affairs and play a role which is helpful to others. We ensure the centrality of ASEAN in the evolving regional architecture, not by force or assertion but by the openness and neutrality of our position and by our usefulness to others'.

ASEAN is open to engagement with all countries and international organisations. The ASEAN Regional Forum brings together the major players in Asia to discuss security issues. Meetings with dialogue partners are a regular feature of ASEAN Summits and Foreign Ministers' Meetings. The 1976 Treaty of Amity and Cooperation in Southeast Asia (TAC) is open to accession by any state, even ones far removed geographically from Southeast Asia.[11] The principal objective of ASEAN diplomacy is to be

---

9 For an early articulation of centrality of ASEAN in the ARF process, *see* the ASEAN Regional Forum: A Concept Paper, adopted by the Second ASEAN Regional Forum in Bandar Seri Begawan on 1 Aug. 1995.

10 Issued in Singapore on 24 July 2008. 'Statement by Mr George Yeo, Minister for Foreign Affairs of Singapore and Chairman of the 41st ASEAN Standing Committee at the Closing Ceremony of the 41st ASEAN Ministerial Meeting and Handing Over of the ASEAN Standing Committee,' ASEAN Secretariat, available at: www.asean.org/.

11 At the time of writing the following have acceded to the TAC (see the ASEAN Legal Instruments list at http://agreement.asean.org): Papua New Guinea (10 Aug. 1989); the People's Republic of China (8 Oct. 2003); India (8 Oct. 2003); Japan (2 July 2004);

friends with everyone but remain in the driver's seat when it comes to matters affecting peace and security in Southeast Asia.

See also Article 41(1) on Conduct of External Relations; Articles 1(15) and 2(2)(m) regarding the centrality of ASEAN.

4. In the conduct of external relations of ASEAN, Member States shall, on the basis of unity and solidarity, coordinate and endeavour to develop common positions and pursue joint actions.

Proposals for ASEAN to develop a common foreign policy were made as early as 1976[12] and championed over time by various member states hoping to enhance ASEAN's international clout. The EPG Report highlighted the need for ASEAN to 'improve its internal coordination and speak with one clear and authoritative voice.'[13] However, there still remains a certain wariness about ASEAN common positions in the style of the European Union, especially on the part of the smaller member states who fear an erosion of sovereignty. ASEAN will not adopt a 'European Union-like common foreign and security policy', as was made clear by Indonesian President Susilo Bambang Yudhoyono[14] early in 2011 when Indonesia took the Chair of ASEAN.

Nonetheless, the Bali Declaration on ASEAN Community in a Global Community of Nations (Bali Concord III) was signed by the Heads of State/Government at the Nineteenth ASEAN Summit.[15] This adopted a common platform on global issues, to be realised by 2022.[16]

Pakistan (2 July 2004); Republic of Korea (27 Nov. 2004); the Russian Federation (29 Nov. 2004); Australia (28 July 2005); Mongolia (28 July 2005); New Zealand (28 July 2005); France (13 Jan. 2007); Timor Leste (13 Jan. 2007); Bangladesh (1 Aug. 2007); Sri Lanka (1 Aug. 2007); the European Communities and European Union (28 May 2009); the Democratic People's Republic of Korea (24 July 2008); the United States of America (22 July 2009); Canada (23 July 2010); Turkey (23 July 2010); Brazil (17 Nov. 2012); the United Kingdom (3 July 2012); Norway (1 July 2013). Serbia has also expressed interest in acceding to the TAC: see the Chairman's Statement of the Twenty-first ASEAN Summit (Phnom Penh, Nov. 2012).

[12] The 1976 Declaration of ASEAN Concord calls for 'Strengthening of political solidarity by promoting the harmonization of views, coordinating position and where possible and desirable, taking common actions': *see* Para A(7).

[13] Report of the Eminent Persons Group on the ASEAN Charter, para 53.

[14] 'Repositioning ASEAN in New World Order', *Straits Times,* 24 Feb. 2011.

[15] Held in Bali from 14 to 19 Nov. 2011.

[16] A Bali Concord III Plan of Action 2013–17 was adopted at the Twenty-first ASEAN Summit in Phnom Penh, Cambodia, on 18 Nov. 2012.

So far, there has been little beyond anodyne statements such as ASEAN's Six-Point Principles on the South China Sea.[17] This followed the very public disagreement between Cambodia on one hand and the Philippines and Vietnam on the other over the latter two countries' disputes with China in the South China Sea. This led to an unprecedented failure to issue a joint communiqué at the conclusion of the Forty-fifth ASEAN Ministerial Meeting held in Phnom Penh from 9 to 13 July 2012. Cambodia came under intense criticism and felt it necessary to issue a press statement on 26 July 2012 defending its chairmanship. The lack of fraternal feeling was again in evidence at the subsequent Twenty-first ASEAN Summit in Phnom Penh,[18] where the Cambodian chair again came in for criticism over the way it handled the South China Sea issue. China has consistently maintained that the bilateral spats it has with individual member states are not an ASEAN-China issue and criticised the Secretary-General for taking sides on account of certain statements he made in May 2014.[19]

The South China Sea problem demonstrates how difficult it is to implement the goal expressed in this Article of developing common positions and pursuing joint actions.

5. The strategic policy directions of ASEAN's external relations shall be set by the ASEAN Summit upon the recommendation of the ASEAN Foreign Ministers Meeting.

From the start ASEAN was driven by the foreign ministries of the member states, the other ministries being kept on the sidelines for the most part. After the First ASEAN Summit (Bali, February 1976) it was clarified that the AMM was the principal organ for the coordination of overall policy direction for ASEAN.[20] The foreign ministers of course have never set policy directions by themselves. Their recommendations go to the ASEAN Summit, which makes the final decision.

As to the ASEAN Summit, *see* Article 7.

---

[17] Issued by the Foreign Ministers in Phnom Penh on 20 July 2012. During the Twenty-fourth ASEAN Summit (held in Nay Pyi Taw, Myanmar) the Foreign Ministers issued a statement expressing their 'serious concerns' regarding developments in the South China Sea. The guarded language points to the difficulty of reconciling the various member states' positions on this explosive issue.

[18] Held in Phnom Penh on 18 Nov. 2012.

[19] *See* 'China demands ASEAN neutrality over South China Sea', *Straits Times,* 19 May 2014: http://www.straitstimes.com/.

[20] This was proclaimed in the Joint Communiqué of the Ninth ASEAN Ministerial Meeting (Manila, June 1976), para 22.

6. The ASEAN Foreign Ministers Meeting shall ensure consistency and coherence in the conduct of ASEAN's external relations.

The ASEAN Foreign Ministers Meeting

The 1967 ASEAN Declaration provided for an annual meeting of foreign ministers, known as the ASEAN Ministerial Meeting (AMM).[21] The ASEAN Standing Committee (ASC) was also established at the same time to support the work of the Foreign Ministers.[22] Initially, this comprised the ambassadors to the host country of the next AMM. In 1992 this was changed to directors-general in charge of ASEAN at the respective foreign ministries, together with the Secretary-General.[23] This was charged with conduct of ASEAN external relations.[24] The role of the ASC has now been taken over by the Committee of Permanent Representatives.[25]

In 1971 senior officials from the ministries of foreign affairs began meeting regularly at the ASEAN Senior Officials' Meeting (ASEAN SOM), a body which was not specifically created by any agreement but which evolved naturally. SOM was established to discuss political issues, especially sensitive ones, before submission to the AMM. The SOM leader was generally the permanent secretary (or his equivalent in countries that did not adopt the British nomenclature) of the ministry. SOM has now been regularised by inclusion in the list of Sectoral Ministerial Bodies in Annex 1.

The AMM is the most durable of the ASEAN institutions and continues to play a significant role in the steering of the organisation. After coming into force of the Charter the AMM was redesignated the ASEAN Foreign Ministers Meeting to reflect its role in the coordination of external relations. Thus, the meeting in Singapore in July 2008 was the last ASEAN Ministerial Meeting.[26] From the next meeting in meeting in Thailand in July 2009 the name was changed to the Foreign Ministers Meeting.[27] The sequence was not broken however, and this meeting is still referred to as

---

21 The very first ASEAN Ministerial Meeting was the one at which the ASEAN Declaration was adopted on 8 Aug. 1967.

22 *See* ASEAN Declaration, Article 3(b).

23 Severino, *In Search of an ASEAN Community*, 22.

24 *See* the Joint Communiqué of the Ninth ASEAN Ministerial Meeting (Manila, June 1976), para 22.

25 *See* the commentary to Article 12.

26 Forty-first ASEAN Ministerial Meeting, Singapore, 17–24 July 2008.

27 Forty-second ASEAN Foreign Ministers Meeting, Phuket, Thailand, 17–23 July 2009.

the Forty-second AMM on the website of the ASEAN Secretariat. There have been annual meetings of the Foreign Ministers since 1967.[28]

In addition to the formal meetings, the Foreign Ministers held special meetings when necessary.[29] The AMM evolved into an occasion for engaging the dialogue partners[30] as well, in the Post-Ministerial Conferences (PMC). In 1999 the ASEAN Foreign Ministers' Retreat was inaugurated to enable frank and open discussion of issues of common interest in an informal setting away from the formal proceedings of the AMM.[31] Initially, the retreats were held in conjunction with the AMM but from 2001 separate retreats were hosted by member states other than the AMM host.[32] There is now an additional annual meeting at the sidelines of the UN General Assembly, the Informal ASEAN Ministerial Meeting (IAMM). From its rather modest beginnings the AMM evolved into one of the main motors of ASEAN. The Foreign Ministers' agenda grew steadily over the years, judging by the length and substance of the communiqués issued after each AMM.

As to the ASEAN Foreign Ministers Meeting as an ASEAN Sectoral Body, *see* commentary on Article 10(2).

Coordination of ASEAN's external relations

While the ASEAN Foreign Ministers continue to be the main body in charge of the conduct of ASEAN's external relations, cooperation with external partners is not their exclusive preserve. The Economic Ministers were initially substantively involved with ASEAN's early dialogue meetings with partners including Japan, the European Economic Community, and the United States. When the foreign ministries sought to take sole control of the dialogue process, the Economic Ministers established

---

28 Except for 1970, when the Philippines was host. The meeting was postponed due to disagreements between the Philippines and Malaysia over Sabah. The AMM met again only in Mar. 1971.

29 For instance, five special meetings of the ASEAN Foreign Ministers were held between 1973 and 1985 to discuss the problems in Indochina. It was decided at a special meeting of ASEAN Foreign Ministers on 10 July 1997 to postpone Cambodia's accession to ASEAN because of the fighting between political factions in the country.

30 At the time of writing the dialogue partners are: Australia, Canada, China, the European Union, India, Japan, New Zealand, the Republic of Korea, the Russian Federation and the USA, together with the United Nations Development Programme. See commentary to Articles 42 and 44.

31 Joint Communiqué of the Thirty-second ASEAN Ministerial Meeting, 23–24 July 1999, para 5.

32 Joint Communiqué of the Thirty-fourth ASEAN Ministerial Meeting, 23–24 July 2001, para 8.

direct consultations with their trade counterparts.[33] An increasing number of ASEAN ministerial bodies have followed suit and conduct their own meetings directly with foreign interlocutors.[34] With the increasing number of meetings there is danger of conflicting initiatives taken by different sectoral bodies. The Foreign Ministers Meeting was therefore delegated the responsibility of ensuring 'consistency and coherence', no easy task given the sensitivity about hierarchy amongst ministers in ASEAN member states. The mechanism for this coordinating function was not spelled out in the Charter.

Accreditation of foreign ambassadors

The ASEAN Foreign Ministers Meeting decides on the accreditation of ambassadors to ASEAN: *see* Article 46.

7. ASEAN may conclude agreements with countries or sub-regional, regional and international organisations and institutions. The procedures for concluding such agreements shall be prescribed by the ASEAN Coordinating Council in consultation with the ASEAN Community Councils.

The 2011 Rules of Procedure for Conclusion of International Agreements by ASEAN (ROP) were adopted at the Ninth ASEAN Coordinating Council meeting in Bali on 17 November 2011.[35] They apply only to agreements that create rights and obligations for ASEAN as an entity distinct from the member states.[36] Any proposal for conclusion of such an agreement goes through the Committee of Permanent Representatives (CPR) to the ASEAN Foreign Ministers Meeting.[37] Either the CPR or the Foreign Ministers will appoint representatives to negotiate the agreement.[38] The

---

33 Severino, *In Search of an ASEAN Community*, 258–9.

34 For example, in the defence ministers convened an ADMM-Plus in Hanoi on 12 Oct. 2010. ADMM-Plus includes Australia, China, India, Japan, New Zealand, the Republic of Korea, the Russian Federation and the United States. It has its own senior officials meeting, the ADSOM-Plus.

35 The text is available in the database of the Centre for International Law, National University of Singapore: cil.nus.edu.sg.

36 2011 Rules of Procedure for Conclusion of International Agreements by ASEAN, rule 2. As to the legal personality of ASEAN, *see* Article 3.

37 2011 Rules of Procedure for Conclusion of International Agreements by ASEAN, rule 3.

38 Ibid.

draft text of the agreement must be submitted to the relevant ASEAN Sectoral Ministerial body at senior officials-level for endorsement.[39] The endorsed agreement is then submitted through the CPR to the Foreign Ministers Meeting for formal confirmation.[40]

Since the Secretary-General is designated as the representative of ASEAN in the Agreement on the Establishment of the ASEAN Secretariat[41], it might be thought that it would be logical to appoint him as representative to negotiate agreements. The Eminent Persons Group envisaged that the Secretary-General would be empowered to sign 'non-sensitive' agreements on behalf of the member states;[42] implicit in this is that he would also be in charge of the negotiations. However, the whole process of concluding international agreements is now subject to oversight by the CPR, which is subordinate in status to the Secretary-General.[43] This may militate against appointing him as the representative for negotiations except for high-level agreements under the direct supervision of the Foreign Ministers or the relevant sectoral bodies.

The Secretary-General may be appointed to sign agreements on behalf of ASEAN,[44] often a purely symbolic act. Thus, for example, the Secretary-General executed the 2012 Agreement on Hosting and Granting Privileges and Immunities between ASEAN and Indonesia[45] and the 2012 Memorandum of Understanding between the Association of Southeast Asian Nations and the Asian Development Bank.[46]

As to the ASEAN Coordinating Council, *see* Article 8; the ASEAN Community Councils, *see* Article 9.

---

39 Ibid., rule 7.

40 Ibid., rule 8.

41 Agreement on Establishment of the ASEAN Secretariat 1976, Article 3(1)(5)(a) as amended by the 1992 Protocol.

42 Report of the Eminent Persons Group on the ASEAN Charter, para 37.

43 *See* commentary to Article 11.

44 2011 Rules of Procedure for Conclusion of International Agreements by ASEAN, rule 8(5).

45 Signed on 2 Apr. 2012 in Phnom Penh, Cambodia.

46 Signed on 4 Apr. 2012 in Phnom Penh, Cambodia.

Article 42. Dialogue Coordinator

1. Member States, acting as Country Coordinators, shall take turns to take overall responsibility in coordinating and promoting the interests of ASEAN in its relations with the relevant Dialogue Partners, regional and international organisations and institutions.

This article formalises the pre-existing practice regarding dialogue coordinators. Each member state remains dialogue coordinator with a Dialogue Partner (of which there are ten plus the United Nations Development Programme) for three years.[47] The status of Dialogue Partner is conferred by the ASEAN Foreign Ministers Meeting: *see* Article 44(1). As exceptions to this system of rotation, the ASEAN Chair coordinates the ASEAN Plus Three and East Asia Summit processes, while the ASEAN Secretariat is the dialogue coordinator for the United Nations Development Programme and Pakistan (which is a sectoral dialogue partner). There are also rotating Coordinators for ASEAN's relations with other regional groupings.

2. In relations with the external partners, the Country Coordinators shall, inter alia:

(a) represent ASEAN and enhance relations on the basis of mutual respect and equality, in conformity with ASEAN's principles;
(b) co-chair relevant meetings between ASEAN and external partners; and
(c) be supported by the relevant ASEAN Committees in Third Countries and International Organisations.

As to the ASEAN Committees in Third Countries and International Organisations, *see* Article 43.

---

[47] The list of dialogue coordinators is to be found on the ASEAN Secretariat website: *see* www.asean.org/asean/external-relations/asean-dialogue-coordinator.

Article 43. ASEAN Committees in Third Countries and International Organisations

1. ASEAN Committees in Third Countries may be established in non-ASEAN countries comprising heads of diplomatic missions of ASEAN Member States. Similar Committees may be established relating to international organisations. Such Committees shall promote ASEAN's interests and identity in the host countries and international organisations.

ASEAN diplomats have found that it is more effective to hunt in packs. A group of ten ambassadors generally has far better access than individual ambassadors alone. ASEAN Committees in Third Countries (ACTC) are a regular feature of diplomatic life in the capitals where the member states have representation. Not every capital has all ten members present, so it is not always the case that an ASEAN Committee will have a full complement of ten.[48] Chairmanship of the Committee rotates alphabetically. The first ACTC was the ASEAN Brussels Committee (1972).

The ASEAN diplomatic community often also includes spouses and children in its non-official activities. Not only diplomats but also non-diplomatic staff from the embassies and consulates participate, fostering a family feeling in a foreign land. This notion of 'family' is often invoked in cooperative ventures by ASEAN missions abroad.

If there is such a thing as an incipient ASEAN identity, it is to be found among the ACTC, especially in collective dealings with the officials of the host country or organisation or with business, cultural and social groups.[49]

The relevant Committees support the Country Coordinator in relations with external partners: *see* Article 42(2)(c).

2. The ASEAN Foreign Ministers Meeting shall determine the rules of procedure of such Committees.

Terms of Reference and Guidelines for the Organization of ASEAN Committees in Third Countries were originally adopted by the ASEAN Standing Committee (ASC) in Kuala Lumpur, Malaysia, on 17 October

[48] At the time of writing there are 37 such committees in various countries and international organisations. In only 12 are all the member states represented. *See* www.asean.org/asean/asean-structure/committees-abroad.

[49] Based on the author's experience as ambassador and a member of the ASEAN Committees in Bonn, Berlin and Brussels.

1979.[50] These were superseded by the 2010 Terms of Reference and Rules of Procedure for the ASEAN Committees in Third Countries and International Organisations.[51]

Article 44. Status of External Parties

1. In conducting ASEAN's external relations, the ASEAN Foreign Ministers Meeting may confer on an external party the formal status of Dialogue Partner, Sectoral Dialogue Partner, Development Partner, Special Observer, Guest, or other status that may be established henceforth.

ASEAN has at present eleven dialogue partners: Australia,[52] New Zealand,[53] Canada,[54] Japan,[55] the European Union,[56] the United States,[57] the United Nations Development Programme,[58] South Korea,[59] China,[60]

---

[50] *See* www.asean.org/communities/asean-political-security-community/category/senior-officials-levels.

[51] Adopted at the Forty-third ASEAN Foreign Ministers Meeting in Hanoi on 20 July 2010.

[52] Australia became the very first formal dialogue partner in 1974. *See* the Overview of ASEAN-Australia Dialogue Relations: www.asean.org/news/item/overview-of-asean-australia-dialogue-relations.

[53] New Zealand became a dialogue partner in 1975. *See* the Overview of ASEAN-New Zealand Dialogue Relations: www.asean.org/news/item/asean-new-zealand-dialogue-relations-2.

[54] The first meeting between ASEAN and Canada took place in 1977. *See* ASEAN-Canada Dialogue Relations: www.asean.org/news/item/asean-canada-dialogue-relations-2.

[55] Japan's informal dialogue partnership began in 1973 and was formalised in Mar. 1977 with the convening of the ASEAN-Japan Forum. *See* the Overview of ASEAN-Japan Dialogue Relations: www.asean.org/news/item/asean-japan-dialogue-relations.

[56] Cooperation with what was then the European Economic Community began in 1977 at the Tenth ASEAN Ministerial Meeting (July 1977) and institutionalised with the signing of the ASEAN-EU Cooperation Agreement on 7 Mar. 1980. *See* ASEAN-EU Dialogue Relations: www.asean.org/news/item/asean-eu-dialogue-relations.

[57] Dialogue relations with the US were established in 1977. *See* the Overview of ASEAN-US Dialogue Relations: www.asean.org/news/item/overview-of-asean-us-dialogue-relations.

[58] The United Nations Development Programme was engaged with ASEAN practically from the start in 1967. It became a dialogue partner in 1977. *See* www.asean.org/asean/external-relations/undp.

[59] South Korea began as a sectoral dialogue partner in 1989 and became a full dialogue partner at the Twenty-fourth ASEAN Ministerial Meeting in 1991. *See* the Overview of ASEAN-Republic of Korea Dialogue Relations: www.asean.org/news/item/asean-republic-of-korea-dialogue-relations.

[60] China's formal engagement with ASEAN began in 1991, when her Foreign Minister attended the Twenty-fourth ASEAN Ministerial Meeting in Kuala Lumpur as a guest of the Malaysian government. China became a full dialogue partner in 1996. *See* the

Russia[61] and India.[62] Pakistan is a sectoral dialogue partner.[63] Each dialogue partnership is coordinated by a member state for three years.[64] The ASEAN Secretariat coordinates relations with Pakistan and the United Nations Development Programme.

Papua New Guinea was accorded the status of special observer in 1976. A delegation from Papua New Guinea first attended the ASEAN Ministerial Meeting in 1976 as an observer and guest of the Philippine government.[65]

2. External parties may be invited to ASEAN meetings or cooperative activities without being conferred any formal status, in accordance with the rules of procedure.

The practice seems to have begun with the Fourth ASEAN Ministerial Meeting (March 1971) in Manila, at which representatives of the South Vietnam and the Khmer Republic were present as guests of the host government. Since then, there have been many instances of guests attending ASEAN meetings, often as a prelude to more formal relations of some sort.

Article 45. Relations with the United Nations System and Other International Organisations and Institutions

1. ASEAN may seek an appropriate status with the United Nations system as well as with other sub-regional, regional, international organisations and institutions.

Overview of ASEAN-China Dialogue Relations: www.asean.org/news/item/asean-china-dialogue-relations.

[61] Russia, like China, began formal engagement with ASEAN in 1991 when her Foreign Minister attended the Twenty-fourth ASEAN Ministerial Meeting in Kuala Lumpur as a guest of the Malaysian government. Russia became a full dialogue partner in 1996. *See* the Overview of ASEAN-Russia Dialogue Relations: www.asean.org/news/item/asean-russia-dialogue-relations.

[62] India started as a sectoral dialogue partner in 1992 and became a full dialogue partner in 1995. *See* ASEAN-India Dialogue Relations: www.asean.org/news/item/asean-india-dialogue-relations.

[63] Pakistan became a sectoral dialogue partner in 1993. *See* the Overview of ASEAN-Pakistan Sectoral Dialogue Cooperation: www.asean.org/news/item/overview-of-asean-pakistan-sectoral-dialogue-cooperation-2.

[64] *See* commentary to Article 42(1).

[65] *See* the Joint Communiqué of the Ninth ASEAN Ministerial Meeting, Manila, para 3.

ASEAN has observer status at the United Nations, though without a permanent mission.[66] The General Assembly resolution conferring this status was adopted on 4 December 2006.[67]

2. The ASEAN Coordinating Council shall decide on the participation of ASEAN in other sub-regional, regional, international organisations and institutions.

As to the ASEAN Coordinating Council, *see* Article 8.

Article 46. Accreditation of Non-ASEAN Member States to ASEAN

Non-ASEAN Member States and relevant inter-governmental organisations may appoint and accredit Ambassadors to ASEAN. The ASEAN Foreign Ministers Meeting shall decide on such accreditation.

This was a recommendation of the Eminent Persons Group on the ASEAN Charter.[68] At the time of writing 77 countries and the European Union have accredited ambassadors to ASEAN.[69] Not all of them are resident in Jakarta.

As to the responsibility of the ASEAN Foreign Ministers Meeting for external relations, *see* Article 41(6).

---

[66] *See* UN website www.un.org/en/members/intergovorg.shtml.

[67] Resolution 61/46 Cooperation between the UN and ASEAN dated 4 Dec. 2006.

[68] Report of the Eminent Persons Group on the ASEAN Charter, para 51.

[69] The ASEAN Secretariat maintains a list at http://www.asean.org/news/item/ambassadors-to-asean.

CHAPTER XIII.

GENERAL AND FINAL PROVISIONS

Article 47. Signature, Ratification, Depository and Entry Into Force

1. This Charter shall be signed by all ASEAN Member States.

All the member states signed the ASEAN Charter at the Thirteenth ASEAN Summit in Singapore on 20 November 2007.

2. This Charter shall be subject to ratification by all ASEAN Member States in accordance with their respective internal procedures.

The dates of ratification of the Charter are as follows:[1] Singapore, 18 December 2007; Brunei, 31 January 2008; Laos, 14 February 2008; Malaysia, 14 February 2008; Cambodia, 2 April 2008; Vietnam, 14 March 2008; Myanmar, 14 July 2008; Philippines, 3 November 2008; Indonesia, 14 November 2008; Thailand, 15 November 2008.

3. Instruments of ratification shall be deposited with the Secretary-General of ASEAN who shall promptly notify all Member States of each deposit.

As to the Secretary-General, *see* Article 11. The dates on which the member states deposited their instruments of ratification are as follows:

---

1 Information taken from the list maintained by the ASEAN Secretariat. 'ASEAN Legal Instruments,' *ASEAN Secretariat, see*: agreement.asean.org.

Singapore, 7 January 2008;[2] Brunei, 15 February 2008;[3] Laos, 20 February 2008;[4] Malaysia, 20 February 2008;[5] Vietnam, 4 April 2008;[6] Cambodia, 2 April 2008;[7] Myanmar, 21 July 2008;[8] Philippines, 3 November 2008;[9] Indonesia, 13 November 2008;[10] and finally Thailand, 15 November 2008.[11] It appeared that for ceremonial purposes some instruments of ratification were symbolically handed over to the Secretary-General at whatever convenient opportunity might have arisen after deposit of the instrument of ratification.[12]

4. This Charter shall enter into force on the thirtieth day following the date of deposit of the tenth instrument of ratification with the Secretary-General of ASEAN.

The Charter came into force on 15 December 2008. A special meeting of the Foreign Ministers was held at the ASEAN Secretariat to mark the occasion.[13] The occasion was graced by President Susilo Bambang Yudhoyono of Indonesia.

Article 48. Amendments

1. Any Member State may propose amendments to the Charter.

---

2 ASEAN Secretariat Press Release dated 20 Feb. 2008, see: www.asean.org/asean/asean-charter/media-releases-on-the-asean-charter.

3 Ibid.

4 Ibid.

5 Ibid.

6 ASEAN Secretariat Press Release dated 10 Apr. 2008: www.asean.org/asean/asean-charter/media-releases-on-the-asean-charter.

7 ASEAN Secretariat Press Release dated 18 Apr. 2008: www.asean.org/asean/asean-charter/media-releases-on-the-asean-charter.

8 ASEAN Secretariat Press Release dated 21 July 2008: www.asean.org/asean/asean-charter/media-releases-on-the-asean-charter.

9 ASEAN Secretariat Press Release dated 12 Nov. 2008: www.asean.org/asean/asean-charter/media-releases-on-the-asean-charter.

10 ASEAN Secretariat Press Release dated 13 Nov. 2008: www.asean.org/asean/asean-charter/media-releases-on-the-asean-charter.

11 ASEAN Secretariat Press Release dated 15 Nov. 2008: www.asean.org/asean/asean-charter/media-releases-on-the-asean-charter.

12 For example, Filipino Foreign Secretary Alberto Romulo symbolically handed over the instrument of ratification to the Secretary-General at the Permanent Representation of the Philippines to the UN in New York on 12 Nov. 2008, more than a week after the deposit of the instrument at the ASEAN Secretariat on 3 Nov.

13 ASEAN Secretariat Press Release dated 9 Dec. 2008: www.asean.org/asean/asean-charter/media-releases-on-the-asean-charter.

Annexes 1 (ASEAN Sectoral Ministerial Bodies) and 2 (Entities Associated with ASEAN) may be updated by the Secretary-General on the recommendation of the Committee of Permanent Representatives without having to go through the procedure prescribed in this Article: *see* Articles 10(2) and 16(3).

2. Proposed amendments to the Charter shall be submitted by the ASEAN Coordinating Council by consensus to the ASEAN Summit for its decision.

As to the ASEAN Coordinating Council, *see* Article 8; the ASEAN Summit, *see* Article 7; decisions by consensus, *see* Article 20.

3. Amendments to the Charter agreed to by consensus by the ASEAN Summit shall be ratified by all Member States in accordance with Article 47.

It took almost exactly a year before all the member states ratified the Charter after signing it. One should not expect the process of amendment to proceed much faster.

4. An amendment shall enter into force on the thirtieth day following the date of deposit of the last instrument of ratification with the Secretary-General of ASEAN.

This is the same as for the entry into force of the Charter itself: *see* Article 47(4).

Article 49. Terms of Reference and Rules of Procedure

Unless otherwise provided for in this Charter, the ASEAN Coordinating Council shall determine the terms of reference and rules of procedure and shall ensure their consistency.

As to the ASEAN Coordinating Council, *see* Article 8. Examples of Terms of Reference (TOR) adopted by the ACC include the TOR of the ACC Working Group (ACCWG) to discuss all relevant aspects related to the application by Timor-Leste as well as its possible implications on ASEAN; TOR of the ASEAN Connectivity Coordinating Committee (ACCC); and TOR for the Initiative for ASEAN Integration (IAI) Task Force.

ASEAN institutions have developed pragmatically in response to the changing regional and international environment. This is amply demonstrated by ASEAN itself, which evolved from an association for building trust to the organisation it is today. Ironically, the current emphasis on rules may lead to a proliferation of red tape which will impede the development of effective ASEAN institutions. Too often the 'rules-based' ASEAN envisaged by the Charter is interpreted by member country bureaucrats as necessitating more rules, rather than putting the emphasis on complying with the existing ones and carrying out prior commitments. There is too much focus on forms and procedure rather than the substance of cooperation.[14] ASEAN risks being strangled by the noodle bowl of new rules, regulations and terms of reference.

Article 50. Review

This Charter may be reviewed five years after its entry into force or as otherwise determined by the ASEAN Summit.

As the Charter entered into force on 15 December 2008 it was due for review after 14 December 2013. A High Level Task Force (HLTF) on Strengthening the ASEAN Secretariat and Reviewing the ASEAN Organs was set up in late 2013,[15] as a prelude to possible changes to the Charter.

The original suggestion was that the Charter should be reviewed every five years; this was not hard-coded into the Charter in the end. The ASEAN Summit will decide when the review is to take place. Significantly, there was no mention of review of the Charter in the Chairman's Statement of the Twenty-fourth ASEAN Summit[16] even though the Heads of State/ Governments welcomed the establishment of the new HLTF.

---

[14] A glaring example is the Rules of Procedure on Interpretation of the ASEAN Charter (*see* commentary to Article 51). This prescribes a procedure while robbing the exercise of all legal value.

[15] *See* the Joint Communiqué of the Forty-sixth ASEAN Foreign Ministers' Meeting (held in Bandar Seri Begawan, Brunei, 29–30 June 2013), para 4 and the Chairman's Statement of the Twenty-fourth ASEAN Summit (held in Nay Pyi Taw, Myanmar, 9–10 May 2014), para 81.

[16] Issued on 11 May 2014 in Nay Pyi Taw, Myanmar.

Article 51. Interpretation of the Charter

1. Upon the request of any Member State, the interpretation of the Charter shall be undertaken by the ASEAN Secretariat in accordance with the rules of procedure determined by the ASEAN Coordinating Council.

It was understood by the High Level Task Force (HLTF) drafting the Charter that clauses 1 and 2 of this Article deal with different situations. Clause 1 covers the case where there is no dispute, but a question of interpretation crops up which needs to be clarified. The next clause deals with situations where the interpretation is disputed. This clause also makes clear that the ASEAN Secretariat (ASEC) cannot unilaterally issue interpretations of the Charter without being requested. This again reflects the member states' reluctance to allow ASEC to develop into anything like an independent institution.

During the Charter-drafting process, several delegations proposed that member states should have the option to request an interpretation of specific articles of the ASEAN Charter in instances where no dispute was involved. Some HLTF members referred to the example of the UN system where the Office of Legal Affairs may be requested to provide interpretation or legal advice.[17] As this article was dealt with only at the penultimate meeting of the HLTF in Bandar Seri Begawan (September 2007), discussion was short due to the looming deadline.

It had been suggested by one delegation that requests for interpretation be dealt with by an ASEAN Legal Committee, consisting of representatives from the member states.[18] However, this was considered to be too cumbersome and it was agreed by the HLTF that a beefed-up legal unit of the ASEAN Secretariat could undertake this task.[19] The understanding was that ASEAN Secretariat would be

---

[17] There is a General Legal Division (GLD) of the United Nations Office of Legal Affairs (OLA), the function of which is inter alia 'Interpreting and advising on certain Articles of the Charter, of General Assembly resolutions and Decisions, of the regulations, rules and mandates of programmes and activities, and of other administrative issuances of the Organization': see the description of the GLD on the website of the OLA http://legal.un.org/ola/div_gld.aspx?section=gld.

[18] This suggestion appears to have been resurrected. The possibility of establishing such a committee to address legal issues in future was mentioned in the Chairman's Statement of the Nineteenth ASEAN Summit (Bali, Nov. 2011), para 109.

[19] On a visit to the ASEAN Secretariat in 2012, the author was told by a senior ASEAN official that ASEC still did not have the resources to interpret the Charter. This is why this author and Jean-Claude Piris (formerly Director-General of the Legal Service of the European Council) have argued for the establishment of a proper ASEAN Legal Service. *See* Woon and Piris, *Towards a Rules-Based Community*.

neutral and had the institutional memory of how the Charter and other implementing documents came into being.[20] However, the member-state representatives subsequently charged with implementation evidently thought otherwise. Rules of Procedure (ROP) for the Interpretation of the ASEAN Charter were adopted by the ASEAN Coordinating Council on 2 April 2012. Rule 2(1) states right at the beginning that the interpretation of the ASEAN Secretariat is non-binding and non-authoritative. It does not even represent the view of ASEAN as an organisation.[21] ASEC is obliged to invite member states to provide their views and take these into account when making its interpretation.[22] Basically, what the ROP has done is to rob ASEC of any real role in interpretation of the Charter, contrary to what has been provided. This is a stark example of procedure frustrating the intent of the Charter and of red tape strangling what should have been an expeditious process.

Given the caveat in rule 2(1) of the ROP, one might perhaps be allowed to ask why anyone would bother getting an interpretation from the ASEAN Secretariat. Any interpretation is non-authoritative, non-binding and does not even represent the view of ASEAN as an entity separate from its members. It is a pity that this was allowed to happen. Requests for interpretation do not arise *in vacuo*; presumably a member state would only make such a request in the context of some disagreement with another member state. ASEC is a neutral body and will not be partial to any member state in its interpretation of the Charter. The suggested alternative is to establish a committee consisting of member-state nominees to interpret the Charter. This will introduce an unwelcome degree of partisanship into the process. The member-state nominees (who are unlikely to be very senior) will be bound by any instructions given by the foreign ministries of their respective countries. The whole exercise will become another occasion for diplomatic negotiation rather than the legal process that it should be. This will hardly help in creating the rules-based law-abiding ASEAN that the Charter is supposed to bring about.

Requests to the ASEAN Secretariat relating to Article 51(1) are currently handled by the Legal Services and Agreements Division (LSAD) in the

---

20 This understanding is confirmed by Termsak Chalermpalanupap in 'Life in ASEAN after the Entry into Force of the ASEAN Charter', in Tiwari, ed., *Life After the Charter*, chapter 3, 58. Dr Termsak assisted the HLTF in its work throughout the drafting process.

21 It is arguable that rule 2(1) goes far beyond procedural matters and impinges on substance. In so far as it is inconsistent with the rights and obligations of the member states contained in the Charter, it may be ineffective because of Article 52(2).

22 *See* rule 4 of the 2012 Rules of Procedure for the Interpretation of the ASEAN Charter.

Community and Corporate Affairs Department of the ASEAN Secretariat. At the time of writing LSAD consisted of a handful of legal officers who not only had to advise on interpretation and drafting of ASEAN agreements but also were given the task of processing all administrative contracts for the ASEAN Secretariat. The lack of resources devoted to LSAD is symptomatic of the attitude of member states towards creating an effective legal framework for ASEAN, despite the pious protestations in the Charter.

Requests for interpretation by other ASEAN organs

ASEAN officials have told the author that it is usually sectoral bodies which request the Legal Services and Agreements Division for an interpretation. No provision exists for such requests. This is a matter of some importance, for example, in the context of whether a proposed agreement or instrument is in conformity with the Charter, since Article 52(2) would render any inconsistent rights or obligations nugatory. Strictly speaking, requests from an ASEAN organ would have to be channelled through a member state, an unnecessarily cumbersome procedure. It may be that the best way to deal with this pragmatically is for such requests to be made informally to the Secretary-General, since one of his roles is to advise on ASEAN activities.[23] The Secretary-General and his deputies are also present at many (though not all) of the meetings of the various organs. The ROP does not apply to requests that do not emanate from member states, so the Secretary-General will not be tied down to the valueless procedure prescribed by that instrument.

Rule 1(2) of the 2012 Rules of Procedure state that 'these Rules shall not prevent request to the ASEAN Secretariat by any ASEAN organ seeking clarification or information relating to matters within the scope of its activities'. However, the Rules of Procedure do not specify how an ASEAN organ may go about making such requests. As a matter of practice, in ASEAN meetings ASEC is often requested to provide background papers on ASEAN instruments or clarification on ASEAN practice. These background papers serve as working documents. They do not amount to interpretation of previous ASEAN instruments or of the Charter.

Similarly, nothing is explicitly said about requests for interpretation from entities associated with ASEAN. Whether ASEC will respond to such requests is a matter of policy and practice. It will be a question of

[23] *See* the 1976 Agreement on Establishment of the ASEAN Secretariat, Article 3(1)(4) as amended by the 1992 Protocol.

resources. As a matter of principle and policy, it would be good if the ASEAN Secretariat were to be the authoritative source from which guidance on the Charter comes.

2. Any dispute arising from the interpretation of the Charter shall be settled in accordance with the relevant provisions in Chapter VIII.

The 2010 Protocol to the ASEAN Charter on Dispute Settlement Mechanisms (DSM Protocol)[24] covers only disputes between member states. There is no provision for the resolution of a dispute over the interpretation of the Charter between ASEC and a member state or between any other ASEAN organs. Unfortunately, the High Level Legal Experts Group did not address this in the DSM Protocol.

If ASEC issues an interpretation of the Charter, a member state has the choice of accepting or rejecting it. Presumably, the fact that ASEC has made such an interpretation would be relevant in any dispute between member states in relation to the particular Article of the Charter in question. They could then formally invoke the dispute settlement procedures in Chapter VIII and the DSM Protocol. However, this is unnecessarily time-consuming and expensive in terms of resource allocation. A more efficient mechanism is required. It is always open to the ASEAN Summit as supreme policymaking organ to designate (or create) some body to make an authoritative decision on interpretion, based on legal and not political principles. This would be vital if ASEAN is to realise its stated ambition to be a rules-based organisation. Clearly, the suggestion of a body consisting of member-state representatives taking instructions from the foreign ministries would not fit the bill. To have credibility, such a body must be independent, neutral, objective and competent.[25]

3. Headings and titles used throughout the Charter shall only be for the purpose of reference.

This is purely for guidance in interpretation. The headings do not always reflect precisely the content of the articles.

---

[24] Signed by the Foreign Ministers at the Sixteenth ASEAN Summit held in Hanoi, 8–9 Apr. 2010. This is not yet in force according to the list maintained by the ASEAN Secretariat. 'ASEAN Legal Instruments,' ASEAN Secretariat, online: agreement.asean.org. *See* commentary to Article 25 of the ASEAN Charter.

[25] The author has argued elsewhere for the creation of a proper ASEAN Legal Service: *see 'Towards a Rules-Based Community.*

Article 52. Legal Continuity

1. All treaties, conventions, agreements, concords, declarations, protocols and other ASEAN instruments which have been in effect before the entry into force of this Charter shall continue to be valid.

There is no definitive list of ASEAN instruments even on the website of the ASEAN Secretariat. The Centre for International Law of the National University of Singapore maintains a database of ASEAN instruments.[26]

2. In case of inconsistency between the rights and obligations of ASEAN Member States under such instruments and this Charter, the Charter shall prevail.

This clause was necessary because it was impossible to reconcile all the various instruments during the short period available for drafting the Charter. The Charter takes precedence over what has gone before.

Nothing is said about subsequent instruments that are inconsistent with the Charter. Given the stringent procedure prescribed for amendments to the Charter in Article 48, such backdoor amendments would not be legal. The Charter should also prevail in such cases. However, there is no procedure for declaring whether a provision in an instrument subsequent to the Charter is inconsistent. The only way a decision can be obtained is either to ask the ASEAN Secretariat for an interpretation (which is non-binding, non-authoritative and does not represent the views of ASEAN as an organisation according to the Rules of Procedure for the Interpretation of the ASEAN Charter)[27] or to invoke the 2010 Protocol to the ASEAN Charter on Dispute Settlement Mechanisms (DSM Protocol)[28] when it finally comes into force.

Article 53. Original Text

The signed original text of this Charter in English shall be deposited with the Secretary-General of ASEAN, who shall provide a certified copy to each Member State.

---

[26] *See* http://cil.nus.edu.sg/.

[27] Adopted by the ASEAN Coordinating Council on 2 Apr. 2012. *See* rule 2(1) and the commentary to Article 51 of the ASEAN Charter (infra).

[28] Signed by the Foreign Ministers at the Sixteenth ASEAN Summit held in Hanoi, 8–9 Apr. 2010. *See* commentary to Article 25 of the ASEAN Charter (infra).

Article 34 states that the working language of ASEAN shall be English. The whole process of drafting the Charter was conducted in English, though that was not an official language in the majority of ASEAN Member States. The oddities of expression are the result of this, as well as of the fact that the Charter was not drawn up by trained legal draughtsmen but rather was the result of compromises among the HLTF members, even regarding matters of legal phraseology.

Article 54. Registration of the ASEAN Charter

This Charter shall be registered by the Secretary-General of ASEAN with the Secretariat of the United Nations, pursuant to Article 102, paragraph 1 of the Charter of the United Nations.

The Charter was registered with the UN on 30 October 2009.[29]

As to the Secretary-General, *see* Article 11.

Article 55. ASEAN Assets

The assets and funds of the Organisation shall be vested in the name of ASEAN.

This is a necessary corollary to the fact that ASEAN now has a legal personality: *see* commentary to Article 4. The funds and assets used to be held in the name of the ASEAN Secretariat.

[29] As number 46745: *see* the UN Treaty Collection database at treaties.un.org.

ANNEX 1

ASEAN SECTORAL MINISTERIAL BODIES

I. ASEAN Political Security Community

1. ASEAN Foreign Ministers Meeting (AMM)
   - ASEAN Senior Officials Meeting (ASEAN SOM)
   - ASEAN Standing Committee (ASC)
   - Senior Officials Meeting on Development Planning (SOMDP)

2. Commission on the Southeast Asia Nuclear Weapons - Free Zone (SEANWFZ Commission)
   - Executive Committee on the SEANWFZ Commission

3. ASEAN Defence Ministers Meeting (ADMM)
   - ASEAN Defence Senior Officials Meeting (ADSOM)

4. ASEAN Law Ministers Meeting (ALAWMM)
   - ASEAN Senior Law Officials Meeting (ASLOM)

5. ASEAN Ministerial Meeting on Transnational Crime (AMMTC)
   - Senior Officials Meeting on Transnational Crime (SOMTC)
   - ASEAN Senior Officials on Drugs Matters (ASOD)
   - Directors-General of Immigration Departments and Heads of Consular Affairs Divisions of Ministries of Foreign Affairs Meeting (DGICM)

6. ASEAN Regional Forum (ARF)
   - ASEAN Regional Forum Senior Officials Meeting (ARF SOM)

II. ASEAN Economic Community

1. ASEAN Economic Ministers Meeting (AEM)
   - High Level Task Force on ASEAN Economic Integration (HLTF-EI)
   - Senior Economic Officials Meeting (SEOM)

2. ASEAN Free Trade Area (AFTA) Council

3. ASEAN Investment Area (AIA) Council

4. ASEAN Finance Ministers Meeting (AFMM)
   - ASEAN Finance and Central Bank Deputies Meeting (AFDM)
   - ASEAN Directors-General of Customs Meeting (Customs DG)

5. ASEAN Ministers Meeting on Agriculture and Forestry (AMAF)
   - Senior Officials Meeting of the ASEAN Ministers on Agriculture and Forestry (SOM-AMAF)
   - ASEAN Senior Officials on Forestry (ASOF)

6. ASEAN Ministers on Energy Meeting (AMEM)
   - Senior Officials Meeting on Energy (SOME)

7. ASEAN Ministerial Meeting on Minerals (AMMin)
   - ASEAN Senior Officials Meeting on Minerals (ASOMM)

8. ASEAN Ministerial Meeting on Science and Technology (AMMST)
   - Committee on Science and Technology (COST)

9. ASEAN Telecommunications and Information Technology Ministers Meeting (TELMIN)
   - Telecommunications and Information Technology Senior Officials Meeting (TELSOM)
   - ASEAN Telecommunication Regulators' Council (ATRC)

10. ASEAN Transport Ministers Meeting (ATM)
    - Senior Transport Officials Meeting (STOM)

11. Meeting of the ASEAN Tourism Ministers (M-ATM)
    - Meeting of the ASEAN National Tourism Organisations (ASEAN NTOs)

12. ASEAN Mekong Basin Development Corporation (AMBDC)
    - ASEAN Mekong Basin Development Corporation Steering Committee (AMBDC SC)
    - High Level Finance Committee (HLFC)

13 ASEAN Centre for Energy

14. ASEAN-Japan Centre in Tokyo

III. ASEAN Socio-Cultural Community

1. ASEAN Ministers Responsible for Information (AMRI)
    - Senior Officials Meeting Responsible for Information (SOMRI)

2. ASEAN Ministers Responsible for Culture and Arts (AMCA)
    - Senior Officials Meeting for Culture and Arts (SOMCA)

3. ASEAN Education Ministers Meeting (ASED)
    - Senior Officials Meeting on Education (SOM-ED)

4. ASEAN Ministerial Meeting on Disaster Management (AMMDM)
    - ASEAN Committee on Disaster Management (ACDM)

5. ASEAN Ministerial Meeting on the Environment (AMME)
    - ASEAN Senior Officials on the Environment (ASOEN)

6. Conference of the Parties to the ASEAN Agreement on Transboundary Haze Pollution
    - Committee under the COP to the ASEAN Agreement on Transboundary Haze Pollution

7. ASEAN Health Ministers Meeting
    - Senior Officials Meeting on Health Development (SOMHD)

8. ASEAN Labor Ministers Meeting (ALMM)
    - Senior Labour Officials Meeting (SLOM)
    - ASEAN Committee on the Implementation of the ASEAN Declaration on the Protection and Promotion of the Rights of Migrant Workers

9. ASEAN Ministers on Rural Development and Poverty Eradication (AMRDPE)
    - Senior Officials Meeting on Rural Development and Poverty Eradication (SOMRDPE)

10. ASEAN Ministerial Meeting on Social Welfare and Development (AMMSWD)
    - Senior Officials Meeting on Social Welfare and Development (SOMSWD)

11. ASEAN Ministerial Meeting on Youth (AMMY)
    - Senior Officials Meeting on Youth (SOMY)

12. ASEAN Conference on Civil Service Matters (ACCSM)

13. ASEAN Centre for Biodiversity (ACB)

14. ASEAN Coordinating Centre for Humanitarian Assistance on Disaster Management (AHA Centre)

15. ASEAN Earthquakes Information Centre

16. ASEAN Specialised Metereological Centre (ASMC)

17. ASEAN University Network (AUN)

ANNEX 2

ENTITIES ASSOCIATED WITH ASEAN

I. Parliamentarians

ASEAN Inter-Parliamentary Assembly (AIPA)

II. Business Organisations

ASEAN Airlines Meeting
ASEAN Alliance of Health Supplement Association (AAHSA)
ASEAN Automotive Federation (AAF)
ASEAN Bankers Association (ABA)
ASEAN Business Advisory Council (ASEAN-BAC)
ASEAN Business Forum (ABF)
ASEAN Chamber of Commerce and Industry (ASEAN-CCI)
ASEAN Chemical Industries Council
ASEAN Federation of Textiles Industries (AFTEX)
ASEAN Furniture Industries Council (AFIC)
ASEAN Insurance Council (AIC)
ASEAN Intellectual Property Association (ASEAN IPA)
ASEAN International Airports Association (AAA)
ASEAN Iron and Steel Industry Federation
ASEAN Pharmaceutical Club
ASEAN Tourism Association (ASEANTA)
Federation of ASEAN Economic Associations (FAEA)
Federation of ASEAN Shippers' Council
US-ASEAN Business Council

III. Think Tanks and Academic Institutions

ASEAN-ISIS Network

IV. Accredited Civil Society Organisations

ASEAN Academics of Science, Engineering and Technology (ASEAN CASE)
ASEAN Academy of Engineering and Technology (AAET)
ASEAN Association for Clinical Laboratory Services (AACLS)
ASEAN Association for Planning and Housing (AAPH)
ASEAN Association of Radiologists (AAR)
ASEAN Chess Confederation (ACC)
ASEAN Confederation of Employers (ACE)
ASEAN Confederation of Women's Organisation (ACWO)
ASEAN Constructors Federation (ACF)
ASEAN Cosmetics Association (ACA)
ASEAN Council for Japan Alumni (ASCOJA)
ASEAN Council of Teachers (ACT)
ASEAN Federation for Psychiatric and Mental Health (AFPMH)
ASEAN Federation of Accountants (AFA)
ASEAN Federation of Electrical Engineering Contractors (AFEEC)
ASEAN Federation of Engineering Organisation (AFEO)
ASEAN Federation of Flying Clubs (AFFC)
ASEAN Federation of Forwarders Association (AFFA)
ASEAN Federation of Heart Foundation (AFHF)
ASEAN Federation of Land Surveying and Geomatics (ASEAN FLAG)
ASEAN Federation of Mining Association (AFMA)
ASEAN Fisheries Federation (AFF)
ASEAN Football Federation (AFF)
ASEAN Forest Products Industry Club (AFPIC)
ASEAN Forestry Students Association (AFSA)
ASEAN Handicraft Promotion and Development Association (AHPDA)
ASEAN Kite Council (AKC)
ASEAN Law Association (ALA)
ASEAN Law Students Association (ALSA)
ASEAN Music Industry Association (AMIA)
ASEAN Neurosurgical Society (ANS)
ASEAN NGO Coalition on Ageing
ASEAN Non-Governmental Organisations for the Prevention of Drugs and Substance Abuse
ASEAN Oleochemical Manufacturers Group (AOMG)

ASEAN Orthopaedic Association (AOA)
ASEAN Paediatric Federation (APA)
ASEAN Para Sports Federation (APSF)
ASEAN Ports Association (APA)
ASEAN Thalassaemia Society (ATS)
ASEAN Valuers Association (AVA)
ASEAN Vegetable Oils Club (AVOC)
Asian Partnership for Development of Human Resources in Rural Asia (AsiaDHRRA)
Committee for ASEAN Youth Cooperation (CAYC)
Federation of ASEAN Consulting Engineers (FACE)
Federation of ASEAN Public Relations Organisations (FAPRO)
Federation of ASEAN Shipowners' Association (FASA)
Medical Association of Southeast Asian Nations Committee (MASEAN)
Rheumatism Association of ASEAN (RAA)
Southeast Asia Regional Institute for Community and Education (SEARICE)
Southeast Asian Studies Regional Exchange Program (SEASREP) Foundation
Veterans Confederation of ASEAN Countries (VECONAC)

V. Other Stakeholders In Asean

ASEAN (National Police) ASEANAPOL
Federation of Institutes of Food Science and Technology in ASEAN (FIFSTA)
Southeast Asian Fisheries Development Centre (SEAFDEC)
Working Group for an ASEAN Human Rights Mechanism

ANNEX 3

ASEAN FLAG

The ASEAN Flag represents a stable, peaceful, united and dynamic ASEAN. The colours of the Flag - blue, red, white and yellow - represent the main colours of the flags of all the ASEAN Member States.

The blue represents peace and stability. Red depicts courage and dynamism. White shows purity and yellow symbolizes prosperity.

The stalks of padi represent the dream of ASEAN's Founding Fathers for an ASEAN comprising all the countries in Southeast Asia bound together in friendship and solidarity. The circle represents the unity of ASEAN.

The specification of Pantone Colour adopted for the colour of the ASEAN Flag are:

Blue: Pantone 19-4053 TC
Red: Pantone 18-1655 TC
White: Pantone 11-4202 TC
Yellow: Pantone 1 3-0 758 TC

For the printed version, the specifications of colours (except white) will follow those for the colours of the ASEAN Emblem, i.e.,:

Blue: Pantone 286 or Process Colour 100C 60M 0Y 6K
Red: Pantone Red 032 or Process Colour 0C 91M 87Y 0K
Yellow: Pantone Process Yellow or Process Colour 0C 0M 100Y 0K

The ratio of the width to the length of the Flag is two to three, and size specifications for the following Flags are:
Table Flag: 10cm x 15 cm
Room Flag: 100cm x 150 cm
Car Flag: 10 cm x 30 cm
Field Flag: 200 x 300 cm

ANNEX 4

ASEAN EMBLEM

The ASEAN Emblem represents a stable, peaceful, united and dynamic ASEAN. The colours of the Emblem - blue, red, white and yellow - represent the main colours of the crests of all the ASEAN Member States.

The blue represents peace and stability. Red depicts courage and dynamism. White shows purity and yellow symbolizes prosperity.

The stalks of padi represent the dream of ASEAN's Founding Fathers for an ASEAN comprising all the countries in Southeast Asia bound together in friendship and solidarity. The circle represents the unity of ASEAN.

The specification of Pantone Colour adopted for the colour of the ASEAN Emblem are:

Blue: Pantone 286
Red: Pantone Red 032
Yellow: Pantone Process Yellow

For four-colour printing process, the specification of colours are:

Blue: 100C 60M 0Y 6K (100C 60M 0Y 10K)
Red: 0C 91M 87Y 0K (0C 90M 90Y 0K)
Yellow: 0C 0M 100Y 0K

Specifications in the brackets are to be used when an arbitrary measurement of process colours is not possible,

In Pantone Process Colour Simulator, the specifications equal to:

Blue: Pantone 204-1
Red: Pantone 60-1
Yellow: Pantone 1-3

The font used for the word 'ASEAN' in the Emblem is lower-case Helvetica in bold.

SELECTED ACRONYMS AND ABBREVIATIONS

AAC	ASEAN Audit Committee
AADMER	ASEAN Agreement on Disaster Management and Emergency Response
ACB	ASEAN Compliance Body
ACC	ASEAN Coordinating Council
ACCT	ASEAN Convention on Counter-Terrorism
ACIA	ASEAN Comprehensive Investment Agreement 2009
ACMB	ASEAN Compliance Monitoring Body (now ACB)
ACT	ASEAN Consultation to Solve Trade and Investment Issues
ACTC	ASEAN Committees in Third Countries
ADMM	ASEAN Defence Ministers Meeting
AEC	ASEAN Economic Community
AECC	ASEAN Economic Community Council
AEM	ASEAN Economic Ministers Meeting
AFMM	ASEAN Finance Ministers Meeting
AFTA	ASEAN Free Trade Area
AFRP	ASEAN Secretariat Financial Rules and Procedure
AHMM	ASEAN Health Ministers Meeting
AHRD	ASEAN Human Rights Declaration
AIA	ASEAN Investment Area
AICHR	ASEAN Intergovernmental Commission on Human Rights
AIPA	ASEAN Inter-Parliamentary Assembly, founded as the ASEAN Inter-Parliamentary Meeting (APM) in 1975, developed into the ASEAN Inter-Parliamentary Organisation (AIPO) in 1978, adopted its current name and format in 2005
ALAWMM	ASEAN Law Ministers Meeting

ALMM	ASEAN Labour Ministers Meeting
AMAF	Meeting of the ASEAN Ministers of Agriculture and Forestry
AMCA	Meeting of ASEAN Ministers Responsible for Culture and the Arts
AMEM	ASEAN Ministers on Energy Meeting
AMM	ASEAN Ministerial Meeting. This has been re-designated the ASEAN Foreign Ministers' Meeting since the Forty-second AMM.
AMME	ASEAN Ministerial Meeting on the Environment
AMMin	ASEAN Ministerial Meeting on Minerals
AMMS	ASEAN Ministerial Meeting on Sports
AMMST	ASEAN Ministerial Meeting on Science and Technology
AMMTC	ASEAN Ministerial Meeting on Transnational Crime
AMRDPE	ASEAN Ministers on Rural Development and Poverty Eradication
AMRI	ASEAN Ministers Responsible for Information
API	Agreement on the Privileges and Immunities of ASEAN 2009
APSC	ASEAN Political and Security Community, previously known as the ASEAN Security Community (ASC) from 2003–07
APT	ASEAN plus Three, viz, China, Japan and the Republic of Korea, also abbreviated as ASEAN+3
ARF	ASEAN Regional Forum
ASC	ASEAN Standing Committee, consisting of foreign ministry officials
ASCC	ASEAN Socio-Cultural Community
ASCCO	ASEAN Coordinating Conference for the ASEAN Political-Security Community
ASEAN-5	Indonesia, Malaysia, the Philippines, Singapore and Thailand
ASEAN-6	ASEAN-5 plus Brunei (i.e., the 'older' ASEAN member states)
ASEAN-ISIS	ASEAN Institutes of Strategic and International Studies
ASEC	ASEAN Secretariat
ASED	ASEAN Education Ministers Meeting
ASLOM	ASEAN Senior Law Officials Meeting
ASOD	ASEAN Senior Officials on Drug Matters
ATIGA	ASEAN Trade in Goods Agreement
ATM	ASEAN Transport Ministers Meeting
AUN	ASEAN University Network

CCI	Coordinating Committee on Investment
CEPT	Common Effective Preferential Tariff Scheme
CLMV	Cambodia, Laos, Myanmar and Vietnam
CPR	Committee of Permanent Representatives
DSG	Deputy Secretary-General
DSM	Dispute Settlement Mechanism
EAS	East Asia Summit, comprising the ASEAN member states, Australia, China, India, Japan, Republic of Korea, New Zealand, Russia and the United States of America
EDSM	Enhanced Dispute Settlement Mechanism
EPG	Eminent Persons Group
HLTF	High Level Task Force
HLEG	High Level Legal Experts Group on Follow Up to the ASEAN Charter
HLP	High Level Panel on an ASEAN Human Rights Body
HPA	Hanoi Plan of Action
IAED	Internal Audit and Evaluation Division
IAI	Initiative for ASEAN Integration
IAMM	Informal ASEAN Ministerial Meeting
JMM	Joint Ministerial Meeting of Foreign and Economic Ministers
M-ATM	ASEAN Tourism Ministers Meeting
PMC	Post-Ministerial Conferences
RCEP	Regional Comprehensive Economic Partnership
ROP	Rules of Procedure
SEAMEO	Southeast Asia Ministers of Education Organization
SEANWFZ	Treaty on the Southeast Asia Nuclear Weapon-Free Zone 1995
SEOM	Senior Economic Officials' Meeting
SOCA	Senior Officials' Committee for the ASEAN Socio-Cultural Community

SOM	Senior Officials' Meeting, comprising foreign ministry officials
SOMRDPE	Senior Officials' Meeting on Rural Development and Poverty Eradication
TAC	Treaty of Amity and Cooperation in Southeast Asia 1976
TELMIN	ASEAN Telecommunications and IT Ministers Meeting
TOR	Terms of Reference
VAP	Vientiane Action Programme
WG-AHRM	Working Group on an ASEAN Human Rights Mechanism
ZOPFAN	Zone of Peace, Freedom and Neutrality Declaration 1971

BIBLIOGRAPHY

Articles and Books

"An Islet for a Sea." *The Economist*, 8–14 Dec 2012.
"Army Invokes Martial Law." *Bangkok Post*, 20 May 2014.
"As It Happened: Thailand Coup." *BBC News*, 22 May 2014.
Anwar, Dewi Fortuna. *Indonesia in ASEAN: Foreign Policy and* Regionalism. Singapore: Institute of Southeast Asian Studies, 1994.
Beckman, R. and J. Ashley Roach, ed. *Piracy and International Maritime Crimes in ASEAN: Prospect for Cooperation*. United Kingdom: Edward Elgar, 2012.
Chalermpalanupap, Termsak. "Promoting and Protecting Human Rights in ASEAN." http://www.asean.org/archive/93-14248-HumanRightsArticle.pdf.
Cheah, B. K. "The MCP and the Anti-Japanese Movement." In *Red Star Over Malaya: Resistance and Social Conflict During and After the Japanese Occupation of Malaya, 1941–1946*. Third edition. Singapore: Singapore University Press, 2003.
"China Demands ASEAN Neutrality over South China Sea." *Straits Times*, 19 May 2014.
Chow, Jermyn. "Indonesian Warship Usman Harun Disallowed from Calling at Singapore Ports and Naval Bases." *Straits Times*, 18 Feb 2014.
Clutterbuck, R. *The Long, Long War: The Emergency in Malaya 1948–1960*. United Kingdom: Cassell & Co, 1966.
Emmerson, D. K. *Hard Choices: Security, Regionalism and Democracy in Southeast Asia*. Singapore: Institute of Southeast Asian Studies, 2009.

European Union. "Co-Chairs' Statement of of the 20th EU-ASEAN Ministerial Meeting." http://www.eeas.europa.eu/statements/docs/2014/140723_03_en.pdf.

Federal Research Division of the Library of Congress Country Studies. "Philippines: Relations with Asian Neighbours." countrystudies.us/philippines/93.htm.

Flores, J. M. and J. Abad. "The Founding of ASEAN." In *ASEAN at 30*. Jakarta: ASEAN Secretariat, 1997.

Government of Vietnam. *Report to the President on the Ratification of the Protocol*
to the ASEAN Charter on Dispute Settlement Mechanisms. 213/TTr-CP, 29 Aug 2012.

Hao Duy Phan. *A Selective Approach to Establishing an ASEAN Human Rights Mechanism in Southeast Asia: The Case for a Southeast Asian Court of Human* Rights. Netherlands: Koninklijke Brill, 2012.

Head, Jonathan. "Asean Fiasco Deepens Thai Stalemate." *BBC News*, 11 Apr 2009.

"I still need Ranariddh." *Asiaweek*, 13 Jun 1997.

International Crisis Group. "Waging Peace: ASEAN and the Thai-Cambodian Border Conflict." *Asia Report*, no. 215 (2011): 1-40.

International Tribunal for the Law of the Sea. "Press Release: Arbitrators Appointed in the Arbitral Proceedings Instituted by the Republic of the Philippines against the People's Republic of China." *ITLOS/Press 191*, 25 Apr 2013.

Iskandar, M. A. "ASEAN Must Address Coup in Thailand: Yudhoyono." *Antara News*, 24 May 2014.

Jayakumar, S. and Tommy Koh. *Pedra Branca: The Road to the World Court*. Singapore: NUS Press, 2009.

Kawilarang, Renne R.A and Harriska Farida Adiati. "New ASEAN Anthem Sung." *Viva News*, 16 Dec 2008.

Koh, T., R. G. Manalo and W. Woon, ed. *The Making of the ASEAN Charter*. Singapore: World Scientific Publishing, 2009.

Kubitscheck, H. S. *Geschichte Malaysias und Singapurs*. Berlin: VEB Deutscher Verlag der Wissenschaften, 1984.

Lee, K. Y. *The Singapore Story: Memoirs of Lee Kuan Yew*. Singapore: Times Editions, 1998.

———. *From Third World to First: The Singapore Story 1965–2000*. Singapore: Times Publishing, 2000.

Leifer, M. ASEAN and the Security of Southeast Asia. London: Routledge, 1989.

"Malaysia Boosts Sabah Security After Lahad Datu Clashes." *BBC News Asia*, 4 Mar 2013.

Ministry of Foreign Affairs. "Remarks by Minister for Foreign Affairs George Yeo in Parliament during Committee of Supply Debate on 3 Mar 2011." http://www.mfa.gov.sg/content/mfa/media_centre/press_room/pr/2011/201103/press_20110303_01.html.

———. "Statement by Minister for Foreign Affairs George Yeo, Singapore, 22 Jul 2008." http://www.mfa.gov.sg/content/mfa/media_centre/press_room/pr/2008/200807/press_20080722_09.html.

"Remarks by Minister for Foreign Affairs George Yeo in Parliament during Committee of Supply Debate on 3 Mar 2011."

"Pembicaraan Soal Ambalat (Discussions on the Question of Ambalat)." *BBC Indonesia.com*, 10 Jun 2009.

"Profile: Surayud Chulanont." *BBC News*, 1 Oct 2006.

"Repositioning ASEAN in New World Order." *Straits Times*, 24 Feb 2011.

Ricklefs, M. C. et al. *A New History of Southeast Asia.* United Kingdom: Palgrave Macmillan, 2010.

Severino, R. C. *Southeast Asia in Search of an ASEAN Community: Insights from the Former ASEAN Secretary-general*. Singapore: Institute of Southeast Asian Studies, 2006.

Singapore Academy of Law. *The Singapore Law Reports (Reissue)*. Singapore: Singapore Academy of Law, 2010.

Southeast Asian Ministers of Education Organization. "The ASEAN Way." Last modified 22 Apr 2012. http://www.seameo-innotech.org/SEAtoolkit/index.php/teaching-materials-images/item/174-the-asean-way-asean-anthem.

Thompson, Eric C and Chulanee Thianthai. "Awareness of and Attitudes Toward ASEAN: Findings of a Ten Nation Survey." www.aseanfoundation.org/documents/FA-New_%20Asean_Convert_lowres.pdf.

Tarling, Nicholas, ed. *The Cambridge History of Southeast Asia Volume 2: The Nineteenth and Twentieth Centuries*. Cambridge: Cambridge University Press, 1993.

———. *Southeast Asia: A Modern History*. Australia: Oxford University Press, 2001.

Tiwari, S, ed. *ASEAN: Life After the Charter*. Singapore: Institute of Southeast Asian Studies, 2010.

Turnbull, C. M. *A Short History of Malaysia, Singapore and Brunei*. Singapore: Graham Brash, 1980.

UNESCO World Heritage Centre. "Temple of Preah Vihear." http://whc.unesco.org/en/list/1224/.

Uy, Veronica. "$20,000 ASEAN Song-writing Contest on." *Inquirer.net,* 11 Sep 2008.

"Vietnam Anti-China Protest: Factories Burnt." *BBC News Asia*, 14 May 2014.
Wong, P. K. and K. K. Ng. "The Competitiveness of ASEAN after the 1997 Asian Financial Crisis." *Asia Competitiveness Institute Monograph Series* (2008): 1-71.
Woon, W. and J-C Piris. *Towards a Rules-Based Community: An ASEAN Legal Service*. Cambridge: Cambridge University Press, 2014.
World Bank. "Countries and Economies." http://data.worldbank.org/country.
World Trade Organization. *Dispute DS1*, 1995.
———. *Dispute DS371*, 2008.
———. *Understanding on Rules and Procedures Governing the Settlement of Disputes*.

Cases

Case Concerning Sovereignty over Pulau Ligitan and Pulau Sipadan (Indonesia/Malaysia) (Judgment) [2001] ICJ Rep 575.
Case Concerning the Temple of Preah Vihear (Cambodia/Thailand) (Judgment) [1962] ICJ Rep 6.
Case Concerning the Temple of Preah Vihear (Cambodia/Thailand) (Judgment) [1961] ICJ Rep 17.
Request for the Interpretation of the Judgment of 15 Jun 1962 in the Case Concerning the Temple of Preah Vihear (Cambodia/Thailand) (Order) [2011] ICJ Rep 537.
Case Concerning Sovereignty over Pedra Branca/Pulau Batu Puteh, Middle Rocks and South Ledge (Malaysia/Singapore) (Judgment) [2008] ICJ Rep 12.
Case Concerning Sovereignty over Pulau Ligitan and Pulau Sipadan (Indonesia/Malaysia) (Judgment) [2002] ICJ Rep 625.
Territorial and Maritime Dispute (Nicaragua v. Colombia) (Judgment) [2012] ICJ Rep 624.
Reparations for Injuries Suffered in the Service of the United Nations (Advisory Opinion) [1949]
Request for the Interpretation of the Judgment of 15 Jun 1962 in the Case Concerning the Temple of Preah Vihear (Cambodia v. Thailand) (Judgment) [2013].
Case concerning Land Reclamation by Singapore in and around the Straits of Johor (Malaysia v. Singapore) (Order) [2003].
Case Concerning the Temple of Preah Vihear (Cambodia v Thailand) (General List No. 4—Judgments of 26 May 1961 and 15 June 1962).

Documents

ASEAN

ASEAN. 1967 ASEAN Declaration.
———. *1971 Zone o f Peace, Freedom and Neutrality Declaration.*
———. *1976 Agreement on the Establishment of the ASEAN Secretariat.*
———. *1976 Declaration of ASEAN Concord.*
———. *1976 Treaty of Amity and Cooperation in Southeast Asia.*
———. *1979 Agreement between the Government of Indonesia and ASEAN relating to the Privileges and Immunities of the ASEAN Secretariat.*
———. *1983 Protocol Amending the Agreement on the Establishment of the ASEAN Secretariat.*
———. *1984 Declaration of the Admission of Brunei Darussalam into ASEAN.*
———. *1985 Protocol Amending the Agreement on the Establishment of the ASEAN Secretariat.*
———. *1987 Protocol Amending the Treaty of Amity and Cooperation in Southeast Asia.*
———. *1989 Protocol Amending the Agreement of the Establishment of the ASEAN Secretariat.*
———. *1992 Agreement on the Common Effective Preferential Tariff Scheme for the ASEAN Free Trade Area.*
———. *1992 Framework Agreement on Enhancing ASEAN Economic Cooperation.*
———. *1992 Protocol Amending the Agreement on the Establishment of the ASEAN Secretariat.*
———. *1995 ASEAN Framework Agreement on Services.*
———. *1995 Declaration of the Admission of the Socialist Republic of Viet Nam into ASEAN.*
———. *1995 Treaty on the Southeast Asia Nuclear Weapon-Free Zone.*
———. 1997 ASEAN Declaration on Transnational Crime.
———. *1997 Declaration on the Admission of the Lao People's Democratic Republic into ASEAN*
———. *1997 Declaration on the Admission of the Union of Myanmar into ASEAN.*
———. *1997 Joint Statement of the Special Meeting of the ASEAN Foreign Ministers on Cambodia.*
———. *1997 Memorandum of Understanding on the Establishment of the ASEAN Foundation.*
———. *1997 Protocol Amending the Agreement on the Establishment of the ASEAN Secretariat.*

———. *1998 ASEAN Framework Agreement on the Facilitation of Goods in Transit.*
———. *1998 Framework Agreement on the ASEAN Investment Area.*
———. *1999 Chairman's Press Statement on ASEAN Third Informal Summit.*
———. *1999 Declaration on the Admission of the Kingdom of Cambodia into ASEAN.*
———. *1999 Protocol for the Accession of the Kingdom of Cambodia to ASEAN Agreements.*
———. *2000 Revised Memorandum of Understanding on the Establishment of ASEAN Foundation.*
———. *2002 ASEAN Tourism Agreement.*
———. *2003 Declaration Of ASEAN Concord II.*
———. *2004 ASEAN Framework Agreement for Integration of Priority Sectors.*
———. *2004 ASEAN Protocol on Enhanced Dispute Settlement Mechanism.*
———. *2005 ASEAN Agreement on Disaster Management and Emergency Response.*
———. *2005 Kuala Lumpur Declaration on the Establishment of the ASEAN Charter.*
———. *2007 Cebu Declaration on the Blueprint of an ASEAN Charter.*
———. *2009 Agreement on the Privileges and Immunities of ASEAN.*
———. *2010 Protocol to the ASEAN Charter on Dispute Settlement Mechanisms.*
———. *2010 Rules of Authorisation for Legal Transactions under Domestic Laws.*
———. *2010 Rules for Reference of Unresolved Disputes to the ASEAN Summit.*
———. *2010 Third Protocol Amending the Treaty of Amity and Cooperation in Southeast Asia.*
———. *2011 Rules of Procedure for the Conclusion of International Agreements by ASEAN.*
———. *2012 Agreement between the Government of the Republic of Indonesia and ASEAN on Hosting and Granting Privileges and Immunities to the ASEAN Secretariat.*
———. *2012 ASEAN Agreement on the Movement of Natural Persons.*
———. *2012 Rules of Procedure for the Interpretation of the ASEAN Charter.*
———. *2012 Rules for Reference of Non-Compliance to the ASEAN Summit.*
———. "Ambassadors to ASEAN." Last modified August, 2014. http://www.asean.org/news/item/ambassadors-to-asean.
———. *Annex for ASEAN Security Community Plan of Action.*
———. *ASEAN Annual Report 2006–07.*
———. *ASEAN Annual Report 2008–09.*
———. *ASEAN Annual Report 2012–13.*
———. "ASEAN Anthem." http://www.asean.org/asean/about-asean/asean-anthem.

———. "ASEAN Centres & Facilities." http://www.asean.org/asean/asean-centres-facilities.
———. ASEAN Charter.
———. "ASEAN Committees in Third Countries and International Organisations (ACTC)." Last modified Mar 2014. http://www.asean.org/asean/asean-structure/committees-abroad.
———. "ASEAN Convention on Counter-Terrorism Completes Ratification Process." http://www.asean.org/news/asean-secretariat-news/item/asean-convention-on-counter-terrorism-completes-ratification-process.
———. "ASEAN Dialogue Coordinatorship." http://www.asean.org/asean/external-relations/asean-dialogue-coordinator.
———. ASEAN Economic Community Blueprint.
———. "ASEAN Emblem." http://www.asean.org/asean/about-asean/asean-emblem.
———. "ASEAN Flag." http://www.asean.org/asean/about-asean/asean-flag.
———. ASEAN Framework Agreement on Mutual Recognition Arrangements.
———. ASEAN Framework for Equitable Economic Development.
———. *ASEAN Framework for Regional Comprehensive Economic Partnership.*
———. *ASEAN Human Rights Declaration.*
———. *ASEAN Leaders' Declaration on Drug-Free ASEAN 2015.*
———. "ASEAN Legal Instruments." http://agreement.asean.org.
———. *ASEAN Plan Of Action To Combat Transnational Crime.*
———. *ASEAN Political-Security Community Blueprint.*
———. *ASEAN Regional Forum: A Concept Paper.*
———. ASEAN Security Community Plan of Action. http://www.asean.org/news/item/asean-security-community-plan-of-action.
———. *ASEAN's Six-Point Principles on the South China Sea.*
———. *ASEAN Socio-Cultural Community Blueprint.*
———. "ASEAN Structure: ASEAN Community Councils." http://www.asean.org/asean/asean-structure/asean-community-councils.
———. *ASEAN Vision 2020.*
———. *Cha-am Hua Hin Declaration on the Intergovernmental Commission on Human Rights.*
———. *Cha-am Hua Hin Declaration on the Roadmap for the ASEAN Community (2009-2015).*
———. *Chairman's Statement of the Tenth ASEAN Summit.*
———. *Chairman's Statement of the Eighteenth ASEAN Summit.*
———. *Chairman's Statement of the Nineteenth ASEAN Summit.*
———. *Chairman's Statement of the Twentieth ASEAN Summit.*
———. *Chairman's Statement of the Twenty-first ASEAN Summit.*
———. *Chairman's Statement of the Twenty-second ASEAN Summit.*

———. *Chairman's statement of the Twenty-fourth ASEAN Summit.*
———. "Deputy Secretaries-General of ASEAN." http://www.asean.org/asean/asean-secretariat/deputy-secretaries-general-of-asean.
———. *e-ASEAN Framework Agreement.*
———. "External Relations." http://www.asean.org/asean/external-relations.
———. *Framework Agreement on Comprehensive Economic Cooperation Among the Governments of the Member Countries of ASEAN and the Republic of Korea.*
———. *Framework Agreement on Comprehensive Economic Cooperation Between ASEAN and China.*
———. *Framework Agreement on Comprehensive Economic Cooperation Between India and ASEAN.*
———. *Framework Agreement on Comprehensive Economic Partnership between Japan and ASEAN.*
———. *Handbook on ASEAN Protocol and Practices*, Jakarta: ASEAN Secretariat, 1995.
———. *Hanoi Plan of Action (1999–2004).*
———. "Historic Firsts: ASEAN Efforts on Cambodian-Thai Conflict Endorsed by UNSC." http://www.asean.org/news/asean-secretariat-news/item/historic-firsts-asean-efforts-on-cambodian-thai-conflict-endorsed-by-unsc?category_id=27.
———. *Joint Communiqué of the First ASEAN Heads of Government Meeting.*
———. *Joint Communiqué of the Second ASEAN Ministerial Meeting.*
———. *Joint Communiqué of the Third ASEAN Ministerial Meeting.*
———. *Joint Communiqué of the Sixth ASEAN Ministerial Meeting.*
———. *Joint Communiqué of the Seventh ASEAN Ministerial Meeting.*
———. *Joint Communiqué Of The Ninth ASEAN Ministerial Meeting.*
———. *Joint Communiqué of the Twelfth ASEAN Ministerial Meeting.*
———. *Joint Communiqué of the Twenty-third ASEAN Ministerial Meeting.*
———. *Joint Communiqué of the Twenty-sixth ASEAN Ministerial Meeting.*
———. *Joint Communiqué of the Twenty-seventh ASEAN Ministerial Meeting.*
———. *Joint Communiqué of the Twenty-eighth ASEAN Ministerial Meeting.*
———. *Joint Communiqué of the Twenty-ninth ASEAN Ministerial Meeting.*
———. *Joint Communiqué of the Thirty-first ASEAN Ministerial Meeting.*
———. *Joint Communiqué of the Thirty-second ASEAN Ministerial Meeting.*
———. *Joint Communiqué of the Thirty-fourth ASEAN Ministerial Meeting.*
———. *Joint Communiqué of the Thirty-seventh ASEAN Ministerial Meeting.*
———. *Joint Communiqué of the Thirty-eighth ASEAN Ministerial Meeting.*
———. *Joint Communiqué of the Forty-first ASEAN Ministerial Meeting.*
———. *Joint Communiqué of the Forty-second ASEAN Foreign Ministers Meeting.*

———. *Joint Communiqué of the Forty-sixth ASEAN Foreign Ministers' Meeting.*
———. *Joint Media Statement of the Thirty-sixth ASEAN Economic Ministers Meeting.*
———. *Joint Press Statement of the Thirty-first ASEAN Economic Ministers Meeting (AEM).*
———. *Joint Press Statement of the Thirty-third ASEAN Economic Ministers Meeting.*
———. *Joint Press Statement of the Thirty-fifth ASEAN Economic Ministers Meeting.*
———. *Joint Statement of the Special ASEAN Foreign Ministers Meeting on the Current Political Development in the Southeast Asia Region.*
———. "Overview of ASEAN-Australia Dialogue Relations." http://www.asean.org/news/item/overview-of-asean-australia-dialogue-relations.
———. "Overview of ASEAN-Canada Dialogue Relations." http://www.asean.org/news/item/asean-canada-dialogue-relations-2.
———. "Overview of ASEAN-China Dialogue Relations." http://www.asean.org/asean/external-relations/china.
———. "Overview of ASEAN-EU Dialogue Relations." http://www.asean.org/asean/external-relations/european-union/item/overview-of-asean-eu-dialogue-relations.
———. "Overview of ASEAN-India Dialogue Relations." http://www.asean.org/asean/external-relations/india/item/overview-of-asean-india-dialogue-relations.
———. "Overview of ASEAN-Japan Dialogue Relations." http://www.asean.org/news/item/asean-japan-dialogue-relations.
———. "Overview of ASEAN-New Zealand Dialogue Relations." http://www.asean.org/asean/external-relations/new-zealand/item/overview-of-asean-new-zealand-relations-2.
———. "Overview of ASEAN-Pakistan Sectoral Dialogue Cooperation." http://www.asean.org/news/item/overview-of-asean-pakistan-sectoral-dialogue-cooperation-2.
———. "Overview of ASEAN-Republic of Korea Dialogue Relations." http://www.asean.org/news/item/asean-republic-of-korea-dialogue-relations.
———. "Overview of ASEAN-Russia Dialogue Relations." http://www.asean.org/news/item/asean-russia-dialogue-relations.
———. "Overview of ASEAN-US Dialogue Relations." http://www.asean.org/news/item/overview-of-asean-us-dialogue-relations.
———. "Press Release: ASEAN Charter Enters into Force Next Month Bangkok." http://www.asean.org/news/item/asean-charter-enters-into-force-next-month-bangkok-15-november-2008.

———. "Press Release: ASEAN Foreign Ministers to Celebrate the Entry into Force of the ASEAN Charter at the ASEAN Secretariat." http://www.asean.org/news/item/press-release-asean-foreign-ministers-to-celebrate-the-entry-into-force-of-the-asean-charter-at-the-asean-secretariat-asean-secretariat-9-december-2008.

———. "Press Release: Brunei Darussalam, Malaysia, and Lao PDR Ratify the ASEAN Charter." http://www.asean.org/news/item/press-release-brunei-darussalam-malaysia-and-lao-pdr-ratify-the-asean-charter-20-february-2008.

———. "Press Release by the Chair of the High Level Panel on an ASEAN Human Rights Body at the Conclusion of the Eighth Meeting of the HLP on AHRB." http://www.asean.org/images/archive/PR-HLP-8.pdf.

———. "Press Release: Cambodia Deposits Its Instrument of Ratification of the ASEAN Charter." http://www.asean.org/news/item/press-release-cambodia-deposits-its-instrument-of-ratification-of-the-asean-charter-asean-secretariat-18-april-2008.

———. "Press Release: Indonesia Becomes Ninth ASEAN Member State to Deposit Instrument of Ratification of the ASEAN Charter." http://www.asean.org/news/item/indonesia-becomes-9th-asean-member-state-to-deposit-instrument-of-ratification-of-the-asean-charter-asean-secretariat-13-november-2008.

———. "Press Release: Philippines Deposits Instrument of Ratification of the ASEAN Charter." http://www.asean.org/news/item/philippines-deposits-instrument-of-ratification-of-the-asean-charter-asean-secretariat-12-november-2008.

———. "Press Release: Secretary-General of ASEAN Dr Surin Pitsuwan's Remarks at the Ceremony for the Deposit of Myanmar's Instrument of Ratification of the ASEAN Charter." http://www.asean.org/news/item/secretary-general-of-asean-dr-surin-pitsuwan-s-remarks-at-the-ceremony-for-the-deposit-of-myanmar-s-instrument-of-ratification-of-the-asean-charter-singapore-21-july-2008.

———. "Press Release: Secretary-General Sympathises with Thai Leaders' Hesitation on Postponement of Fourteenth ASEAN Summit." http://www.asean.org/news/asean-statement-communiques/item/press-release-secretary-general-sympathises-with-thai-leaders-hesitation-on-postponement-of-14th-asean-summit-office-of-the-secretary-general-asean-secretariat.

———. "Press Release: Viet Nam Hands Over Instrument of Ratification for ASEAN Charter to Secretary-General of ASEAN." http://www.asean.org/news/item/press-release-viet-nam-hands-over-instrument-of-ratification-for-asean-charter-to-secretary-general-of-asean-10-april-2008.

———. *Report of the Eminent Persons Group on the ASEAN Charter.*
———. *Singapore Declaration of 1992.*
———. *Statement of ASEAN Foreign Ministers on the Recent Developments in the Rakhine State.*
———. "Statement by the Chairman of ASEAN Following the Informal Meeting of the Foreign Ministers of ASEAN." http://www.asean.org/images/archive/documents/N110222.pdf.
———. "Statement by Mr George Yeo, Minister for Foreign Affairs of Singapore and Chairman of the 41st ASEAN Standing Committee at the Closing Ceremony of the 41st ASEAN Ministerial Meeting and Handing Over of the ASEAN Standing Committee." http://www.asean.org/news/item/statement-by-mr-george-yeo-minister-for-foreign-affairs-of-singapore-and-chairman-of-the-41st-asean-standing-committee-at-the-closing-ceremony-of-the-41st-asean-ministerial-meeting-and-handing-over-of-the-asean-standing-committee-singapore-24-july-2008.
———. *Terms Of Reference and Guidelines for the Organization of ASEAN Committees in Third Countries.*
———. *Terms of Reference of the Committee of Permanent Representatives to ASEAN.*
———. *Terms of Reference of the Eminent Persons Group (EPG) on the ASEAN Charter.*
———. "Terms of Reference of ASEAN Intergovernmental Commission on Human Rights." http://aichr.org/?dl_name=TOR-of-AICHR.pdf
———. *Vientiane Action Programme (2004–10).*
———. *Work Programme to Implement the ASEAN Plan of Action to Combat Transnational Crime.*

International Court of Justice (ICJ)

International Court of Justice. *Reparations for Injuries Suffered in the Service of the United Nations*, 1949.
———. "Application by the Philippines for Permission to Intervene." http://www.icj-cij.org/docket/files/102/7698.pdf.
———. "Application Instituting Proceedings and Pleadings: Case Concerning the Temple of Preah Vihear." http://www.icj-cij.org/docket/files/45/9249.pdf.
———. "Case Concerning the Temple of Preah Vihear, Merits, Judgment of 15 Jun 1962." http://www.icj-cij.org/docket/files/45/4871.pdf.
———. "Case Concerning the Temple of Preah Vihear, Preliminary Objections, Judgment of 26 May 1961." http://www.icj-cij.org/docket/files/45/4857.pdf.

———. "Request for the Interpretation of the Judgment of 15 Jun 1962 in the Case Concerning the Temple of Preah Vihear, Order dated 18 Jul 2011." http://www.icj-cij.org/docket/files/151/16564.
———. "Request for the Interpretation of the Judgment of 15 Jun 1962 in the Case Concerning the Temple of Preah Vihear, Judgment dated 11 Nov 2013." http://legal.un.org/ICJsummaries/documents/english/203_e.pdf.
———. Rules of Court.
———. "Sovereignty over Pedra Branca/Pulau Batu Puteh, Middle Rocks and South Ledge (Malaysia/Singapore), Judgment." http://www.icj-cij.org/docket/files/130/14492.pdf.
———. "Sovereignty over Pulau Ligitan and Pulau Sipadan (Indonesia/Malaysia), Judgment." http://www.icj-cij.org/docket/files/102/7714.
———. "Special Agreement: For Submission to the International Court of Justice of the Dispute between Indonesia and Malaysia Concerning Sovereignty over Pulau Ligitan and Pulau Sipadan." http://www.icj-cij.org/docket/files/102/7177.pdf.
———. "Special Agreement: For Submission to the International Court of Justice of the Dispute between Malaysia and Singapore Concerning Sovereignty over Pedra Branca/Pulau Batu Puteh, Middle Rocks and South Ledge." http://www.icj-cij.org/docket/files/130/1785.pdf.
———. Statute of the Court.
———. "Territorial and Maritime Dispute (Nicaragua v Colombia), Judgment." http://www.icj-cij.org/docket/files/124/17164.pdf.

United Nations (UN)

United Nations. *1946 Convention on the Privileges and Immunities of the United Nations.*
———. *1961 Vienna Convention on Diplomatic Relations.*
———. *Charter of the United Nations.*
———. "General Legal Division." http://legal.un.org/ola/div_gld.aspx?section=gld.
———. "Permanent Observers." http://www.un.org/en/members/intergovorg.shtml.
———. "United Nations Treaty Collection: Chapter III Privileges and Immunities, Diplomatic and Consular Relations, etc." https://treaties.un.org/Pages/ViewDetails.aspx?src=TREATY&mtdsg_no=III-3&chapter=3&lang=en.
———. "United Nations Treaty Collection: Charter of the Association of Southeast Asian Nation." https://treaties.un.org/Pages/showDetails.aspx?objid=080000028025f1e4

Online Resources

The following sources are from *Encyclopaedia Britannica Online*; the online version of *Encyclopaedia Britannica.*

"ASEAN." http://global.britannica.com/EBchecked/topic/556542/ASEAN#ref227052.

"Cambodia: Cambodia since 1990." http://global.britannica.com/EBchecked/topic/90520/Cambodia/52491/The-1990s.

———. "Cambodia: Independence." http://global.britannica.com/EBchecked/topic/90520/Cambodia/52487/Independence.

———. "East Timor: History."http://global.britannica.com/EBchecked/topic/596313/East-Timor/326338/History.

———. "Indonesia: History." http://global.britannica.com/EBchecked/topic/286480/Indonesia.

———. "Indonesia: Japanese Occupation." www.britannica.com/EBchecked/topic/286480/Indonesia/22819/Japanese-occupation.

———. "Laos: History." http://global.britannica.com/EBchecked/topic/330219/Laos.

———. "Malaysia: History." http://global.britannica.com/EBchecked/topic/359754/Malaysia.

———. "Malaysia: Political Transformation." www.britannica.com/EBchecked/topic/359754/Malaysia/52562/Political-transformation#ref509484.

———. "Myanmar: History." http://global.britannica.com/EBchecked/topic/400119/Myanmar/214472/History.

———. "Papua: History." http://global.britannica.com/EBchecked/topic/293960/Papua/303094/History.

———. "Philippines: World War II." www.britannica.com/EBchecked/topic/456399/Philippines/23718/World-War-II.

———. "Thailand: History." http://global.britannica.com/EBchecked/topic/589625/Thailand.

———. "Thailand: The Phibunsongkhram Dictatorship and World War II." http://global.britannica.com/EBchecked/topic/589625/Thailand/52682/The-Phibunsongkhram-dictatorship-and-World-War-II.

———. "Vietnam: History." http://global.britannica.com/EBchecked/topic/628349/Vietnam.

INDEX

ABOUT THE AUTHOR

Professor Walter Woon read law at the National University of Singapore on a Development Bank of Singapore Scholarship, graduating with First Class Honours in 1981 and winning the Adrian Clark Memorial Gold Medal for being the top student. He then proceeded to Cambridge University on a Commonwealth Scholarship, graduating with an LL.M (First Class Honours) in 1983. He was awarded the Whytehead Scholarship and the Wright Prize by St John's College Cambridge.

He attended the Postgraduate Practice Law Course in 1981 and was awarded the Aw Boon Haw and Aw Boon Par Memorial Prize as top student. He was called to the Singapore Bar in 1984 and appointed Senior Counsel in 2007.

Professor Woon is currently David Marshall Professor at the Law Faculty and Deputy Chairman of the Centre for International Law (CIL), National University of Singapore. He is concurrently Dean of the Singapore Institute of Legal Education (SILE), which conducts the Bar Examinations and Foreign Practitioner Examinations for entry into the legal profession. Professor Woon also is chairman of the Society of International Law Singapore (SILS), as well as an Executive Council Member of the Asian Society of International Law (Asian SIL). In addition he is a member of the Criminal Practice Committee of the Law Society of Singapore and the Chancery Bar Association of England and Wales.

Between 1988 and 1995 he was Sub-Dean and Vice-Dean of the Law Faculty of the National University of Singapore. He was a Nominated Member of Parliament from 1992 to 1996. From 1995 to 1997 he was Legal Adviser to the President and Council of Presidential Advisers. He served as Solicitor-General from 2006 to 2008 and subsequently became Attorney-General from 2008 to 2010. He has also been Judge Advocate-General and a member

Signing ceremony of the ASEAN Charter at the Thirteenth ASEAN Summit in Singapore, 20 November 2007. The author is fourth from the left in the second row, between the flags of Indonesia and Laos.

of the Presidential Council for Minority Rights and the board of directors of the Monetary Authority of Singapore.

From 1998 to 2006 Professor Woon was Singapore's ambassador to Germany, Greece, the European Communities, the European Union, Belgium, the Netherlands, Luxembourg and the Holy See. In 2007 he was Singapore's alternate member on the High Level Task Force for Drafting of the ASEAN Charter, serving as Singapore delegation leader during the later half of the process. He presented the completed Charter to the ASEAN Foreign Ministers for signature by the Heads of State/Government at the Thirteenth ASEAN Summit in November of that year.